THINKING AND REASONING IN HUMAN DECISION MAKING:

THE METHOD OF ARGUMENT AND HEURISTIC ANALYSIS

PETER A. FACIONE, PH.D.   NOREEN C. FACIONE, PH.D.

PUBLISHED BY THE CALIFORNIA ACADEMIC PRESS LLC, MILLBRAE, CA

WWW.INSIGHTASSESSMENT.COM

ISBN 1-891557-58-0

The authors may be contacted through the publisher, The California Academic Press LLC.

The California Academic Press
217 La Cruz Avenue
Millbrae, CA. 94030
United States of America

Cover design and cover art © Measured Reasons LLC, Hermosa Beach CA

ISBN 1-891557-58-0

Printed in the United States of America

10   9   8   7   6   5   4   3   2

Contents

Tables

Figures

Acknowledgements

We want to thank all of you who, over the past many years, have supported and encouraged us to complete this decade long project. Thinking out loud with you and explaining our goals was a vital ingredient for this project. We especially thank those of you who posed difficult questions at seminars, workshops, conferences, and consultations. Many of these challenging questions about how better to understand real life decisions made in high stakes contexts pushed our research efforts and drove the development of this new methodology. Some of you must have special mention here for your particularly patient interest. We appreciate the support shown for this project by the partners at Insight Assessment, and we are grateful for the enthusiasm shown for this work by our good friend and colleagues, Dr. Isiaah Crawford, Dr. Christine Miaskowski, Dr. Marylin Dodd, and Dr. Carol Giancarlo. Finally we thank Jennifer Stripe and Gregory Wolcott for assisting with the copyediting of the manuscript.

Forward

Over the course of two generations, we have witnessed the unprecedented development of structured, useful, relevant, and operational methodologies for modern critical thinking, well adapted to our second millennium ways of practicing it, problem understanding and decision-making. We appreciate the achievements of numerous brilliant minds in the area and this book is a standout among such contributions. Here is why.

Let me frame this discussion in consideration of the health sciences, as this is my area of expertise. I think readers will be easily able to generalize from this context, as there seems to have been parallel evolutions is other professional fields. In health sciences, we have generally dealt with fragments of epistemology, hermeneutics, logic, critical thinking and other domains of philosophy: Heuristics has seeped into our clinical teaching. Causal reasoning is now well rooted in epidemiological research and clinical trials. Informal logic and hopefully fallacy-free modern argumentation have found their way into daily communication with our peers and patients. These important and often vital tidbits of higher order thinking have been sprinkled into our teachings and practice for decades through epidemiology, biostatistics, even bedside teaching, and now evidence-based and anchored health sciences of medicine, public health, nursing and dentistry. It always takes courage, if not guts, to present to practicality-oriented health professionals focused mainly on pragmatic decision-making and doing, a distinct volume devoted to a particular branch of philosophy. An additional challenge is to spread the word without yet having a credited course number.

It is much easier to convey a structured explanation and guide to categorical syllogisms, scientific method, research project proposals or medical article writings. To write about heuristics is much more challenging if the message is to be equally structured, focused, useful, usable and relevant for its practitioners. This is where the Authors of the book have remarkably succeeded by combining both reflective and reactive reasoning in problem understanding and decision-making.

Readers who are already familiar with the essentials of modern philosophy will benefit most from Peter and Noreen Facione's book since it is built on such foundations. So, what new insights does the book feature then?

Today, thinking can be seen not only in light of classical Aristotelian or ancient Nyaya philosophy. Stephen E. Toulmin proposes an equally universal model of argumentation particularly relevant for research, practical understanding and decision making in health sciences and elsewhere. To improve upon such understanding and decision-making, the Authors highlight in this book their method of argument and heuristic analysis, the A & H Method, stemming from the already established domain of argumentation, taking into account the reality of life. Within the context of heuristics in the health sciences, for example, a busy physician in the midst of a frantic hospital emergency service simply does not have enough time to base his or her decisions on a full blown argumentation and analysis of its building blocks and their interconnections. He or she must make mental shortcuts while preserving the correct essence of clinical problem solving. Algorithms are just one of the decision making tools where appropriate. Researchers in artificial intelligence and computer sciences face similar problems.

In addition to "direction giving" paths in decision-making, Peter and Noreen Facione offer us a "direction searching" alternative and complement based on the reality of daily work: clinical situations, political and legal decisions and others. Their framework is much broader than health sciences, in focus in this foreword. The A & H method enriches this second alternative by taking into account the heuristic process of reasoning. In its application, the book shows how both "laypersons" (patients) and "professionals" (in health care, in this example) think, speak about their experience, and arrive at their interpretations and claims, whether it be an exploration of the patient's attitude towards a health problem or a diagnostic and therapeutic decision chosen by the health professional. A similar double view may exist in other domains such as in the study of ways in which the public reasons compared to ways in which legal, political or administrative bodies interpret and explain situations to propose justified decisions about them.

The Authors show us how to "map" the flow of the natural language of proponents and consumers of information, how to understand them better. They explain how to translate the process of reasoning into some manageable concept map giving direction within such a map to better understand the problem. Can we compare and integrate the views of proponents and consumers in these maps?

What did I like the most in this book? I was particularly impressed with the drawing and analysis of situations as they occur in daily life and in their natural language rather than the creation of oversimplified models. These models are often necessary for even the basic understanding of more complex problems and approaches. I also found Chapter Six systematically covering heuristic thinking to be a fascinating read! Very few others deal with the problem of heuristics in such an original manner, especially for the benefit of less philosophically experienced readers. A limited number of texts currently available compare favorably to this book's systematic and structured approach to the explanation of these thinking strategies.

It is usually very difficult to propose something new that brilliantly refines tested and proven ways. This A & H book enriches our current armamentarium of searches for the best evidence, critical appraisal of evidence in its largest sense and the uses of the best evidence in further rational decision making. Putting into practice its message and testing its uses in various domains of human endeavor will further show its value. How will it work and develop in health sciences and elsewhere? What benefit from its practical uses and applications will it bring? Interesting times are coming and I wish these pages good and well- deserved luck!

Professors Peter and Noreen Facione belong to those rare and exceptional intellectual powerhouses (and power households) where a union of hearts, souls and spirits leads to important contributions. Another couple in health sciences that instantly comes to mind is Robert and Suzanne Fletcher, Professors at the Harvard School of Medicine and former Editors-in-Chief of the Annals of Internal Medicine and among the fore-parents of clinical epidemiology. Elsewhere, spouses David Marks and Julia Barfield, British architects built the London Eye observation wheel. Are there other such relationships between readers leading to the achievement of similarly good deeds? They would be most welcome!

Milos Jenicek, MD
Rockwood, July 2007.

Truthseeking:

The habit of mind characterized by a courageous desire to achieve the best possible knowledge in any given context; the disposition to follow reason and evidence wherever they lead, even if the results are inconsistent with one's cherished beliefs.

The American Philosophical Association
Delphi Research Study

Chapter 1: Overview of the Method of Argument and Heuristic Analysis

At times smart, informed people make unwise decisions, putting themselves and others at needless risk. The examples are as obvious as they are familiar: Knowing the risks, some people smoke, allow themselves and their children to grow morbidly obese, continue to add to mounting debts, make unnecessarily risky financial investments, promise things they know they are unlikely to deliver and socialize in settings prone to sudden violence.

Mindful of the unfortunate consequences of decisions such as these, four questions naturally stir curiosity and motivate inquiry: (1) How is it that sane, informed, responsible and rational people make risky, uncertain, high stakes decisions which appear to other equally sane, informed, responsible and rational people to be unwise, if not simply foolish? (2) Why do the explanations people offer for these decisions appear to them, and at times to others, to be plausible and rational? (3) How do people find the courage to sustain and act on these decisions, given their knowledge of the counter-arguments, the alternatives, the uncertainty and the risks? And, (4) for those cases when the judgments are indeed foolish, are there interventions, respectful of autonomy and informed decision making, which would guide those decision makers to make better judgments?

Criteria for a Method of Decision Analysis

It has proven difficult for scientists to answer these four questions. To answer them satisfactorily one's methodology must, at a minimum, be strong enough to analyze risky high stakes judgments into their constituent elements, to explain how these elements are integrated into a final judgment about what to believe or what to do, and to evaluate the quality of that judgment. Such an analytical methodology would satisfy at least these three criteria:

The Method of Argument and Heuristic Analysis (A&H Analysis) emerged though many years of endeavor aimed at capturing and displaying more and more of the decision process. A&H Analysis captures the flow of the decision maker's reasoning, the major options as the decision maker perceives them, the reasons the decision maker relies upon or considers and discards, and the influences of biases or heuristics on the decision making.

Thus, the results produced by A&H Analysis contain an integrated internal authenticity, as contrasted to the externalities that demographic studies, cross sectional attitudinal studies, or algorithmic mathematical modeling approaches afford.

TABLE 1: CRITERIA FOR A SUITABLE METHODOLOGY

Analyze and map the structure of a decision	First, the method should enable investigators reliably to analyze and to map the decisions people make, revealing their reasons and how those reasons relate to the options being considered, revealing the heuristics and identifying the biases which influence their reasoning, and holistically revealing the preponderance of reasons for and against the chosen option.
Evaluate the strength of the reasoning	Second, the method should enable investigators to assess reliably the decision making under investigation on the basis of established standards of sound reasoning and good thinking.
Predict and guide decision making	Third, the method should enable investigators to use reliably those decision maps and assessments to guide predictions and interventions to aid decision making.

A&H supports comparisons of the decision making of many individuals facing essentially the same problem. And, thus, it offers the potential to inform individual and community intervention studies. If an empirically discernable pattern can be found in decisions which many individuals make with regard to essentially the same problem, and if that pattern repeatedly results in undesirable outcomes for a number of those individuals, we should then seek to examine that decision pattern and set about finding ways to prevent it from recurring or ways to limit its persuasive power. A&H Analysis also supports the detailed comparison of several decisions made by the same individual. Knowing that a person or a group of people may be prone to making a given mistake, a skillful coach will recognize the opportunity to assist that individual or that group to improve. This is as true with regard to decision making as it is for any other domain where guided practice can aid in achieving better results.

In designing and refining this new method we intend A&H Analysis to focus on decision making as humans engage in that process, not on decisions as may be made by machines or by other species. The purpose of A&H Analysis is to explicate in a deep, complete, and integrated way the process of human decision making so that these decisions can be studied scientifically. We see the primary object of the A&H Method as being to generate an analysis of the decision making which ordinary, rational, sane, and physiologically unimpaired persons engage in when deciding what to do in contexts involving some degree of risk or uncertainty. This includes making the initial decision involving risk and uncertainty as well as the decision making processes involved in reconsidering or sustaining that initial decision.

Risky Decisions Abound

Consider the following relatively commonplace examples of situations involving high stakes decision making in contexts of risk and uncertainty. In some of these examples, there is time for deliberation. In others the decision must be made almost instantaneously.

- An elderly widower sits alone in his silent house. He is short of breath and sleeping is difficult because aortic heart valve stenosis has caused fluid to accumulate in his chest. The cardiologist he saw earlier in the week recommended surgery. Yes, he knows he must decide whether to have the operation before it is too late. The doctor said in a year or so without an operation his heart will fail completely, and he will die. His children, now all middle-aged and living far away, have phoned to urge him to have the surgery. He knows they are worried about him and that they are trying to talk some sense into him. Ah, but they are young. Is it really worth all the pain and bother of heart surgery just so that afterward he can return to his current life? He'll still be alone most days. He'll still be struggling with the problems of old age. He might not survive the surgery. He thinks not.

- Impatient with the traffic, a bicycle messenger dodges and zigzags between the cars, busses, and pedestrians crowding the busy city street.

- Knowing it will probably mean layoffs and possibly a strike, a management team wrestles with whether to cut its financial losses by discontinuing an unprofitable product line.

- Wanting to do what's right, scientifically supportable, and politically acceptable, a politician seeks the advice of experts and reads agency reports and public opinion polls in the process of deciding what position to take on complex and sensitive questions like foreign aid, undocumented workers, capitol punishment, health care reform, or the latest ethically controversial biogenetic discovery.

- Glimpsing a possible enemy combatant rushing past an open door, the sergeant fires his automatic rifle into the building.

- An inline skater, eager to begin his exercise, realizes that he has left his kneepads, wrist guards and helmet in the trunk of his car. Instead of returning to the car, he decides to skate without wearing the protective gear.

- A young woman who lives alone hears that a neighbor's house was broken into. She decides to purchase a gun and keep it, loaded, in the top drawer of her nightstand.

- Aggrieved workers meet to decide whether to strike because of low pay and dangerous working conditions.

- As they decide whether the breadwinner should take the company's early retirement program, a couple considers their finances, health, hopes and worries about the future.

Every thoughtful analyst recognizes that decisions like these involve a multiplicity of interrelated elements. For example, the way an individual or the group frames a problem often opens up one cluster of potential solutions while closing off others. The observations, beliefs, attitudes, training, salient experiences, intentions, obligations, expectations, interests, priorities, values, and emotions of the decision maker(s) influence, to a greater or lesser extent, the final outcome. These kinds of things are often cited by decision makers when giving explanations of how they decided as they did. While cogent to the decision maker(s) themselves, the explanations offered for risky decisions might not stand up to careful analysis. Any number of problems may impact the decision making process negatively. For example, flaws in logic, reliance on vague or misapplied similarities to other unrelated events, overestimations of chances for success, errors in comprehending the character or the scope of the initial problem, incomplete data gathering, failures of imagination in conceiving of reasonable options, inadequate examinations of viable alternative solutions. Human decision making, regardless of how deliberative or non-deliberative it might be in different contexts, is influenced by a great many elements which must be accounted for in the analysis.

> We can learn more about how to express the complexity of human reasoning by exploring the flaws in decisions which seem ill-advised, rather than those which seem obviously correct.

Two Powerful Cognitive Factors – Argument Making and Heuristic Thinking

The complexity of human decision making in high stakes contexts of risk and uncertainty can be mapped as the interplay of two cognitive drivers: the human propensity toward self-explanation known as argument making and the influence of cognitive heuristics. Let us briefly consider each in a very preliminary way.

Argument Making is the effort to be logical; that is, to rely on the relevant reasons and facts as we see them when making our decisions. In general, humans endeavor to go about decision making as rationally as the circumstances, significance, and content of their judgments permit. This is not to say that we are always successful in this effort. In fact, we often are not. And yet we explain our choices and judgments to ourselves, if not to others, in terms of the relevant reasons and facts – again, as we see them. Humans like to think that their decisions are well thought out and based on sound arguments. When they are, we can rest assured that we have made the best judgment that the context allowed. But sometimes decisions are based on unsound arguments that include groundless assumptions and poorly drawn inferences. Both mistaken beliefs and flawed reasoning can result in suboptimal decisions.

Heuristic Thinking is the tendency, at times quite useful, of relying on cognitive heuristics, which are highly efficient mental maneuvers, to reach a conclusion. The cognitive maneuvers are as much a part of the human reasoning process as argument making. Cognitive heuristics often enable us to make judgments and decisions more expeditiously and efficiently. Their influences are often positive, but they can introduce errors and biases into decision making.

Unlike computers, human decision making is not algorithmic. Faced with the need to make an important decision, humans are often unclear or in conflict about the nature of the problem, attracted by a given, perhaps mistaken, notion of their intended outcome, and unaware of all of their alternatives, opportunities, or risks. We often do not give due consideration even to all of the alternatives which come to mind. We overestimate our ability to control events, underestimate our chances for failure, and we are affectively drawn toward some options and repelled by others. We mistake superficial resemblances for fundamental structural similarities; we trap ourselves in false us-versus-them dualisms; we generalize from the one to the many; and we readily eliminate options, even good ones, because we perceive a single flaw in them. We settle for "good-enough" when better is available, and we privilege the familiar and the status quo.

Machines, list-processing strategies, rational game theory, formal logic, inferential statistics, Bayesian techniques, computer generated syntactical analyses, and decision tree schema do not, generally, engage in those sorts of things. The A&H Method, described in detail later in this book, takes human decision making as it actually is and enables the investigator to display it in sufficient detail to see how the decision maker's judgment emerges. Using A&H Analysis the investigator can empirically capture, analyze, display, and explain *both good and bad human decision making*.

Progression of the Book – Theory to Method to Applications

Intended only to provide a first look at how the A&H Method can be applied, the remainder of Chapter 1 offers an extended example with minimal explanation. As the book progresses, the A&H methodology is presented in greater detail, beginning with the theoretical orientation in Chapter 2. Then Chapters 3 and 4 explain how to capture, analyze, and manage the data manifested in complex decision making, and how to construct decision maps to display those data and their relationships. Chapters 5, 6, and 7 address the evaluation of the quality of the decision making. Chapter 5 addresses the logical soundness of the arguments used; Chapter 6 speaks to the heuristic influences manifested in various strands of reasoning; and, Chapter 7 explains how to make an integrated holistic evaluation of the entire decision making experience. Chapter 8 discusses how to array and present the findings of A&H Analysis for scientific study and publication.

Before getting into the details, consider the extended illustration in the next section of this chapter. This example illustrates the application of A&H Analysis to one person's decision of whether or not to donate a kidney to a friend in kidney failure. The purpose of this example is to provide an overview of the output of A&H Analysis; subsequent chapters explain each step in the methodology.

An Extended Illustration of the Use of the A&H Method

To illustrate the A&H Method in a scientific research project, consider the decision made by a live organ donor to donate a kidney to someone in kidney failure. Review of this example will provide an immediate sense of the potential use and value of the A&H Method.

Three days before the planned organ donation surgery, this potential donor, let's call him Howard, was interviewed regarding how he made the decision to donate one of his kidneys to a friend who was facing dialysis.[*] Howard was interviewed as part of a larger research study of kidney donation aimed at learning whether live organ donors understand their risk and have realistic expectations about their recovery after organ donation. This type of decision is meant to be purposeful, sufficiently well-informed, reflective, and open to reconsideration right up until the donor begins sedation for surgery.[1,2,3] In making such a decision to become a live organ donor, a person necessarily incurs a measure of personal risk and experiences some uncertainty regarding the anticipated and hoped for outcomes.

Howard's interview was collected using a *talk-aloud* approach, which is described in detail in Chapter 3. This approach calls on the interviewer to prompt minimally and never to judge Howard's thinking.[4] As a result, Howard's is a relatively spontaneous account of his decision, not only retrospectively with regard to his initial decision to donate but as an on-going commitment to sustain that decision beyond the current interview.

In response to the question, "How did you make this decision to become a kidney donor?" Howard began by telling a story about how he had heard that his friend needed a kidney. Howard spoke about his reasons for deciding to donate a kidney and how he reconciled that decision with the concerns or objections he or others may have brought forward. Howard's interview lasted 40 minutes, during which he spoke roughly 2500 words, revealing 18 reasons leading to his decision to donate and 6 reasons why he should not.

---

[*] This interview was collected in accordance with an approved human subjects protocol in a study of organ donation and the physiological recovery of the live donor: Painter and Facione, University of California San Francisco, 2002.

Howard's recorded interview, once completed, was first transcribed so that the decision making content could be identified and readily accessed. Typically, there is a non-linearity in a spontaneous oral presentation of human reasoning. For instance, someone might say "I need to leave. My son is waiting and my parking meter is running out." In this case the conclusion comes first, and reasons – in this case two of them – come later. More reasons to leave may be given later in the dialogue. Thus, a speaker's arguments often require systematic explication in order to provide an accurate interpretation of what the person intends as reasons for the various claims being made and also in order to show the progression of the person's argument strands toward his or her ultimate conclusion. Most often complete argument strands are found in close proximity, but subjects frequently return to embellish an argument that they had advanced earlier in the interview.

As one would expect, non-linearity was evident in Howard's interview. All the arguments, pro and con, that Howard considered in coming to his decision to donate his kidney were examined. At this point the focus of A&H is on understanding and analyzing Howard's reasoning *on his own terms*, not on amending or evaluating his final conclusion. If Howard considered something relevant or persuasive, it is the responsibility of the analyst to identify that part of Howard's thinking and to map it into the description of his network of arguments.

The following argument strand, mapped as Figure 1 below, occurred near the beginning of Howard's interview. This strand includes a pause where Howard recalls his assessment of the problem by imagining his friend in kidney failure. Howard finds it unacceptable that his friend should have to wait for a donor. Howard asserts that he made his initial decision to donate one of his kidneys in less than 60 seconds.

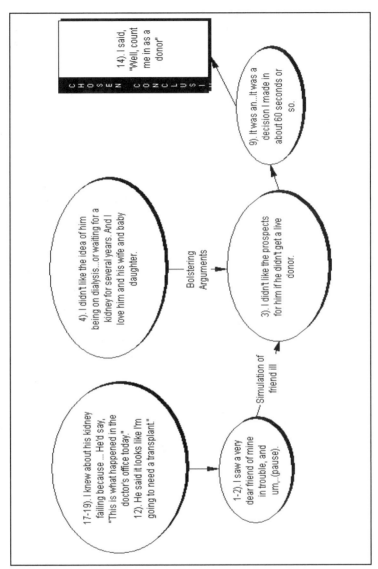

FIGURE 1: "IT WAS A DECISION I MADE IN 60 SECONDS ..."

Figure 1 displays only a part of the map of Howard's decision.[†] The complete map would show the flow of all of the argument strands, pro or

---

[†] Concept mapping software (Inspiration Software, Inc., 1997) was used to depict the argument structure within this interview. This software allows the researcher to introduce and move data segments and designate their relationship to argument strands. Color, shape, and directional arrow coding can be used to record categorizations and the results of analyses visually within the maps.

can, which Howard considered in reaching his decision. In this case there were 18 strands like the one displayed in Figure 1 which culminated in Howard's affirmative and sustained decision to donate. The themes (not the full argument) of these affirmative strands are displayed in Table 2.

TABLE 2: THEMES OF HOWARD'S ARGUMENTS FOR DONATING

Argument strands	Themes
1	I didn't like the prospect of him waiting for a kidney.
2 – W	I'm terrified of doctors, hospitals, and surgery. but that won't stop me from donating a kidney.
3 – W	People are asking, "Who are you giving it to?" He's not a relative, just a friend. but he needs a kidney.
4 – W	My close friends are saying, "We'll pray for you." But it's the guy who's getting my kidney who they should pray for.
5 – W	If people said something that caused me to hesitate, then I would not donate my kidney.
6	There were no other donors.
7	I'd rather give him a gift of love from someone he knows than for him to have a kidney from someone he does not know.
8	It's pretty easy to take the kidney out of me.
9	If professional athletes can donate a kidney and then continue to play sports, then I can certainly give my kidney to a friend that needs it.
10	I don't like being in the spotlight, but I'm comfortable with what I'm doing.
11	I'm going to be determined to get back to my current physical condition.
12	Friends or family who need help will view me as someone to come to.

13	Even if the kidney fails, I'll feel good that at least I tried to help.
14 – W	They are going to cut me open and there is going to be some pain. But It's not going to be as drastic or as painful as I thought.
15 – W	There are downsides. But It's not as scary as you think.
16	The decision was made strictly from the heart.
17	I'll be okay, but just pray for him that the kidney takes.
18	My sister and daughter think it's a great idea.

For Howard, the first argument seemed to carry more weight, for during the interview he returned several times to this summative statement about finding unacceptable the prospect of his friend waiting for a kidney.

When mapping a person's arguments, one often finds some considerations have the potential in the speaker's estimation to lead both toward as well as away from the ultimate conclusion. Our kidney donor regarded some ideas to be part of his basis for deciding to donate a kidney; and yet he also considered those same ideas, but from another perspective, to be potential reasons not to donate. We identify those considerations as *watershed* ideas. Like a physical watershed on a map, from that point one will find one or more argument strands flowing, but in different directions.

For certain research or intervention purposes, the watershed ideas themselves can be the focal points, since these are the ideas the decision maker implicitly acknowledges as potentially leading toward a decision other than the one she or he makes. Hence, there is reason to believe that these ideas are more provocative for the decision maker. To comprehend the resiliency of the final judgment, an investigator is well advised to attend carefully to the decision maker's watershed ideas and how that decision maker resolves their potential to lead to diverging outcomes. When an A&H Analysis reveals watershed ideas, this is an indication that the decision maker has taken the time to explore to a greater or lesser extent the implications of these ideas for the choice or choices not made. Quite often we observe that one or another of these considerations are abandoned or minimally elaborated as argument strands. Figure 2 below exhibits such an abandoned argument.

Consider themes 2, 3, 4, 5, 14, and 15 in Table 2. Each was a watershed issue for Howard. And in each case he argued both sides of the issue, but always concluded that he would/should donate his kidney. Table 3 synopsizes six possible arguments, one based on each watershed issue, which lead toward a decision not to donate a kidney.

Unfortunately we shall never really know how Howard himself would have used the watershed statements to reason toward a decision not to donate, for in his interview Howard abandoned each of the six considerations before completely developing arguments for not donating. But in each case Howard shared how he resolved each concern. In each case he introduced a consideration which led him in the direction of donating. Argument strand 5 – W indicates that Howard did talk with relatives and friends about his decision. Figure 2 illustrates how Howard abandoned consideration of the concerns raised by his mother, using the comments of his sister and daughter to affirm his decision to donate.

TABLE 3: HOWARD'S SIX REASONS NOT TO DONATE

Argument strands	Possible Rationale Leading Toward Not Donating a Kidney
2 – W	I'm terrified of doctors, and hospitals and surgery. And that fear is enough to make me decide that donating is not a good idea.
3 – W	People are asking, "Who are you giving it to?" He's not a relative, just a friend." certainly I'm under no obligation to donate to non-relatives.
4 – W	My close friends are saying, "We'll pray for you." They are smart people and if they are that worried, maybe I should reconsider.
5 – W	If people said something that caused me to hesitate, then I would [not donate my kidney]. And my mother said, "Don't let them get into your body." Maybe she has a point there. I should heed her concerns.
14 – W	They are going to cut me open, and it is going to involve some pain. I can easily avoid all that by not donating.
15 – W	There are downsides, like risk of infection or being given the wrong medications. I can easily avoid these risks by not donating.

In Figure 2, below, the main options of donating or not donating are indicated by the rectangles. [‡] The diamond contains the watershed statement. From there, two ovals reveal Howard's ideas as he moves toward the possibility of not donating. Howard never made an argument that his mother's concerns were unfounded or mistaken. That is, he never refuted her concerns; rather, he put them aside. The hexagon, like a stop sign, indicates that he put them aside. But, as the large arrow shows, he did make a counter-argument that moved his reasoning toward becoming a kidney donor.

[‡] The various shapes used in the A&H Method of decision mapping make it easier for the analyst to recognize the functions of the different elements in the reasoning process. Decision mapping conventions are explained in detail Chapter 4.

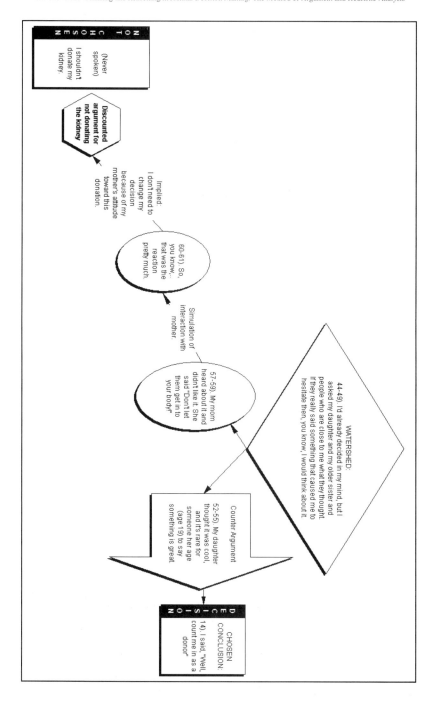

FIGURE 2: WATERSHED "EVERYBODY IS SAYING ..."

Figure 3, below, shows how Howard's reasoning progressed outward from another watershed. Howard tells us that his close friends worry that the surgery entails risk for him. He minimizes their concerns in his recounting of them, actually substituting "blah, blah, blah" at the end of the sentence where their actual concerns would have been listed.

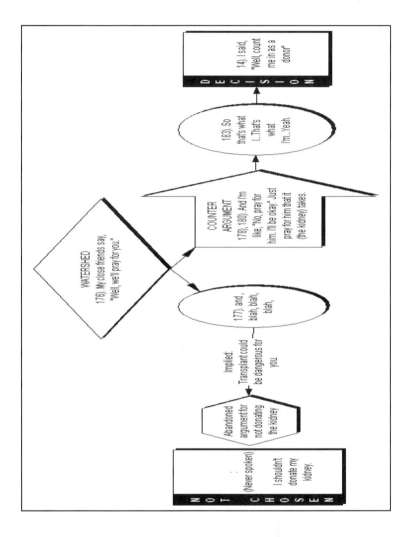

FIGURE 3: WATERSHED -- "MY CLOSE FRIENDS WORRY ..."

For ease of reference, some A&H Analysis mapping conventions for the use of various shapes to indicate reasoning elements and their function in the human decision making process are displayed in Figure 4, below.

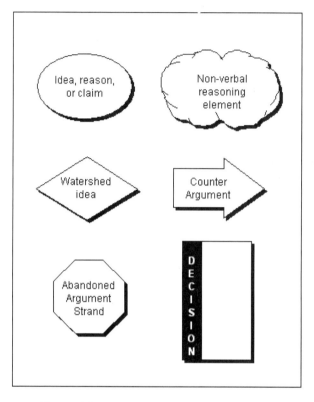

FIGURE 4: SHAPES USED IN A&H DECISION MAPPING

What accounts for Howard's confidence that these concerns can be dismissed? Henry Montgomery[5] investigated how humans make and sustain risky, uncertain decisions to act (or not to act). According to Montgomery, people form early preferences for how they would like to respond to high stakes dilemmas. Then they structure their argument for the value of their chosen alternative while minimizing the values of the other alternatives that will not be chosen. In the course of this process, they may seek selectively for facts that support their choice. While this process may sound curious and lacking in maximal fair-mindedness, there is considerable evidence that this type of mental maneuvering is needed in order for humans to find sufficient confidence in a risky uncertain judgment to allow themselves to act on their decision.[6] The *dominance structure* supporting the chosen alternative bolsters confidence in the uncertain judgment. This is particularly so when the negative consequences of error are high.

While we know of no research to date that explains how to gauge the durability of the dominance structure around any given judgment, there is evidence to suggest that dominance structures are resilient and difficult to override even when new information draws the judgment into question. Viewed holistically, the decision map displaying the arguments considered by Howard revealed a dominance structure around his judgment to donate a kidney to this friend of 20 years who was in kidney failure.[§]

That dominance structure is displayed in Figure 5 which depicts, using only numbers and shapes, all of Howard's arguments: the 18 ovals representing his 18 affirmative arguments, connecting by the line arrows to his chosen conclusion to donate a kidney, and the other 6 ovals indicating the negative arguments which would connect to not donating the kidney had Howard not abandoned all six of them (indicated by the hexagons). In this particular case we found one abandoned argument coming from each of Howard's watershed considerations (the diamond shapes), although in other maps we have found arguments for the "not-chosen" conclusion brought forward from watershed considerations and independent of watershed considerations. That people understand and consider arguments that connect to a not-chosen conclusion suggests that they often endeavor to reason carefully about their choices and can make decisions even in situations where they have not refuted or even abandoned all the considerations which they perceive as leading in a different direction.

[§] Chapter 7 discusses dominance structuring and the holistic examination and evaluation of decision maps.

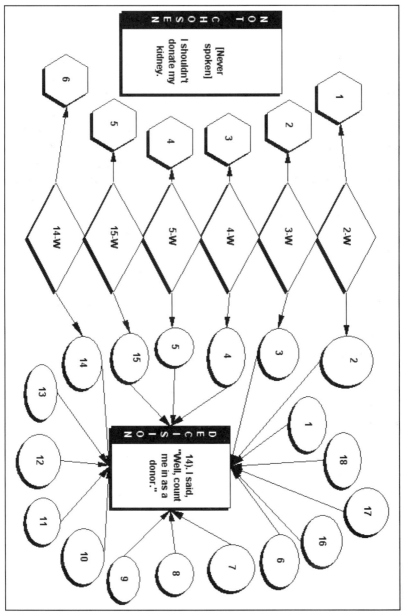

FIGURE 5: DOMINANCE STRUCTURE EVIDENT - 18 TO 6

That a dominance structure appears to be supporting Howard's decision seems reasonable and not at all surprising. The dominance structure represents the confidence needed to sustain a relatively high risk decision in a man who is knowledgeable of the uncertain threat posed by the surgery and any post-operative consequences which might occur to him as a living donor.

Having fully mapped the decision, A&H Analysis proceeds to an evaluation of the reasoning. The first A&H evaluative dimension focuses on the soundness of each of the subject's arguments. Soundness is evaluated in two ways: first, for the truth or falsity of the informational content of the reason given; and, second, for whether the claim being made is logically entailed, justified, or warranted by the reason given. Typically arguments are determined to be *warranted* only if they rely on accurate statements of fact and on relevant and reasonable generalizations regarding those facts.[7] Using contemporary argument evaluation categories, arguments which pass these two tests are labeled as *sound*. But if the argument was based on misinformation or if the reasoning is inferentially incorrect, not justified, or invalid, the argument is evaluated as *unsound.*[**]

The second A&H evaluative dimension considers the heuristic thinking evident in the decision making. In addition to his network of arguments, as captured and revealed in the mapping, Howard's uses of heuristic reasoning (cognitive maneuvers) are also displayed on that full decision map. Figure 1 above, for example, indicates reliance on a cognitive heuristic "Simulation," described in Chapter 6. A&H Analysis examines each reasoning strand a second time to discern how the heuristic thinking involved may have influenced the flow of that argument toward which ever conclusion the speaker drew from it. [††]

An overview of the full protocol for the Method of A&H Analysis is presented in Table 4 below. It summarizes the methodological steps used in the kidney donor illustration and previews the material detailed in later chapters.

[**] Chapter 5 addresses the process of evaluating arguments for soundness in much greater detail.

[††] Chapter 6 presents a number of specific cognitive heuristics and biases, and addresses the evaluation of the influences on decision making.

TABLE 4: PROTOCOL FOR ARGUMENT AND HEURISTIC ANALYSIS

1. Prepare Data for Analysis	The data is parsed, retaining its ordered chronology, into units of analysis (typically a single communication: assertion, belief, comment, proposition, pause/silence, or question). These units may be complete sentences, parts of sentences or incomplete sentences, each contextually understandable (even if not entirely grammatical) as revealing an element in the reasoning process. For example, these elements may be an expression of a claim or a reason for a claim, explicitly asserted or contextually implicit. Or they may be expressions of beliefs, values, or feelings which the decision maker deems relevant enough to mention in connection with explaining his or her rationale for the decision. These elements may be repetitions or summaries of ideas expressed earlier in the data gathering, or they may be inferences based on claims made earlier. Or they may be expressions intended to indicate the decision maker's backing or warrant for an assertion, or to show how the decision maker imagines responding to a rationale, genuine or imagined, which would otherwise lead toward an alternative decision.
2. Identify Main Conclusions	Identify the issue, problem, or dilemma which is central to the decision maker's thinking process and each of the chief alternative conclusions being considered. Often the central problem is a readily perceived dyadic divergence: the choice between doing X or not-doing X. On occasion more than two main conclusions might be found – as, for example, deciding between a very small number of alternatives. Identify the subject's final conclusion, if the decision maker expresses a final judgment in the matter.
3. Identify All Relevant Arguments	Claims and the reasons presented for them are arranged to represent the decision maker's rationale, with the progression of any given claim used as a reason in support of another claim as an argument strand flowing toward one or another of the main conclusions. argument strands are examined for redundancy and related content. Each argument strand is retained, regardless of how underdeveloped it may appear to be. This process continues until all relevant data is accounted for as a component of an argument supporting one of the identified alternative conclusions.
4. Evaluate Arguments for Logical Soundness	Each argument is then analyzed for soundness (quality of reasoning process and accuracy of information content). Sound arguments rely on accurate premises and assumptions and warranted inferences to reach justified conclusions. Unsound arguments rely on false statements, misinformation, unwarranted

	inferences, misapplied analogies, fallacies, mistaken estimates or other reasoning errors to reach unjustified conclusions.
5. Identify Heuristic Influences and Evaluate for Possible Heuristic Errors	Examine each argument strand for the use, or reliance, or influence of heuristic reasoning strategies. These have often been identified in the previous steps, but the data should be searched comprehensively specifically for cognitive heuristics and biases again at this point. The appropriateness of relying on the heuristic to make the decision is evaluated in each instance.
6. Identify Dominance Structuring and Map Related Argument Strands	Argument strands are clustered into similar content areas to create sets of related reasons supporting each of the main conclusions. All argument strands are visually mapped to permit a holistic examination of the flow and progression of the decision process. The mapping should also indicate the points at which the influences of cognitive heuristics and biases entered the flow of the decision making in any of the argument strands. Watershed statements that lead to arguments for more than one decision/conclusion, expressions of counter-arguments, and the connections of each argument strand to the main claim which it supports should all be entered into the map. This map is then examined for evidence of a dominance structuring around the final (chosen) conclusion.

Potential Uses of Argument and Heuristic Analyses

The Method of Argument and Heuristic Analysis offers investigators a tool which goes beyond the merely descriptive or evaluative exploration of human decisions considered individually. The A&H Method bridges the qualitative and quantitative dimensions of behavioral research.

A&H Analysis has the potential to explain and predict human decision making. When many people must make essentially the same decision in roughly the same circumstances, then the analysis of their decision making should produce patterns with sufficient structural similarities that one could predict, with some reasonable level of confidence, what others faced with the same decision will decide. If that turns out to be the case, as it has, for example, in our initial applications of this method to research on chronic health care situations,[8,9] then such knowledge could readily become the basis for intervention research.

Some potential uses of A&H Analysis include:

- Research studies of decisional behaviors (health risk, voting, job choice, major purchases, professional practice decisions, business and leadership decisions, etc.)

- Analyses of public discourse and policy, historical documents, persuasive media presentations

- Development of improved training programs for professionals who have major decision making roles, individually and as thinking teams

- Individual self-awareness and improvement of one's own decision making

- Therapeutic analysis of one's thinking and reflective decision making processes

- Individual or community intervention projects aimed at influencing decision making.

Chapter 2: The Two-System Model of Human Decision Making

This chapter outlines the theoretical understandings which ground the A&H Method for analyzing and evaluating human judgments and decision making. We begin with a model of human decision making as the parallel functioning of two integrated decision making systems, one reactive, the other reflective.[10] Depending on the context of the decision, a decision maker may rely more heavily on one system or the other; or one system may override or reinforce the other. Cognitive heuristics, understood as highly efficient human decision making maneuvers, may aid or may bias the decision making of either system. Decision makers offer arguments, that is, claims and reasons, to explain their decisions. The A&H Method is intended to enable investigators to study authentic examples of human decision making, to display the sound and unsound argument making as well as the use or misuse of heuristic maneuvers in human decision making, and to reveal the integration of both the reactive and reflective decision making systems. In this chapter we describe briefly this theoretical model of human reasoning.

The Science of Humans Decision Making

The comprehensive consideration of novel and difficult problems demands much of our cognitive resources. Capability of this type of reflective thought accounts for the human ability to consider multivariable phenomena and arrive at complex explanations. However, given the choice, simpler explanations are more attractive to humans than increasingly complex explanations.[11] Humans tend to make decisions non-algorithmically. Humans are not always mindful of long term consequences. More often we pursue options perceived as sufficient to handle the problem at hand. Being focused on the issues and problems at hand, humans tend not to seek more sophisticated and integrative explanations when simpler, context-relative judgments seem adequate, and as a result our judgments are not always consistent at a deeply theoretical level.

Some hypothesize that this preference for simpler, more expeditious decisions is related to the management of limited cognitive resources; others suggest it is a product of natural selection.[12,13] All of us know from personal experience that there are limits to the amount, variety, and complexity of the decision making our human brains can handle at any given time. And it seems clear that lacking claws, fangs, skeletal armor, protective fur, poisonous secretions, natural camouflage, strength, or speed, the human species has survived and flourished because of some other evolutionary advantage. As it turned out, it was the fast, efficient, and effective problem solving made possible by our oversized brains and our development of language. Physically nearly powerless against larger predators, had humans needed to analyze exhaustively every immediate threat or had they needed to delay decisions to consider fully all foreseeable consequences of every potential option, the species might well have assured itself an early extinction.

Human decision making in time-limited contexts of risk and uncertainty is often carried on with a relative dearth of information and reflection, and by relying upon less than valid estimations of probability.[14] Often it is not possible to consider calmly even the more probable outcomes of options. This is not to say that our decisions are unreasonable. We offer no evaluation at this point, for we are seeking now to describe human decision making in order to analyze it accurately. One of its central elements is its efficiency. Human decision making is not combinatorially exhaustive of every possible option and all foreseeable consequences. Rather, it is, in general, quick and efficient, even if at times mistaken and unwise.

An acceptable method of analysis targeting human decision making must enable descriptions which taken into account these kinds of distinguishing features. While a complete analysis will inevitably include an evaluative component, the analysis *per se* must be distinguished from those insights which can be expected to emerge from that analysis regarding how humans might go about improving their decision making.

Two Decision Making Systems: Reactive and Reflective

How do we judge whether is it wise to cross a busy street, issue a policy, trust a friend to safeguard a secret, or take our employer's buyout offer when the stakes are high, the outcomes uncertain, and the need to make a decision is now? Most of these judgments are likely to have been influenced at least in part by one or more cognitive heuristics.[15,16,17,18,19]

Cognitive heuristics can be understood as expeditious cognitive maneuvers used during decision making, in some cases consciously. For example, a tactic often consciously invoked in group decision making is to drop from consideration all options which include a feature the group regards as a disqualification. Called "elimination by aspect," this heuristic maneuver simplifies decision making by pruning down the number of options requiring detailed consideration.[‡‡] As with any tactical maneuver, results may vary.

Theories which attempt to explain naturalistic decisions, like the kidney donor example in Chapter 1, describe the interaction of two overlapping systems of reasoning that are active in human decision making.[20,21,22,23] One is often described as reactive, instinctive, quick, and holistic (System-1), and the other is more reflective, deliberative, analytical, and procedural (System-2).

System-1 thinking is believed to rely heavily on heuristics, key situational cues, and salient memories to arrive quickly and confidently at judgments, particularly when situations are familiar and immediate action is required. Many freeway accidents are avoided because drivers are able to see and react to dangerous situations quickly. Often good decisions that feel "intuitive"[§§] are really the fruit of expertise. Decisions good drivers make in those moments of crisis, just like the decisions practiced athletes make in the flow of a game or the decisions that a gifted teacher makes while interacting with students, are born of expertise, training, and practice.

System-2 thinking is believed to be useful for judgments in unfamiliar situations, for processing abstract concepts, and for deliberating when there is time for planning and more comprehensive consideration. Humans use heuristic maneuvers in System-2 thinking as well, often integrated as components of their logical arguments.

Both systems are believed to be valuable, simultaneously functioning processes often checking and balancing each other. The exact nature of the

---

[‡‡] This heuristic and others, along with their related potential advantages and disadvantages, are described in detail in Chapter 6.

[§§] We wish to put on the table our bias against "intuition" as this word is most commonly used. We are puzzled by claims of justified true beliefs ("knowledge") which go beyond observations or direct personal experience and yet are not preceded or preconditioned by some degree of interpretation, analysis, or inference – reflective or unreflective. Perhaps there is such a thing as intuitive knowledge, ineffable, immediate, mystical, and true. Even so, by definition such knowledge, if it is indeed knowledge, is beyond the scope of inter-subjective verification and science – it is "meta"-physical in the true sense. And if so, that which is "known" by intuition is placed outside of possible connections with other evidence-based, replicable, or falsifiable knowledge. Hence, other humans can not, in principle, know that what is asserted to be known by means of intuition is in fact true. One other reason we have deep concerns about appeals to "intuition" as a basis for justifying beliefs as true or decisions as reasonable is that we seek accountability. Unfortunately in matters of importance too often people appeal to intuition because they are either unable or unwilling to explain their judgments and to be held accountable for those explanations and judgments.

interactive functioning of these two aspects of human reasoning has yet to be definitively demonstrated, but regardless of whether there are two reasoning systems or one complexly integrated reasoning system, it is clear that humans do use both types of decision making and that therefore our methodology must account for both the argument-based and the heuristic-based factors which together result in our confident naturalistic decisions to believe and to act. However, the "two-systems" approach does not entail that normal human decision making is schizophrenic or psychologically disordered. Rather, this approach reflects more completely the pushes and pulls which normal human beings often describe as part of their decision making, and this approach accounts for the rapid fire decision making at times and the more reflective decision making at other times experienced by normal human beings.

In describing the "two-systems" approach, we wish to avoid harsh, rigid, stereotypic, divisive, commercialized oppositional over-simplified pop-culture dichotomies characterized by expressions and false-dichotomies such as: "emotion vs. reason," "head vs. heart," "feeling vs. judgment," "intuitive vs. logical," "expansive vs. linear," "creative vs. critical," "right brained vs. left brained," "warm vs. cold," "from Venus vs. from Mars," "blink vs. wide-eyed," etc. Human decision making is neither this superficial nor this simplistic. It is not thought to be the case that some people are only System-1 thinkers while others are only System-2 thinkers. We all have and use both systems in problem solving and decision making. But it is very useful to understand the potential strengths and weaknesses of these two systems as they interact in each of us every day.

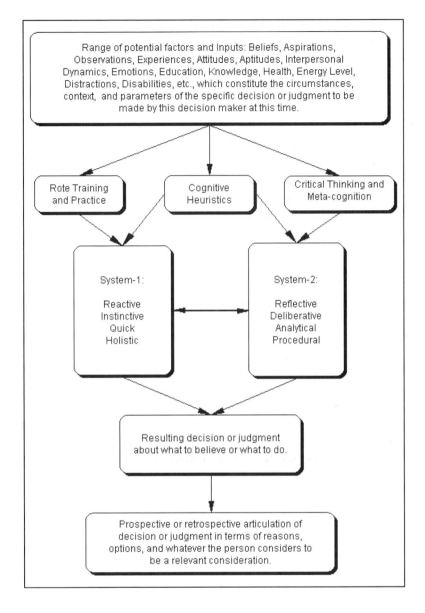

FIGURE 6: MODEL OF TWO SYSTEM HUMAN DECISION MAKING

System-2 decision making is deliberative and conscious. Because it is considered more useful for addressing novel and complex problems in a reflective and methodical way, it is the mode of problem solving and decision making most often addressed – although not necessarily by the name "System-2" – in the liberal education component of one's undergraduate studies and in the evidence-based practice and research methods components of professional or graduate studies. Education aimed at improving one's critical thinking, that is, at improving ones skills and dispositions to engage successfully in purposeful reflective judgment, is education focused directly on strengthening one's System-2 problem solving and decision making.[24]

The two systems are hypothesized to be operating in parallel and interactively. Figure 6 attempts to depict these relationships. While immersed in the constant minutia and unreflective processing of System-1 decision making needed to go about our daily routines, we often find ourselves actually thinking about other things. Perhaps an issue at work or personal relationship is weighing on our minds. We may anchor relatively early in the process on a desired outcome. We decide on seeking that result and then turn our attention to how it might be achieved. We may fret and worry, thinking about what this person or that person will say or do. We may gather some information or give some attention to one or two other options for achieving what we desire – more or less. We might think about how we will present and explain our decision to other people, perhaps even rehearsing an anticipated conversation or two in our minds. We may eliminate some possibilities because of one or another problem they might generate. Sooner or later we gravitate toward a given choice, and it begins to look better and better as compared to other options.[...] Having made a System-2 decision, we take action.

The characterization of System-2 decision making above is intended to illustrate that "deliberative and conscious" should not be confused with "optimal."[†††] At its best, System-2 thinking is reasoned judgment based on interpretation, analysis, evaluation, explanation, and self-correction. Optimally this is the system which values intellectual honesty, analytically anticipating what happens next, maturity of judgment, fair-mindedness,

---

[...] This phenomenon of human decision making, known as "Dominance Structuring," is discussed in Chapter 7.

[†††] To improve deliberative decision making we recommend these strategies: (1) Suspend judgment when possible about specific outcomes or choices until a fuller range of possibilities can be developed and considered. (2) Systematically attempt to expand the number of options for consideration. (3) More thoroughly research relevant information regarding main options, their actual costs, the genuine likelihoods for success, etc. (4) Before making a final decision review the assumptions, evidence, options, and reasons to be sure that nothing important has been missed. (5) Be sure that the timing is right, seeking not to decide too hastily but not to delay too long if a decision is needed. (6) Be meta-cognitive, think about your thinking seeking always to apply appropriate methods and standards, and to self-correct for potential errors. These habits of mind have been identified as critical thinking dispositions. Advice about cultivating good habits of reflective thought can be found in the writings of many of the great philosophers from Aristotle and Plato to the present. Notable insights, for example, are offered by no less a figure in the history of American philosophy than John Dewey. See, *How We Think*, first published in 1910 by D. C. Heath and Company of Boston, reprinted in 1997 by Dover Publications of Mineola, New York.

elimination of biases, and truth-seeking. But our System-2 thinking is not always at its best. For example, our reasoning skills may not be keen, our inferences may not be warranted or justified, our assumptions and beliefs may not be true, or we may fail to anticipate consequences or approach issues with the necessary precision and systematicity.

Uncertainty and Error

System-1 and System-2 are believed to be vital decision making tools when stakes are high and when uncertainty is an issue. We can often rely on System-1 to get us through the day-to-day while engaging System-2 on some other topic of concern. People report they can drive from home to work without remembering any of the hundreds of routine automobile operating decisions necessary to make the trip. Others report being able to drink a cup of coffee and finish a bowl of breakfast cereal almost without noticing because they are so engrossed in the morning newspaper. Engaged in their individual cell phone conversations, great numbers of shoppers meander along through a busy mall without bumping into one another or dropping the bags containing the things they just purchased.

Each of these two cognitive systems is believed to be capable of functioning to monitor and potentially override the other. Conflicted decision making contexts have, through the ages, been described in different ways – "temptation" being only one example. We are drawn one way, but at the same time, pulled the other way. Our "gut" says, do X; but our "brain" says, do Y. We looked at all the evidence and all the options and yet we "don't feel comfortable" with where our deliberative decision is heading. Some theorists suggest these common experiences are evidence that in certain kinds of ambiguous or complex situations the two systems might conflict, drawing the decision maker in different directions. In general, this is thought to be an advantage which reduces the chance of making poor, sub-optimal, or even dangerous errors in judgment.

Even a good thinker makes both System-1 and System-2 errors from time to time. We misinterpret things, overestimate or underestimate our chances of succeeding, rely on mistaken analogies, reject options out of hand, trust feelings and hunches, judge things credible when they are not, etc. Often biases and mistakes like these are directly related to the influences and misapplications of cognitive heuristics. Because we share the propensity to use these heuristics as we make decisions, and because at times they seem as to be hardwired into our species, we shall examine several in closer detail.

Both System-1 and System-2 can be helpfully influenced or negatively biased by the application or misapplication of one or more cognitive heuristics. Simply put, cognitive heuristics are maneuvers which expedite human decision making. Cognitive heuristics are not beliefs, although they can influence what one comes to believe. Neither are they procedural rules with clear conditions of application, although many of them are tactical in the sense of suggesting how to proceed expeditiously. There may be ecological validity to our species' general reliance on heuristically expedited decision making. While individual members of the species may make mistakes from time to time because of this, arguably the net overall impact at the species level has generally been beneficial. It seems plausible to speculate that when a hungry predator was spotted approaching, more of those who instinctively fled lived to pass along their DNA, whereas those who could not make up their minds about what to do were more likely to have been taken as prey.

For the past fifty years, cognitive scientists have been observing, describing, naming, and differentiating these maneuvers under the generic rubric of cognitive heuristics and biases. The semantic territory may not yet be mapped entirely. The precise boundaries between one heuristic and another may not always be crisp; some heuristics may not have been identified or investigated definitively yet. That being said, there is sufficient consensus and enough published science to move forward.

Because our method of analysis requires attention to the content of the decisions and the reasons adduced for those decisions, it is essential to take note of the influences of cognitive heuristics operating individually or in tandem to enhance or to bias specific decision outcomes. To name but a few possibilities, a person's reason may turn out to be based on an erroneous association of ideas, an unfortunate affective response, an unreasonable fear of loss, an overly optimistic estimation of control, or an easily imagined but mistaken simulation of future events. By focusing on each heuristic's enabling cognitive maneuver, which we will do in detail in Chapter 6, we can become adept at detecting and evaluating the influences of that maneuver on a specific human judgment and decision making process.

Given the model of human decision making outlined above, to look at argument making alone would be to knowingly truncate the data available to an investigative analysis of human decision making.

Human Argument Making and Reason Giving

For human beings, reasoned judgment and decision making depend on our capacity for argument making. That is, they depend on our being able, at least in principle, to give ourselves reasons for or against what we decide, or have decided, to do or to believe.

Reason giving behavior is a natural part of human judgment and decision making. We supply reasons to ourselves, and often to others when asked, regarding why we made the choice we made. In the paradigmatic situation, human reasons are the evidentiary beliefs we rely upon when explaining the claim that a given judgment or decision is, in our estimation, justifiable. That is, with certain obvious qualifications, such as given our understandings of the problem, the options, the context of judgment, the relevant facts, the applicable principles, values, and criteria for the adequacy of the judgment. But in giving our reasons for our claims, we ordinarily do not explain all the contextual qualifications. Our communication behavior is far more expeditious. Typically humans give a reason simply by stating the specific belief or data they think is relevant, leaving the listener to fill in all the gaps, including how that specific piece of information connects with the claim being made.

Consider this argument expressing a typical System-2 judgment: "Why do I believe that Bill will default on his mortgage payments? Because he lost his job last week." In giving his reason, the speaker references only one specific fact, namely, that Bill lost his job. The generalization, "When people do not have a steady source of income they often default on their loan payments," is not provided. Nor is the conceptual connection, "a mortgage payment is one example of a loan payment." Nor are the assumptions, such as "Bill has no other financial resources he can use to make the mortgage payment," or "Bill has a mortgage insurance policy which will cover his payments if he becomes unemployed," supplied. In fact, like an iceberg, most of the elements which make this apparently simple example argument work are hidden below the surface of what is actually articulated.

Reason giving is not confined to explaining our System-2 thinking only. We can give reasons for our reactive System-1 judgments. For example, suppose you are driving your car along a two lane highway and an oncoming vehicle suddenly starts to cross the center line into your lane. You break and swerve on to the shoulder of the roadway to avoid a collision. In a split second the other car rushes past and, adrenaline pumping, you angle your car back onto the roadway and continue along. In this System-1 scenario, there is plenty of evidence of reasoned judgment.

You could easily express in words, now that the sudden and unexpected emergency has been managed, the reason why you believed you were in imminent danger and why you decided to drive onto the shoulder of the highway. That the human mind can work so speedily and reactively does not entail that it functions without having reasons for coming to judgments about what to believe and what to do.[‡‡‡]

Reason giving and argument making are primarily intended to demonstrate that a judgment is correct, that is to explain why we are correct or right to believe what we believe or to have decided to act as we did. But humans are complex in their social interactions. And any method of analysis which seeks to explicate human judgment and decision making must provide for that complexity. Thus the A&H methodology extends the analysis of human reason giving beyond the paradigmatic case of explaining why one's judgments are justified.

Unlike machines, humans are socially and politically complex animals capable of using reason giving and argument making in a number of less than completely forthright ways. For example, at times people offer excuses; that is, they make arguments and give reasons for why they should not be held accountable for something. "I didn't know all the facts," "I was distracted," or "I couldn't understand the instructions," are common examples. People use excuses to explain why they should not be blamed for the unwanted outcomes of actions or decisions. When analyzing a person's arguments and explanations, we can often (but not always) code excuses as something the person believes to be true. Another human behavior which relies on the fundamental social convention of giving reasons is known as "changing the story." This behavior also involves argument making and reason giving. Changing the story may be motivated by the need to seek approval, or for other motives, and can be observed when people offer new, more palatable, reasons for their past decision when the original reasons have been found wanting. A third situation is intentional deception. There

---

[‡‡‡] Unless an individual is purposefully being disingenuous the difference between "having reasons" and "giving reasons" often comes down to the practical matter of taking the time to put ones thinking into words. How? By trying to answer in a forthright way questions like "Why did I do that?" or "Why do I believe that?" But there are caveats worth noting: There is always the possibility that the person could be mistaken about his or her own reasons either though a lack of self-understanding or, worse, through self-deception. With groups of people making decisions, the difference between "having a reason" and "giving a reason" can be more complex. Some of the reasons individual member of the group may have for supporting the group's final decision may not be among the group's reasons. In fact, one can imagine a case where a group would have made a different decision if it had known the concealed reasons one or more of its members had for supporting what was being decided. The group, when it articulates its consensus view, will offer its reasons. And, again, some members of the group, including those who endorse that final decision, may not accept all of those reasons. For the moment, however, we shall focus on individuals and on paradigm cases of truthful and forthright reason giving.

are times when people give reasons which are not their true reasons, wishing instead to conceal these from the listener. The motivations for deception range from the beneficent to the malevolent, from innocent to sinister.

In scientific investigations of every kind there are potential threats to the validity of the data being gathered, and A&H Analysis is not an exception. To understand human decisions A&H Analysis gathers data from human beings who are willing to share their reasons for their decisions. To maximize the potential for forthrightness, the investigator must maintain objectivity, being a patient, non-threatening and non-judgmental listener who is not a stakeholder in the outcome of the decision being examined. We will describe these techniques in detail in Chapter 3. However, if there is good reason to believe that one or more of the subjects provided unreliable information, the investigator should exclude those data from the analysis just as scientists working in other empirical domains would exclude unreliable data from their research. At times an investigator may be analyzing an argument or a decision process for the specific reason of determining whether the decision maker is being forthright. Using A&H Analysis does not reliably identify deception, however the mapping of the argument or decision process as well as the chronology of the reason-giving may provide the investigator additional insight into this determination.

Argument, Claim, Reason, Datum, Warrant and Argument Strand

The A&H Method starts by capturing human decision making at the level which most reflects how persons would describe their own reasoning. That is, A&H Analysis focuses on the decision maker's principle claim and his or her reasons for making the claim. It will be helpful to use certain words with a modest level of precision, but not in ways that are fundamentally inconsistent with their ordinary usages.

The word **_argument_** will be used to refer to the reason-claim combination.[25,26] If a person makes a claim and others inquire as to why the person feels justified in holding that view, the person in response can offer his or her reason or reasons. We shall consider each reason-claim combination as one argument. If the person offers three independent reasons for the same claim, then the person shall be said to have made three arguments. For example, "I decided to have the foot I injured playing basketball last Saturday checked in the emergency room because I was worried when the swelling didn't go down, because my wife told me to have it checked, and because if I broke my ankle the emergency room doctors could put a cast on it."

A&H Analysis is not about reforming how people express or explain their reasoning, how they use arguments in their reasoning or in their rhetoric, or how they present or reflect their points of view. Rather, A&H Analysis is an effort to interpret these processes as accurately as possible. Hence, the critical element in identifying a person's arguments is the interpretation of the speaker's intentions in a given context.

Consider this example: A parent tells her child, "Our airplane to Chicago tomorrow will likely be delayed." The child asks "Why?" meaning by that to inquire about the parent's reason for making that predictive claim. The parent explains by stating her reason, "The weather forecast calls for heavy rain and fog." This reason-claim combination is the parent's argument. But suppose that the child does not see the connection and asks what the bad weather has to do with things. The parent could amplify her reason by saying, "When it's rainy and foggy the people in charge of the airport do not allow the airplanes to take off." In this case the parent's reason now contains two statements which together form one reason, and, thus, according to our terminology, the parent is still making one argument. However, the argument is now more fully articulated because of the parent's desire to explain herself more fully to the child.

Typically a person's ***claim***, as we are using the term, is a statement by which the person asserts the judgment that something should be believed or should be done. The ***reason***, as we are using the term, is the basis the person has for believing that the claim is true. Since often a reason references a specific observation or fact the argument maker believes to be true, it will become convenient to refer to that observation or fact as a ***datum***. Often a more fulsomely presented reason includes a generalization which the argument maker relies upon to authorize the inference from the datum to the claim. We shall call that generalization a ***warrant***. In the example above the generalization, "When it's rainy and foggy the people in charge of the airport do not allow the airplanes to take off," is the warrant. The warrant, together with the datum, "The weather forecast calls for heavy rain and fog," form the parent's reason for her claim that, "Our airplane to Chicago tomorrow will likely be delayed."[§§§]

[§§§] The terms "argument," "datum," "claim," "reason," and "warrant," as defined here readily connect with the words like "premise," and "conclusion," as these terms are used in traditional approaches to logic and logical analysis. A "reason," as we are using the word, is simply the set of beliefs, spoken or unspoken, which form the basis in the mind of the person making the argument

In almost all cases the data a speaker explicitly presents will not express everything that the speaker believes to be relevant to establishing the claim. Human argument making, like other human behaviors, is engaged in only to the extent that the speaker believes it is minimally necessary to achieve her or his purpose. In the case of argument making, the purpose is explaining. And when the speaker believes that the explanation is sufficient, he or she typically will end the process. Unless acceding to a request for clarification or further explanation, argument makers generally do not present more than is needed to make their claims. Much that could be said is left unspoken in most human decision making and explanation giving situations; it is presumed culturally and contextually. The time, trouble, and conscious effort saved by not having always to make every relevant statement explicit represents a tremendous conservation of cognitive resources for both the argument maker(s) and those whom they are addressing.

Often people support their claims with more than one reason. In fact, it is not uncommon to hear people give two or three independent reasons for a claim that they believe strongly or for claims they think others may doubt. People use expressions like "There are lots of reasons why I decided such-and-such," with the presumption that each reason independently offers additional impetus to the person's having decided as they did.

Suppose, for example, a parent argues, "I think we should talk to the kids about the possibility that you could be laid off. They're old enough to appreciate that we all are going to have to be careful about our family finances. And it's time they learned that the world of work can be quite brutal." Figure 7, below, illustrates how this speaker uses two reasons to argue in support the claim being made.

---

for drawing the inference that a given claim is true. That claim in the terminology of the discipline of logic is known as a "conclusion." Those beliefs, implicit or explicit, which comprise the reason for that claim, are known in the terminology of traditional logic as "premises."

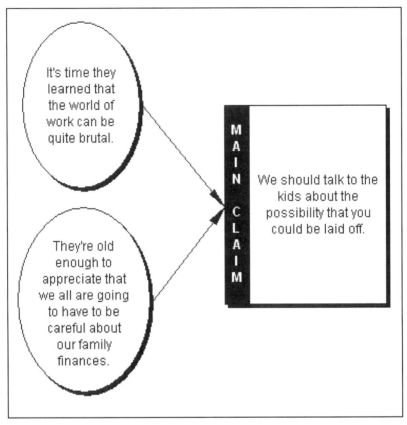

FIGURE 7: "WE SHOULD TELL THE KIDS"

Simple arguments like the two reason-claim combinations represented in Figure 7 are not uncommon. But equally common is human argument making which relies on linked reasoning where each claim is a step along the way to a further claim. Figure 8, below, illustrates how a speaker explained falling stock prices using linked reasoning. From an initial starting point the speaker's reasoning progresses through two intermediate claims to reach the main claim. For convenience we refer to a linked set of reasons and claims, such as shown in Figure 8, as an ***argument strand***.

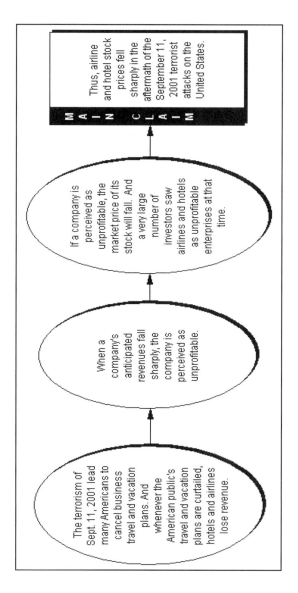

FIGURE 8: WHY THE STOCK PRICES FELL

Patterns like those illustrated in Figure 7 and Figure 8 are frequently combined to show the reasoning of a speaker who is relying on multiple independent argument strands to support his or her final conclusion. Figure 9 below illustrates this. The speaker uses three argument strands to support the main claim that late November 2001 was a good time to purchase stock in airline and hotel companies. The first strand is based on the idea that airline and hotel revenues were increasing at that time. The second on the belief that these were fundamentally sound businesses. And the third on the idea that their stock price at that time was undervalued, which turned out to be true given the all time highs the market reached a few years later. If asked to present his or her reason for believing "Most airline and hotel stocks lost 60% of their value in the sixty days following September 11, 2001," the speaker might cite the argument strand expressed in Figure 8.

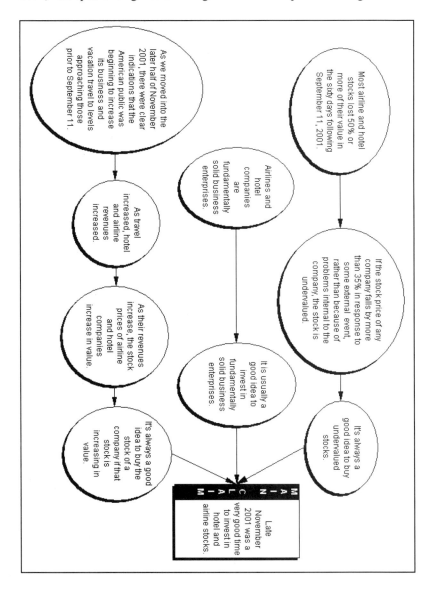

FIGURE 9: NOVEMBER 2001 WAS A GOOD TIME TO BUY

The A&H Method maps the argument strands which comprise a person's reasons for reaching a given decision or conclusion. In the next two chapters, we present the analytical steps in the A&H Method which culminate in the conventions and techniques for A&H decision and argument mapping.

Chapter 3:
Capturing Complex Decision Data

A potentially superior source of data for A&H Analysis is the non-judgmental, in-depth interview. Designing the interview guide which the interviewer will be following in order to externalize the interviewee's decision process is the first necessary step to collecting data that captures a decision process. Carrying out the interview with skill, tolerance, clarification of ambiguity and thoughtful probing completes the process. This chapter begins by describing the Think Aloud technique for conducting such an interview. Those research questions for which this technique is most useful are then presented. In addition to interviews, another source of data is textual material. This chapter concludes with a discussion of the use of documentary materials to study decision processes.

The Think Aloud Interviewing Technique

The Think Aloud technique builds on the usual guidelines which describe a good in-depth interviewing process. A setting well suited to collecting verbal data, tape recording the interview, and establishing trust are key points. The Think Aloud interview technique has been well described by Svenson,[27] although she referred to it as a "Talk Aloud" interview. McCracken[28,] and Michler[29] also discuss this technique in detail.

When the focus of the interview is on decision process, it is important that the subject be oriented to the type of questioning that will occur in the Think Aloud interview, as this experience will be somewhat different than any previous interview process that she or he may have encountered. It will help to provide the subject with the term "Think Aloud" as you explain that you will be asking them to talk with you about a number of topics (those in your interview guide). Depending on your research design, you may want to the interviewee them that you will be asking him or her to think aloud about a particular decision or action that they have taken or is about to take.

To capture the thinking involved in a decision process most *ideally*:

- The interview questions invite an actual decision process, or a revisiting of the decision process (these are my reasons for deciding to do or not to do this) or evaluation process (these are my reasons for what I think about this issue).

- The respondent is made as comfortable as possible about sharing their thinking details. No idea is beyond expression. No conclusion too unimportant, too dangerous, or too embarrassing to voice.

- The goal is to obtain evidence of as many considerations contemplated by the decision maker as possible.

- The interviewer strives throughout not to influence the thinking process, or to be as minimal an influence as possible on the thinking process.

- The interviewer begins by asking the subject to speak about the first topic in the topic list. One good opening question format is: "I am interested in your views on (first topic). Can you begin by telling me something about that?"

- Possible frames:
    "Did you say (repeat a phrase)?" Clarify or confirm a claim.
    "Can you say more about that?" Encourage further development of a stated idea.
    "Why do you think this is so?" Elicit more reasons for a stated claim.

- Follow-up questions should invite reflection on how and why the decision or the evaluation is being made.

- The interviewer must not evaluate, critique, or ever appear to pass judgment on the responses of the interviewee.

- Use caution not to interrupt a subject in the middle of a narrative account of a past decision process (See section below: Elicit Memories: Narratives). While the relevance of the narrative may not be immediately apparent, it may have critical importance to the analysis.

- Accurate descriptions of a judgment process include more than a few reasons and a conclusion. The interviewer should note observed evidence of unspoken thoughts and feelings used to arrive at the judgment. These might be revealed as pauses and unfinished sentences, or as emotions expressed and ideas conveyed by face and body movement, as well as statements implicit in the voiced data. Pauses when relating one's reasons for a decision may indicate that the speaker is self-censoring or "filtering."

Some would argue philosophically that the very act of inviting the interviewee to revisit the decision making will, of necessity, influence or affect the person's decision, and, therefore, one can never be certain that one is gathering valid data. Like Heisenberg's Uncertainty Principle, a decision is something that is influenced simply by being observed, they would maintain. In response we propose four considerations. (a) There are many examples of interviewees who maintain that they are truthfully and accurately describing their decisions without changing them. Thus the *a priori* philosophical concern must also entail that these persons are mistaken about themselves and their knowledge of their own decisions. We find that unlikely as a universal proposition about all interviewees in all times and places. (b) Even if we were to agree that there may be some nuances lost in the recounting, the decision reported remains the same in all essential respects, including the main reasons considered pro and con; or, (c) that while one might hypothesize that talking about a decision necessarily affects that decision, that hypothesis has not been established empirically; or, (d) were it true that talking about a decision might affect it in some important way, that specific concern needs to be addressed in each data gathering instance separately as would any other threat to validity in the research design.

Usually the questions on the investigator's interview guide are presented for review by the institutional review board that oversees the ethics of research involving human subjects. In order to characterize correctly a Think Aloud interview for institutional review board review, we recommend listing the topic areas of the interview concerning which the subject will be probed for comment, and including a short paragraph (or the bullet list above) to indicate the likely questioning format. See the example, Figure 10, below.

Think-Aloud Interview Topic: To Separate or Divorce

Subject will be asked to talk a bit about each of the following areas:

Perceived flaws in the relationship

Physical attraction – Change?

Trials to mend the relationship

Meaning of a failed relationship

Anger issues

Other confidants

Financial issues

Children?

Perceived causes for the relationship problems

Feared consequences? Violence?

Timetable for the decision

The subject will be asked to discuss each of these areas using very broad opening questions.

Follow-up questions will focus on elaborating, clarifying, and expanding the description of what is being considered in the judgment process in accordance with the following considerations: [Insert here, for example, the bullet points listed in the body of the text above.]

FIGURE 10: EXAMPLE "THINK ALOUD" INTERVIEW TOPIC GUIDE

In common discourse, people are not often asked to explain exhaustively their thinking aloud. More often they are asked "Why?" only once, and they provide only one or two thoughts. If there is follow up, it may be to argue the point or to evaluate the person's thinking in some way; or the conversation may simply move on. So the experience of being invited to explain fully one's reasons to another person who will listen attentively without judging is not a common one. To avoid appearing inattentive, impatient, intolerant, or making any other negative impression on the subject, the interviewer should prepare the subject for the experience of being invited to keep talking about their decision longer than usual. For instance, the interviewer might prepare the subject for this in-depth Think Aloud interview by saying, "I'll be asking you to say more about some ideas you have. I might say something like this, 'What else did you think about?' It won't mean that I thought your first answer was wrong. I'll just want you to tell me as much as you can about what you're explaining to me."

Beginning the interview itself

Most interviews which inquire about a decision that is still in process, that is, where a culminating event has not yet occurred or an irrevocable action has not yet been taken, will begin by inviting the subject to talk about how the decision was initially made and then talk about his or her current, real-time thinking regarding the decision. But, as in the case of many interview approaches, asking one or two preliminary questions to orient the subject to the topic of interest and to establish some level of trust remains an excellent way to begin. It is usually a good idea to be direct with the subject, explaining that what is of interest is their *thinking process* about the topic. For example, if the topic is a decision to change jobs, one might say, "As you know, this is a study of career decisions that people make, and I am most interested in how you decided to leave your job at the bank and go to work in the automobile industry."

Elicit memories: Narratives

People often store prior decision processes as episodic memories that can be accessed and verbalized as narratives. Narratives are stories people tell one another to explain *what happened* and *why it happened.* Episodic memories translated to narratives are subjective accounts of events, and that is exactly what we require when inviting people to tell about decisions made in contexts of uncertainty and risk. Narratives tend to be most vivid when the remembered event entailed a conflict or was an occasion where life events deviated in some way from the storyteller's perceived ideal or expectations.[30,31,32]

Not everything in a Think Aloud interview is a narrative. But narratives are common and we find that they tend to come early in the interview. This is particularly true when the topic of the interview is an account of a high stakes decision that was made in the past.

Narratives typically tell a story that begins with an introduction and includes a cast of characters and a setting. The introduction always sketches the key players in the story and orients the interviewer as to time and place. A narrative often contains a dramatic complication and its resolution. In a decision narrative, the complicating event of concern to A&H Analysis is the mental push and pull associated with the decision itself.

It is in the telling of the complication and the resolution that we expect to find the most central data explaining the decision process. For this reason, it is often preferable to ask the subject to tell you about a particular event by beginning anywhere they might wish to begin, rather than by asking them specific questions. Beginning by asking, "Tell me the story about how you came to buy your new car," will usually provide an interviewer with a richer domain of data than the more specific question, "Why did you buy a Lexus?" While both questions may elicit the same narrative from an excellent subject, the first question is more likely to assist a respondent to recall the situation surrounding the decision, and the thoughts, emotions, and other people who may have influenced their decision. The second question might be responded to with only a curt, "The styling."

Consider, for example, the decision to take a new job. The interviewer might invite a narrative by asking, "Tell me the story about how you decided to take a new job." The subject's narrative about this decision will probably begin by talking about a time before the new job was a central focus, perhaps even with considerations about the past job. It will likely continue until we are told what led them to think about seeking a new job, how they found out about the new job opportunity, why they thought it might or might not be a good idea, and eventually why they decided to take the job and how they see themselves dealing with whatever downsides that might have first concerned them. But if the subject stops prior to the resolution or speaks minimally in this "why and why not" part of the narrative, it is the job of the interviewer to ask a question that encourages the telling of the remaining part of the story. The question should be inviting rather than critical, argumentative, or evaluative, lest the speaker abandon the story, become defensive, or withhold relating all of their thinking – pro and con – about the decision in question.

Narratives reflect past personal experiences and the way in which the individual interprets and internalizes the meaning of those experiences. It is for this reason that they are so valuable when they are offered as part of the subject's response in a think aloud interview. They include an individual's attributions and the meaning they make of events and issues, information that is fundamental to understanding the reasoning that supports their motivation toward initiating and sustaining behaviors.

It is important to allow the subject to tell you the complete decision story without interruption, because the subject is verbalizing a stored account and may skip, forget, or omit portions of their mental record if the accounting is interrupted. There is usually a chronological orientation to a narrative account, so that the interviewer can know when the narrative has finished. Some highly embellished narratives include a coda that brings the narrator and the interviewer back to the present and that indicates a readiness to move to the next topic of discussion.[33,34,35] For example, a subject may conclude the job Think Aloud by saying something like, "So, that's how I came to be working here today."

After the complete story has been told for the first time, the interviewer can return to each aspect of the story for additional explanation and clarification. The subject may tell some aspects of the story again spontaneously later in the interview, particularly if they sense that they have left out something important. All of this is in the interest of the interviewer as well. All spontaneous narrative is free of contamination by the interviewer. While a story is going on, the interviewer's job is to examine the narrative for the decision process and structure follow-up questions about the decision process that were not already anticipated in the interview guide.

In the course of recounting the decision process, it is typical for the subject to re-make the decision as a function of explaining it to the interviewer. The subject may muse about what is known and not known, displaying his or her uncertainty about potential key facts relevant to the decision. The subject may state what she or he believes is normative or express a guess about what others would want her or him to decide or do.

Strive to remain neutral

Asking a person why he or she made certain decisions or holds certain beliefs is unlikely to elicit much of a response if the question appears judgmental or even subtly hostile. A pointed question from the interviewer that is perceived as criticizing the wisdom of a subject's stated opinion or judgment will often cause the subject to withhold information or even to alter his or her thinking to conform with that of the interviewer. At a minimum, the subject may feel the need to abandon his or her own considerations to defend ideas in the face of the interviewer's critique.

The use of silence

An in-depth interview that successfully achieves the Think Aloud objective might result in the subject becoming lost in his or her thoughts and at times unaware of the interviewer. Describing a decision process to one's self or to another person involves "meta-analysis" within the subject. That is, the subject is thinking about his or her own thinking and perhaps also evaluating the quality of that thinking. The adept interviewer will anticipate this occurrence and have the ability to remain unobtrusive for some moments of silence to allow the thinker to carry out this meta-analysis. This evidence of introspection should be regarded as valuable. After some time, the interviewer should then ask the subject to say something about the thoughts they were just having during the period of silence.

Silence can be difficult for the interviewer to endure. One technique to pace the time allowed to the subject is to count seconds silently, not by glancing at a watch. Do not be surprised if a silence lasts for 15 to 20 seconds if the subject is pondering an issue. Newell's research documents this to be the timeframe needed to consider a novel or complicated point.[36] As indicated in the discussion below about data analysis, these silent periods and the comments made by the subject immediately afterward a silent period are often of particular importance to the analysis.

Dealing with social desirability response bias

Both immediately after a period of silence or after a shorter hesitation or pause, the subject may provide a filtered response to the interviewer regarding his or her thinking process. Filtering is a cognitive process which occurs when a speaker says only part of what they had been thinking, withholding other content as a result of social consciousness about how their thoughts will be received by others. At times filtering even results in the subject's speaking a falsehood. More often filtering simply moderates the account of the thinking process to make it more socially acceptable.

Changing one's response because of a concern about how one's thoughts might be judged (social desirability response bias) is a familiar threat to the validity of research data. The researcher must consider whether the influence of social desirability response bias on the analysis is a factor that will require control. If so, adding a measurement scale, such as one of the short forms of the Marlowe Crowne[37,38] to an instrument packet to be completed by one's potential subjects for in-depth interview, will aid the researcher in detecting and estimating the influence of that potential source of bias.

Certainly narratives replete with social desirability response bias can be analyzed using the A&H Method, but if one has such a measure, one might use it to eliminate subjects from the interview portion of a study that requires more candid accounts. But unless one was interested in studying social desirability response bias, there might be little value to an interview with a subject who says only what he or she believes the interviewer wants to hear. What would be the value of a false argument map?

So, what to do if, during the interview itself, the interviewer begins to suspect that the subject may have a high social desirability response bias? There may well be nothing that can reset a given interview, but in some cases reiterating to the subject that their true thoughts are valuable to the research study does elicit more candor. This is a delicate moment in the interview, and this comment by the investigator must be made artfully. But, if done so, there is a high likelihood that the subject will return to the topic and nuance their first response in a way that is more internally consistent with other comments that they have made on the topic. Another tactic is to wait until the narrative section of an interview is completed and then, toward the end of the process, to ask cautiously that the subject say more by way of clarifying earlier ambiguities, vague generalizations, apparent exaggerations, and the like. This often results in the subject becoming more candid about his or her real perspectives on the issue.

At times it helps to acknowledge the subject's desire to be perceived as acting appropriately even as one seeks the clarification which would give the more accurate picture. Here is an actual example from a study of non-compliance in health care utilization. In this case the person was asked a specific question: "How often do you see your physician?" The subject's response is replete with apparent social desirability response bias. Sensing this, the interviewer uses the tactics described above to elicit a more candid response of the subject's actual argument:

> Subject: "And of course I see my doctor annually because those are the guidelines and I always listen to those guidelines. You know....I always do. I always know how important it is to take care of myself."

Interviewer: "I appreciate your talking to me about this. And I hear that you care about your health. And I can think of lots of reasons why someone may not always follow the guidelines."

Subject: (said without a pause): "Yeah, that's right. That's me too. Sometimes I just let it go because I have other stuff that's more important. Or I don't want to think about spending the money. I don't like my doctor much, and I don't think she cares whether I come in to see her or not."

In this case the interviewer simply went on with the interview, realizing but not commenting on the inconsistency of the responses regarding whether the subject usually followed guidelines, and then, some moments later, the interviewer asked, "Can you tell me a bit more about your last visit to your doctor?"

Forming Research Questions Appropriate to A&H Analysis

The A&H Method is best applied to the analysis of human judgments regarding matters considered to be of consequence to the individual or to the group making those judgments. To appreciate exactly where A&H Analysis might be the data analysis method of choice, consider a list of possible research questions with regard to cigarette smoking:

1) What proportion of Americans smoke?

2) Is this proportion increasing or decreasing?

3) Is smoking bad for your health?

4) What are the health risks of smoking?

5) Would you support an additional tax on cigarettes?

6) Are you trying to stop smoking?

7) Do you intend to join a smoking cessation program sometime soon?

Questions 1 and 2 are epidemiological questions one would answer by collecting frequency data over time about who smokes and who does not. The A&H Method does not apply here. Questions 3 through 5 might be asked of smokers and non-smokers as a way to assess attitudes about cigarette smoking or knowledge of the potential health consequences of cigarette smoking. One might ask a number of questions like these on a structured survey. And learning the answers to these questions would be important, but the analysis of responses to these questions would not require an A&H Analysis.

Questions 6 and 7 enter the domain of predicting individual behavior. Questions like number 6 and 7 would engender a scientific investigation grounded in theories like Prochaska's Transtheoretical Model,[39] Triandis' behavioral model of subjective culture,[40] or Ajzen and Fishbein's Theory of Reasoned Action.[41] Researchers might ask questions like 6 and 7 to study how the intention to quit smoking comes about, or to study the effectiveness of a smoking cessation program that is based on readiness to quit smoking or that is based on the formed intention to stop smoking. There have been lots of valuable studies about cigarette smoking that take this approach. It is possible that a subject might offer an account of a decision process in response to these questions, but it is not likely to require the A&H Approach.

But the investigator could choose to ask questions 6 and 7 this way:

> 6a) What are your reasons for deciding to try [or not to try] to stop smoking?

> 7a) Why did you decide to begin [or not to begin] a smoking cessation program sometime soon?

Reframed in these ways, the questions ask the individual specifically to identify ideas that they had which served as reasons for their deciding to take action (or not to take action) to stop smoking. The A&H Method could be used for questions like 6a and 7a. Another approach would be to supply the subjects with a list of possible reasons and invite the subject to identify those that applied in his or her case. Studies relying on questionnaires of this kind have generated useful results. However, supplying the subject with a checklist of possible reasons will not yield the person's reasons as they might have been supplied spontaneously in their own words. And the checklist will not provide much insight regarding the alternative considerations which influence the final judgment. To learn this, the investigator needs an in-depth interview, one which maximally captures as much of the subject's thinking process as possible.

An investigator seeking the richest decision relevant data for analysis could ask:

6b) How did you make the decision to try [or not to try] to quit smoking?

6c) Talk a bit about your decision to try [or not to try] to quit smoking.

7b) What was your thinking about beginning a smoking cessation program sometime soon?

7c) Would you think out loud a bit about the idea of beginning a smoking cessation program sometime soon?

Patiently, respectfully and non-judgmentally asking "Why?" can often evoke an authentic reason giving response. For example:

8) Why did you start smoking again?

9) Why did you begin smoking in the first place?

10) Why do you continue to smoke?

In-depth interviews which fully elicit the answers to any of these questions would provide excellent data for A&H Analysis. Using the A&H Method gets to the heart of the judgment process and provides insights as to the System-1 and System-2 factors that the decision maker is relying upon to become confident in the decision itself.

Other Data Sources for A&H Analysis

Public Documents and Historical Material

The A&H Method is useful for the analysis of private and public documents which record key decisions, if the documents go beyond simply recording the end product of the decision process to include a description of the actual reasons for the decision. This is not always the case. Some documents record the judgments a group or an individual has made but exclude some or all of the reasons, either pro or con, which were considered significant in coming to that decision. Others record only the decision and such particulars as when, where, and by whom the decision was made. At times documents include the formal procedures which were followed by the individual or the group in coming to its decision, but not the thinking process itself. Instead these documents indicate, for example, that fact-finding hearings were held, that various stakeholder groups were invited to have input, that draft recommendations were then formulated and made public, that opportunities were provided for additional comment or input on those recommendations, that there was a discussion by a relevant committee or advisory panel, and that after all of that a decision was made a duly authorized individual or group. But none of this formal procedural information describes the thinking process itself. The A&H Method would not be applicable in such cases because the reasoning is missing.

If President Abraham Lincoln had recorded his thinking with regard to whether or not to issue the Emancipation Proclamation, then one could apply the A&H Method to those records. They might take the form of personal notes, public speeches, memoirs, letters, or secondary sources such as the notes or memoirs of someone in whom Lincoln confided his reasons.

Speeches and public documents written specifically to explain one's thinking can be a rich source of data for A&H Analysis. The statement California's Governor Arnold Schwarzenegger issued in 2006, on the eve of the execution of Stanley Williams, is one such document. In his denial of clemency for Mr. Williams, at a time of high public interest given the circumstances surrounding Mr. Williams' case, Governor Schwarzenegger posted his statement publicly for the people of California to read. This public account is reproduced in Appendix A. An analysis of the account is included in Chapter 8.

A decision analysis based solely on published text may contain limitations: considerations deemed too sensitive to be shared might be withheld, additional bolstering considerations may be added, key issues or fundamental questions might be sidestepped, and elements intended to make the document more persuasive than descriptive might be added. In addition, heuristic thinking is less apparent than explicit argument making. Thus, when reporting or publishing the analysis as an account of the judgment process, the source of the data should be cited and the potential limitations associated with the source of the data duly noted.

In the case of historical documents where the writer/orator may not have been expecting to provide a complete description of an important historical decision or may not have been attempting to justify a decision, there will be other potential limitations to consider. These will be a function of the completeness of the evidence of the decision process contained in the available documents. These limitations could be overcome if the decision maker were willing and able to respond to additional questioning. Again, as with all good research, the analyst has the responsibility to discuss the limitations of the analysis and report on the source of the decision data.

Gathering Group Decision Making Data

The basic Think Aloud technique, with the appropriate A&H Method question frames to elicit information about the thinking process, can be applied to the gathering of data about a group's decision making. The cautions mentioned above, such as not appearing to be judgmental and controlling for social desirability response bias, are relevant in the case of gathering and analyzing group decision data. There are numerous accounts of focus group interview technique. One reliable standard is Kreuger,[42] with examples focusing on marketing. Another fine discussion is Gibbs.[43]

While focus groups are most often used to gather data about opinions, attitudes, satisfaction, preferences, or potential participation in planned services or events, they have, in some cases, been used to collect community attitudes and narratives. For an example, we point you to our paper on breast health behavior and decisions to seek care for breast symptoms.[44] While this paper does not report an A&H Analysis of the focus group data, it does demonstrate how one might obtain the interview to elicit data that could be analyzed using the A&H Method.

One additional precaution, however, must be noted. Although a focus group participant may share a personal narrative during a group discussion, for the most part, data collected in a group session context should be treated as the thinking *of the group*. It would be a mistake to attribute that thinking to each member of the group. The opinions, choices, and reasons of the group may or may not be the opinions, choices, or reasons of its members. Group decision data is best collected and used to study the thinking process of groups, *not of the individuals who are the members of the group.* And, since so many important decisions which affect either themselves as a collective or others outside the group are, in fact, made by groups, the application of the A&H Method to these data can reveal the influences of heuristic thinking and argument making as factors influencing the outcome of group decision making.

Chapter 4:
Data Management and Decision Mapping

This chapter continues the methodological discussion in two parts: first, how to organize and code the decision data, and second how to array those data for visual inspection in a "Decision Map." Decision mapping conventions communicate the content and the relationships of the ideas the decision maker considered in coming to a judgment about what to believe or what to do. We will use an extended case example to illustrate decision mapping conventions. We begin this chapter with the management of the decision data gathered using the approaches presented in the previous chapter.

Describing the Decision Makers

As with all analyses of interview data, the demographic statistics of the sample should be tracked for the eventual report of the study or research project. The investigator using the A&H Method will be reporting analyses of the thinking process of the individuals or groups who provided the in-depth Think Aloud or documentary data. A clear description of the sample assists others to determine whether others might also share similar thinking patterns. We would predict more variance in the reasoning of individuals within each demographic category than might be described by the group membership itself. Even when people agree on the final judgment, they may have come to that conclusion with very different reasons in mind. Not only might their interests be divergent or the responsiveness to the influences of various cognitive heuristics be different, but their reasoning skills can be quite varied as well. Our research in critical thinking skills and habits of mind indicates that there can often be great variance in the reasoning abilities of the members of groups which, on other demographic variables, such as education, might appear rather homogenous.[45] Decision maps and A&H Analysis techniques bring these variations to light and thus enable investigators to analyze and to evaluate their impacts on human decision making.[46,47]

Preparing Data for Analysis

The recorded in-depth Think Aloud interviews are first transcribed into text files.[****] An accurate transcription is of fundamental importance, as the A&H Method of analysis relies heavily on the capture of decision relevant data from auditory to text. Most interviews are conducted in 60-90 minutes, and this typically provides a transcription of 12-20 single spaced pages of data, or about 5,000 -10,000 words.

In our own research to date we have come to think of the familiar notion of an *__idea__*[††††] as providing a fine enough starting point for the initial unit of measurement. In this we are using the word 'idea' in its ordinary meaning. For example, a person may say that he or she has an idea, wants to share an idea, likes or does not like an idea, understands or does not understand another person's idea, or agrees or disagrees with someone else's idea. A precondition for saying any of these things is that the idea in question can be articulated as a meaningful phrase or short sentence, that there is a potentially understandable content to that sentence, and that the content can be evaluated as true or false, wise or unwise. We do not take the "phrase" as the unit of analysis because a purely syntactic approach will fail to capture the full richness of the human reasoning involved in complex decision making. We do not take the "theme" as the unit of analysis because that approach fails to capture the reasoning and the relationships between reasons and the inferences drawn from them. We do, however, take a liberal view with regard to including among the data a wide variety of other communicative elements observed during the interview. These may include gestures, facial expressions, off-hand remarks, pauses, expressions of emotion, body language, etc.

Parsing the Data

We begin, then, by parsing the subject's interview data into its meaningful, and thus analyzable, data-segments, which are the person's own ideas

---

[****] At the time of this publication, commercially available voice-to-text software is not sufficiently reliable, and transcription remains the only option a careful investigator can rely upon, even though it is a time-intensive step in the data management process. Hopefully more accurate, broadly applicable, affordable, and easily used voice-to-text equipment and software will yield improvements in the near future.

[††††] Yes, we are aware of the long and treacherous history of the concept of an "idea" in philosophy and psychology. However, it is a useful starting point, for it has a reasonably well entrenched common sense meaning in ordinary usage. Because we move quickly into argument analysis in the next sections of the A&H methodology, this common, everyday concept of an "idea" is sufficiently durable, in spite of its rugged history, to accomplish the work at hand.

expressed in their own words as phrases or sentences. It will be important to maintain the links between these data phrases in order to maintain the integrity of the person's own arguments as the subject made them. We do that by noting the order in which data phrases occur in the interview and by retaining the clustering of data phrases around a given argument strand as the interviewee spoke them. Here are some practical suggestions for how to do this expeditiously:

- We have found it works quite well to import the entire electronic file of the transcribed interview into our favorite word processing program.[‡‡‡‡]

- We recommend the analyst then review the transcription while listening to the taped interview, recording any missed pauses or other verbalizations, as well as making any needed corrections in the transcript for completeness and accuracy.

- After activating the software's automatic line numbering function, we read through the interview text using the "enter" key to break out each idea as a separate data segment. Other communicative elements, like pauses, are also broken out, as will be seen in the examples below. The line numbering function gives each data-segment its own reference number and maintains the order of the data segments for later analysis.

- If we decide that we need to revise the coding of the data segments – either by dividing a more complex one into simpler units or by combining two incomplete ideas – this can be done very quickly and easily using the "enter" or the "back" key and the software will automatically renumber each data segment from that point to the end of the transcript, thus maintaining the chronology of the interview.

- When we judge that we have made a good first pass at demarcating the data segments with sufficient accuracy to move on to other steps in the analysis, we turn off the automatic line numbering function. This stops the

---

[‡‡‡‡] Researchers who have previously analyzed text data have preferences as to the choice of data analysis software packages to use. None are yet designed to offer menu driven A&H analysis, but these packages do offer considerable assistance in data management. If you are new to text data analysis, and do not have skills with these data management software programs, you will find that most word processing programs offer all the functions that are needed to carry out the demarcation of text data that we describe here.

renumbering and prevents inadvertent shifting of the chronology as we manipulate the data for other purposes.

- One can always turn the line numbering function back on in order to revise and improve the demarcation of data segments to capture the speaker's thinking as accurately as possible. This is not an infrequent occurrence, as it often happens that a segment which initially was seen as one idea turns out actually to have been intended by the speaker to be interpreted as two ideas.

Once the data has been parsed and you are ready to begin analyzing and mapping the argument, it is advisable to archive a permanent record file of the parsed data so nothing will be lost in the analysis. Working from a copy of this electronic file as you carry out the analysis will allow you to export segments of the data directly to analysis tables for comment. Similarly, an electronic file can be used to copy and paste segments of data into decision map software to create figures summarizing the decision process. We have also found it's helpful to search the electronic copy using the word find function of your software program as you complete the analysis. At the same time the printed copy provides a quick reference when one wishes to check an analysis by revisiting the full transcript of the interview.

Let us consider two examples to illustrate the data parsing phase of A&H Analysis. First, recall the kidney donation example in Chapter 1. Here is an example of parsing some of the data from the interview with our subject kidney donor, to whom we gave the name Howard. These were the first words Howard actually spoke in the interview:

Howard: "Um, well, I found that, um, I saw a very dear friend of mine in trouble and, um, I didn't like the uh, the uh, prospects for him if he didn't get a live donor. I didn't like the idea of him being on dialysis or waiting for a kidney for several years. And I love him and I love his wife and his baby daughter. And I felt that I've got two kidneys, I don't need both and it was an, it was a decision that I made in about sixty seconds or so. Yeah. ... So, as soon as I found out from him, ... He said, "And it looks like I'm going to need a transplant," I thought about it for maybe sixty seconds and said, "Well count me in as a possible donor if you want to have a test done on me."

FIGURE 11: HOWARD'S RESPONSE TO A FRIEND IN NEED

---

1). "Um …

2). well …

3). I found that …

4). um …

5). I saw a very dear friend of mine in trouble and …

6). um …

7). I didn't like the … uh,

8). the uh…

9). prospects for him if he didn't get a live donor.

10). I didn't like the idea of him being on dialysis

11). or waiting for a kidney for several years.

12). And I love him and I love his wife and his baby daughter.

13). And I felt that I've got two kidneys,

14). I don't need both

15). and it was an …

16). it was a decision that I made in about sixty seconds or so.

17). Yeah … (pause)

18). So, as soon as I found out from him, …

19). He said, "And it looks like I'm going to need a transplant,"

20). I thought about it for maybe sixty seconds

21). and said, "Well, count me in as a possible donor if you want to have a test done on me."

FIGURE 12: PARSING OF HOWARD'S RESPONSE

The initial step in A&H Analysis is to demarcate these data and all that comes after, separating and indexing with line numbers each cognitive component of the Think Aloud process. Not every component will necessarily be a complete idea. For example, there are many pauses in Howard's discourse as recorded in Figure 11, in fact one after each of Howard's initial utterances. In Figure 12 these are shown in Lines 1 through 8. This is typical of the beginning of a Think Aloud interview, when the subject is composing his or her account of a decision process which they may either be describing based on their recollection of how the decision was made or which they may still be engaged in making or reinforcing.

Whether the decision is being reaffirmed at the time of the interview or being recalled, it is likely to be remade in the course of the interview. The examples below will provide evidence of this claim, and you can and should remain skeptical about this until you are able to examine your own decision making data.

At this point in the interview, the subject may pass quickly over the reasoning behind the decision, arriving rapidly at a statement about the final judgment he or she has made. Here we can observe a "thumbnail" account of the decision in the first portion of the interview (Lines 5-16). The important thing with this first step is to separate individual cognitive components in the data to make room for the later analysis.

Consider this second example: The transcript in Figure 13, below, is from an interview with a person who was contemplating a job change. The excerpt, a spontaneous account of some of the events which cause this employee frustration at work, occurred about midway in the interview. This is captured below by retaining the sequence of the data from the beginning of the interview.

Speaker: "We can't have the meeting this week. Three managers are out of town until Monday. so they can't make a meeting this week. …. The staff can't have the budget proposals ready in time anyway..... My bet is it will take the staff until next Tuesday to get those to me, and I still don't know what the revenue target for our division is going to be for next year. John said something about getting the info to me this week late, or maybe first thing on Monday. So … let's reschedule the managers' meeting for Wednesday next week."

FIGURE 13: WORKPLACE FRUSTRATION

These data, which are presented in Figure 13 above, occur in phrases positioned from 251 through 261 of the actual interview. It would be reasonable to parse these data in the fashion expressed in Figure 14.

251). We can't have the meeting this week.

252). Three managers are out of town until Monday,

253). so they can't make a meeting this week.

254). … (pause)

255). The staff can't have the budget proposals ready in time anyway

256). … (pause)

257). My bet is it will take the staff until next Tuesday to get those to me,

258). and, I still don't know what the revenue target for our division is going to be for next year.

259). John [the speaker's supervisor] said something about getting the info to me this week late, or maybe first thing on Monday.

260). So … (pause)

261). let's reschedule the managers' meeting for Wednesday next week.

FIGURE 14: PARSING OF THE WORKPLACE FRUSTRATION DATA

Six things about the data presented in Figure 14 should be noted:

- The unit of analysis for capturing the reasoning is the verbalized communication separated into basic ideas which indicate the claims being made and the reasons for them which the speaker gives.

- Although many of the lines are not grammatically complete sentences, each line is meaningful and can be understood and interpreted.

- This example contains a progression of ideas which are reasons the speaker uses in forming the judgment to reschedule the meeting. We can see that the order of the phrases is important. It reflects the unfolding of that reasoning in the mind of the speaker. To conserve this order, there is a running line counter that indexes, displays, and preserves the order of the appearance of each data phrase in the transcribed data (line numbers 251 through 261 in Figure 14).

- Other communicative elements are noted as well, however. These might include a sigh, laugh, groan, facial expression, body movement, laugh, etc... In the case of Figure 14, lines 254, 256, and 260 indicate where the transcription in Figure 13 indicates that the speaker pauses.

- The investigator's clarification – that John is the speaker's supervisor – is added in line 259. The speaker's relationship to John's may have importance in interpreting what the speaker says elsewhere in the interview.

- The speaker's own emphasis is preserved by the investigator, as shown using underlining in line 258. This communicates more than the simple content of the idea, it reveals some of the speaker's frustration with the workplace situation. Different investigators will have different ways of noting for themselves these affective elements in the communication.

There are two decisions in this small piece of data: Decision 1) not to have the meeting this week as scheduled, and 2) to reschedule the meeting for Wednesday of next week. The second decision is, of course, moot if the first decision is not made. In this interview the speaker was thinking about when to reschedule the meeting. He was making the decision as he spoke, rather than recounting for us how he previously made that decision.

Organizing the Data

Having parsed the interview text into data segments – the speaker's ideas – using this technique, the next step is to analyze the data segments in three ways:

1. Intended role or function of each data phrase. (E.g. functioning as the speaker's main claim, or as an intermediate claim, warrant, observational datum/belief/assumption, watershed idea, or counter-argument. Or, multiple phrases that cluster as one theme or argument strand).

2. Intended logical relationship of the phrases. (Viz., indicating which phrases the speaker appears to regard as inferentially following from or as inferentially leading toward which others. The evaluation of the soundness of this reasoning is described in Chapter 5.)

3. Apparent influences of heuristics (Viz. indicating where the speaker's reasoning appears to have been influenced positively or negatively by any of the heuristic maneuvers mentioned in Chapter 1 or 2 and described in detail in Chapter 6.)

If one uses qualitative analysis software, these analyses codes can be attached to the data phrase and the functions of the software used to table data with respect to each of these considerations. If regular word processing software is being used, the process is more cumbersome. However, one can craft a table to record subsequent analyses of each of these data segments. Table 5 is an example of how we record this.

TABLE 5: EXAMPLE LAYOUT OF DATA SEGMENT ANALYTICAL GRID

Name of Research Project Identification Number of Interview Subject OTHER DESCRIPTORS OF THE PROJECT AS NEEDED			
1) This cell is where we would insert the first data phrase, numbered '1' to conserve its chronological order in the interview.	One or more adjacent column(s) are used to code aspects of individual argument strands (role of each phrase as claim or warrant or datum etc., phrases that are part of the same argument strand or theme, or any other key considerations)	One column is always needed to record whether claims are true or false and whether arguments are sound or unsound.	Another is needed to record the speaker's use or misuse of heuristic thinking strategies.
2) Each subsequent data phrase would be analyzed in its own row.			
3) The table would have as many rows as there were data segments	The information in these columns is then collected and presented in a variety of other formats.		
4) Unimportant rows, if any, can be elminated later in the analysis			

The first column of Table 5 contains a data segment in each row, and each column to the right of this box records a part of the analysis. If one were using spreadsheet software, this is the type of listing one could generate, store, retrieve, and amend. To assure accuracy and improve reliability, the analysis resulting from one analyst's work can be compared with a table another independent analyst produces in order to identify, examine, and resolve differences.

Decision Maps

Decision maps[§§§§] illustrate the progression of a person's thinking, revealing how reasons flow into claims, how intermediate claims flow into main conclusions, how some thoughts are powerfully influential and how others are perhaps considered and abandoned. Decision maps are intended to show all the reasoning involved, which includes the influences of cognitive heuristics on both the System-1 and the System-2 elements of the decision maker's reasoning process. Ultimately the test of the quality of a decision map is how well it represents the inferential relationships as that reasoning was carried out by the decision maker. A decision map, therefore, like a geographer's map, is intended to chart all the relevant features of the reasoning terrain, however smooth or rough they may be.

Fundamentally, a ***decision map*** is a graphically arrayed interpretative analysis of what a person intends should be taken as their claims and their reasons for those claims in a given context. The decision map will include those ideas which the decision maker judged to lead toward his or her final judgment as well as some decision other than the one which was made, and how the decision maker dealt with those ideas. Thus a decision map reflects both the pros and the cons as those were conceived of in the mind of the decision maker, leading toward or away from the chosen option.

Decision maps are only as good as the interpretive and analytical skills of the investigators who are drawing them. If the interpreter understands the subtleties of a given situation and the significance of what is being communicated verbally and nonverbally in that situation, then she or he has

---

[§§§§] Some may prefer the term ***argument maps***, however, this nomenclature may lead one to devalue the influences of cognitive heuristics on the outcome of the decision making process. Thus, we prefer "decision maps" for we are seeking to join both argument and heuristic analyses into a unified approach to understanding in a deep and accurate way all the reasoning which goes into making complex decisions and judgments, particularly in contexts of risk and uncertainty.

the potential to draw a fuller and more accurate map. The A&H Method depends on the ability of the analyst to interpret wisely and correctly what is being communicated when a subject relays how she or he came to a given judgment or made a given decision. If they seek to make refined and accurate decision maps, novice map makers are well advised to gain as much experience as possible, under the guidance of a wise mentor, in order to sharpen their listening skills and open their minds to the subtleties of how humans communicate about their reasoning. Collaborative map making often yields superior results for it provides the opportunity for two or more interpreters to compare their understandings of the reasoning being explicated.

What level of analysis is necessary for achieving sufficient accuracy and completeness? As will be evident in working with the complexity of real cases, the answer depends on the purpose we have in mind. Humans give reasons or supply analyses to the level they believe to be sufficient to achieve a given purpose and not further than that. That is, unless, for some reason, the initial analysis turns out to be inadequate or less sophisticated than first appeared to be necessary. Figure 9 in Chapter 2, for example, displays the three strands of reasons which flow toward its main claim. The person making those arguments regarded them as sufficient. But if asked about it, the person could and should be able to explain more of their thinking, for example, by showing why they believe the reasons that initiate each of the argument strands are true. Figure 8 showed how the person might explain, if asked, why he or she thinks that the initial reason for the first argument strand pictured in Figure 9 is true.

Even given a level of sophistication thought to be appropriate to a given purpose, an analysis can still be evaluated as being more or less accurate and more or less complete. The goal of the analytical phase of the A&H Method is to represent as accurately and as objectively as possible the decision maker's reasoning. If the decision maker's reasoning happened to be inadequate or insufficient in some way, revealing that will be a matter for the evaluative steps in the A&H Method, not the analytical steps.

Excavate the Main Claim First, Then Reason Backward

When explaining their thinking, people typically do not list their reasons like mathematical demonstrations or present them in clear, orderly, and systematic ways. Instead people may give a chronology of events, or make comparisons of things that happened to themselves and to other people they know. They may simply describe their experiences as a way of saying why they decided something. Or, they get side tracked or repeat themselves or offer only cryptic, oblique, and incomplete expressions of their reasons. Also, people often do not actually articulate their main claim, but, knowing from the context that the listener already understands what the choice was, they may speak about it without repeating aloud the obvious. At other times, perhaps out of fear or lack of clarity, they may even obscure it.

The analyst is responsible for identifying what the speaker is attempting to communicate. The speaker may use an analogy, or a story, or may be indirect, confused, vague, etc. Consider how ordinary people explain why they are divorced, why they have no car insurance, why their boss is unfair to them, or why their finances are a mess. For example, the main claim might be "My partner never gave me a chance to fix our relationship." "Who can afford car insurance? I sure can't!" "My boss heard me say our company policy on office decorum is bogus." "I like to visit the sports book in Vegas." And yet, the person may never actually say, in so many words, "My main point is: ..." In crafting useful maps to explicate the reasoning behind high stakes decisions, analysts should expect to be challenged to apply all their interpretive skills.

So, as the analyst beginning the examination of the parsed data, it is often very useful to begin by first identifying the speaker's or the writer's main claim. What did they decide, what is the conclusion they are driving at? And then, from there, reason backward with the speaker or the writer noting the argument strands which lead toward that main claim and those which lead toward alternative end points. Once one knows where the speaker went with his or her reasoning, it is easier to see how the speaker got there. The basic conventions of A&H Analysis decision mapping, first illustrated in Chapter 1 and described there in Figure 4, are reprised in expanded form in Table 6.""""

"""" The maps shown in Figures 1, 2, and 3, (Chapter 1) include notations on the lines which connect some of the shapes. These notations represent the investigator's observation regarding the reasoning elements and their relationships. Appendix B discusses the mapping conventions for adding these enhancements.

TABLE 6: A&H MAPPING CONVENTIONS

Conventions for A&H Analysis Decision Maps (and Argument Maps)	
Labeled Rectangle	Main Claim, Main Alternative, Conclusion
Oval	Datum, Warrant, or Intermediate Claim
Two or More Overlapping Ovals	Datum(a) + Warrant
Connecting Lines with Arrow Heads	Direction of the Flow of the Reasoning
Data Segment Line Numbers	Temporal Order of the Speaker's Presentation of Information about the Decision Making Process and Reasoning
Diamond	Watershed Consideration
Large Arrow Containing Text	Counter-argument Pointing Toward the Claim it Supports
Cloud	Non-verbal Reasoning Element
Hexagon	Abandoned Argument Strand
Information in [Brackets] or {Braces}	Analyst's Clarification, Note, or Evaluative Comment

Display Claims, Reasons, Data, Warrants and Argument Strands

Some systems for capturing part of the logical structure of certain limited classes of arguments, like truth tables, Venn diagrams, and syntactically based Symbolic Logic,[48,49] useful as they are for other kinds of analyses, will not be helpful for our purposes. They fail to capture many of the conceptual and interpersonal complexities humans depend upon in reasoning to their decisions. The decision mapping conventions used in A&H Analysis have been developed, refined and adapted specifically for the demands of representing the inferential relationships among the linked and clustered arguments found in complex human decision making.[†††††] As indicated in Chapter 2, Stephen Toulmin proposed many of the initial ideas for this approach to describing human argument making,[50,51] and there have been improvements over the decades.[52,53,54,55,56]

In Chapter 2 we defined the terms "claim," "reason," "argument," "datum," "warrant" and "argument strand." Figure 4, presented in Chapter 1, indicated that we will be using certain shapes to represent specific elements, for example, an oval for a claim, datum, or warrant. With these basics in mind the interpretation of Figure 15 should be readily apparent. It displays three argument strands leading toward a decision. Recall that the frustrated manager quoted in Figure 13 effectively made two decisions. The first was to cancel the meeting scheduled for this week, and the second was to reschedule the meeting for a specific day next week. The speaker articulates the initial decision before explaining the three reasons for it. This decision, once made, along with the speaker's estimation of how long it would take the staff to prepare necessary materials, then leads to the second decision. Figure 15 displays these reasoning relationships using the basic A&H Analysis decision mapping conventions.

Instead of thoughtfully weighing the pros and cons of various alternatives, speakers may present reasons for only one option or argue for only one conclusion. Like Figure 15, a map illustrating that kind of a thinking process need include only the one main claim which is the true singular focus of the speaker. In such cases the analyst's map might well be thought of as an ***argument map***. Figure 15 is an argument map which shows three reasons for the intermediate or preliminary conclusion, "We can't have the meeting this week," and two reasons for the main decision or conclusion, that the meeting should be rescheduled for next Wednesday.

[†††††] The conventions introduced here will work equally well for preparing "argument maps" intended to display the flow of reasons and intermediary claims toward a conclusion which a person may draw from them.

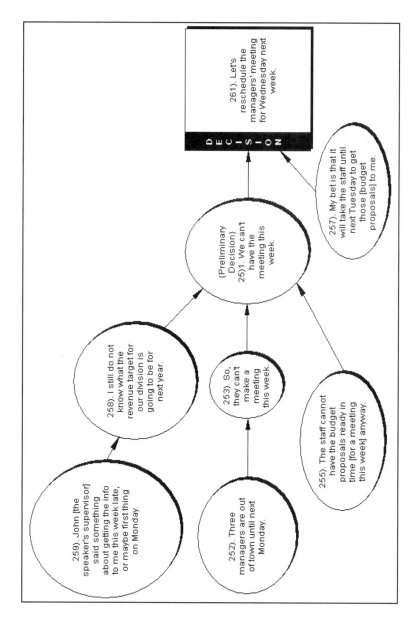

FIGURE 15: "RESCHEDULE THE MEETING FOR NEXT WEDNESDAY" – FIRST PASS

A feature of A&H Analysis is its capacity to reveal the number of different argument strands that lead toward one or another of the decision maker's main options. Not every argument strand will connect directly to a main claim; some will support intermediate claims. Figure 15 illustrates this, with three argument strands flowing into an intermediate claim, rather than connecting directly to the main conclusion.

Revisit to Refine, Clarify and Nuance the Reasoning

Notice that Figure 15 does not account for the pauses evident in the text of Figure 13 and captured by the analyst in the parsing of lines 254, 256, and 260 in Figure 14. There is more to the reasoning than what Figure 15 displays. That is why Figure 15 is labeled a "First Pass." The analyst revisited it and refined it into the map shown in Figure 16.

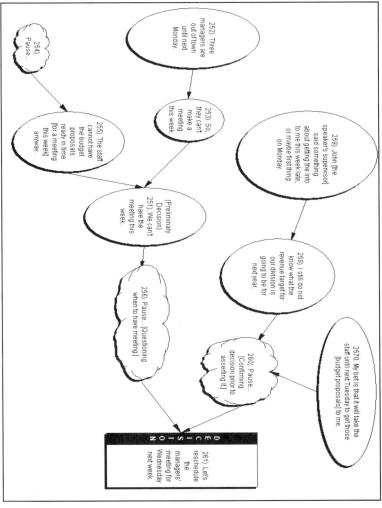

FIGURE 16: "RESCHEDULE MEETING FOR WEDNESDAY" – SECOND PASS

Drawing accurate and complete decision maps is an iterative process. In Figure 16 the analyst offers interpretations of lines 256 and 260 as well. Line 256, a pause coming just after the realization that the staff cannot have the budget proposals ready this week, is interpreted as a moment when the speaker could have been considering when the meeting might reasonably be held. The speaker then answers his own unspoken question by noting in the next line that Tuesday would be the earliest. The third pause, line 260, was interpreted as indicating the moment when the speaker confirmed in his own mind the decision to set the meeting for Wednesday. True, there might be other plausible interpretations of non-verbal elements, such as laughs, pauses, gestures, etc. For example, one could speculate that the pause in line 260 indicated a second of self-doubt, rather than decisiveness. There are a number of ways to resolve interpretive questions: For example, one may review the audio recording, seek more information about the speaker, or look for evidence in other interview segments. Notice that Figure 16, labeled "Second Pass" to show that it is a revision of an earlier map, now depicts the speaker as having two reasons for canceling the meeting this week and two reasons for rescheduling it to Wednesday next week. The analyst's consideration of how best to interpret the speaker's pauses resulted in rethinking the reasoning relationships in the explanatory statements which the speaker did verbalize. We have emphasized that the A&H Method calls for wise and accurate interpretive analyses. There are a number of situations which call on the analyst to make sensible and sophisticated interpretations, and not to be naïvely literal. Below are a few examples.

Irony, Humor, and Sarcasm

When drafting decision maps, it is wise to rephrase irony and sarcasm, switch the statement from the positive that might have been spoken to the negative that was intended, or switch from the negative that might have been spoken to the positive that was intended. For example, in one context "He was wonderfully diplomatic" is meant as sincere praise. It would be a reason in favor of something like, "Let's have him represent our organization." But in another context that same assertion can be intended sarcastically, and so it would imply that we should not even consider having him represent our organization. In this latter case it should be mapped as the person intended, namely as "He was [not at all] wonderfully diplomatic." Witty people often use irony, hyperbole, and humor to make their points. Typically when someone says something like, "The last thing I want is another email address," they are not ranking an email address among the things they want, although that would be the literal truth of what their assertion means. Obviously, an email address would have no place on such a list for that person. Rather, the person is saying, "I do *not* want another email address."

People may offer some vivid and even outlandish comparisons in order to emphasize the strength of their convictions. The analyst's role in decision mapping is to cut through to the reasoning that the argument maker is relying upon and to make that reasoning explicit in the decision map. It may at times be necessary to add interpretative comments to conserve the speaker's meaning. For example, in analyzing "He was a deer in the headlights" or "It was a no-brainer," one might have to clarify by adding the interpretive comments "{He said nothing when he should have spoken up to his boss.}" or "{Without doubt, that was the only possible choice in that context.}"

Misspoken Assertions

Consider the example of a person who says something like "All non-custodial parents are not up to date on their child support payments. We should garnish the wages of the deadbeats." The most reasonable interpretation of the speaker's main claim is not that we should garnish the wages of every non-custodial parent, but only of those who are behind on their child support payments. This makes it very likely that the person simply misspoke in asserting the reason. The speaker meant to have said, "Not all non-custodial parents are up to date on their child support payment." There is, of course, a big difference between "All are not..." and "Not all are..." Yet, the sensible analyst and sophisticated interpreter will make the clarification that attributes to the speaker what she or he very probably intended to communicate in the given context, even if that differs from the words taken in a naïve and strictly literal way. Our purpose, in the end, is to understand decision making. To do this we must be as true as possible to the person's reasoning, even if the person is not fully or accurately expressing that reasoning.

Implicit and Obvious Words and Warrants

It is often helpful to reword modestly and extend the statements in an argument for clarity's sake, as long as one remains faithful to what the argument maker intended in the given context. The use of bracketed words in the ovals serves to record the analyst's interpretation. This clarifies, but does not alter, the speaker's reasoning. The warrants the speaker relied upon in Figure 16 very likely include "It is pointless to have managers' meetings if not all managers can possibly be present." Or, "I don't like to go into budget meetings without vital information. Revenue targets are vital pieces of information." However, we elected in this case not to include the warrants because even without them the map is accurate and sufficiently clear as an expression of the speaker's reasoning. There are at least three situations, however, which would require that the warrants be included in the map: (a) If the speaker had explicitly articulated them; (b) if the analysis were unclear without the speaker's implicit warrants being included; or, (c) if our purpose for making the map had necessitated an explication of a speaker's implicit assumptions. When it is necessary to display an implicit warrant, we shall use **overlapping ovals**, one with datum and the other with the warrant, to exhibit the reason more fully.[‡‡‡‡] See Figure 18 in a new example below.

Shared Cultural Understandings and Linguistic Conventions

Some elements essential to understanding the reasoning are so basic and commonly understood that they need not be replicated in the decision map. Unless there is some reason to believe that those who will be reading the final results of the A&H Analysis or viewing the decision map will fail to understand something important, it is neither necessary to include in the map every cultural detail nor to replicate the conventions of standard language usage. So we need not add to the map that there are five days in a work week, and that they occur in a given sequence, and that the English words 'Monday,' 'Tuesday,' 'Wednesday,' 'Thursday,' and 'Friday' are the names we use to refer to those five days, and that that is their proper sequence in the standard work week. On the other hand, an understanding of the cultural context of the decision will be vital for an analyst to fully comprehend the arguments being made. The reminder here about cultural understanding when analyzing decision data is no different than when it is raised for other types of qualitative research.

[‡‡‡‡] For example, Figure 14 illustrates the use of this convention.

Unspoken Warrants and Intermediate Claims

Having said that there are some unspoken things which need not be included, we now caution that there are other unspoken things which do need to be included. A decision map should include key assumptions the speaker is making when they function as reasons and claims implicitly relied upon, but not overtly expressed. Human discourse is economical. We simply do not say everything that we think is relevant to our main claim if we are talking with friends and colleagues with whom we share a good deal of contextual, cultural, and experiential knowledge. As a result, when we make arguments we move very quickly from a datum to the main claim without asserting the warrant. Or, we omit a series of intermediary claims that we assume everyone in the conversation takes for granted. We may omit or not restate data, if we think those with whom we are conversing already know and appreciate those data.

Text data also pose interesting challenges for the analyst. First, text does not provide the rich set of non-verbal cues that interviews offer. Second, text data may be as spontaneous as email, but more often it has been edited at least once, which suggests that things have been added or cut out, and that ideas may have been rearranged. This can make the author's reasoning clearer or it can obscure matters, depending on the purposes behind the edits. Consider the argument in the following letter, Figure 17, which appeared in the *San Francisco Chronicle* shortly after the punch card voting system failed in Florida during the presidential election in November of 2000.[57] It is typical of argumentative reasoning expressed in written form. And, as often happens with published letters to the editor, it may have been revised for brevity's sake by the newspaper which published it.

Dear Editor,

"I read a lot of moaning about how much money it would take to revolutionize and make foolproof our system of voting. Whatever the cost, the government should fix it and fix it fast. If we have the money to send aid to the rest of the world, surely we can find enough to install voting machines that accurately record the will of the people. The Florida debacle should never happen again."

San Francisco Chronicle, July 13, 2001

FIGURE 17: LETTER TO THE EDITOR

Parsing the four sentences which comprise this letter into the data segments, adding unspoken but implicit and important assumptions, and rewording the text modestly to clarify but preserve the author's intended meanings, we generate the following:

1. Saying we cannot afford the cost of revolutionizing and making foolproof our system of voting is moaning.

2. Whatever the cost [might be, the government should not delay or deter the project].

3. The government should fix [make foolproof] our system of voting [and do it] fast. {Conclusion}

4. We have the money to send aid to the rest of the world.

5. If we have money for the rest of the world, then we can find enough money to install voting machines that accurately record the will of the people.

6. The Florida debacle [with the voting in the 2000 Presidential Election] should never [be permitted] to happen again.

Line 1 shows that we interpret the author as acknowledging in his first line that, yes, it will take a lot of money to fix the voting system. Line 5 indicates that we interpret the author as believing that the nation does have the money to fix the voting system but is spending it on other things.

To reveal more fully this writer's reasoning, Figure 18, below, includes elements which go beyond the explicit data segments. The analysts have included implicit intermediary claims and warrants which they judge that the writer intends as part of the flow of reasoning from the stated data segments to the main conclusion. On this analysis, which is a first pass, the analysts attribute to the writer three implicit warrants, four implicit intermediate claims, and the implicit assumption of one datum.

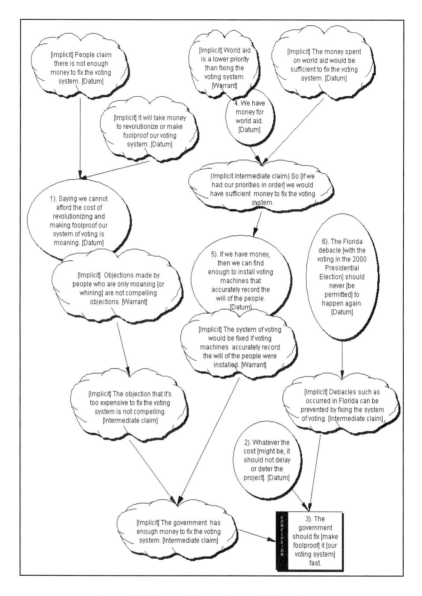

FIGURE 18: "FIX THE VOTING SYSTEM" - FIRST PASS

Notice that the letter writer's conclusion comes in line 3, with arguments above and below it in the text's data segments. In line 1, the writer does intimate that he understands that, yes, it will take a lot of money to fix the voting system. But he never actually says this. So it becomes the first implicit assumption made even before the jumping off point of the written argument – in this case, line 1. A second statement is also implied, namely, that people claim that there is not enough money. Line 1 functions as the starting point for an argument intended to discredit and refute the view that we cannot afford the money needed to fix the voting system. Were he not to prevail in this, the writer would feel that due to prohibitive costs, the voting system should not be fixed. However, the writer, anticipating an objection on the grounds of costs by those who would disagree, offers two counter-arguments. The first is that there is enough money, if we decided to use the funds which are now being spent on foreign aid to fix the voting system instead. The second counter-argument made is the *ad hominem*, suggesting that those who say we do not have enough in the budget are simply moaners or whiners who, therefore, can and should be ignored.

It is important that we not dismiss this letter to the editor as superficial or flippant in spite of its tone or the tactic of opening with an *ad hominem* assault on those who might disagree. The decision map generated by A&H Analysis reveals that the author of the letter did offer an affirmative argument for the importance to our democracy of fixing the voting system, namely, that we need an accurate way of recording the will of the people.§§§§§ Decision mapping the speaker's full argument assists in achieving a fair-minded evaluation because full and accurate decision maps reveal the complexity of a person's thinking. Thus they aid the evaluator to avoid overly simplistic interpretations.

Responsibility and Reliability

The analyst is responsible for the explication of the speaker's reasoning, including rewording statements and making explicit what is relevant and implicit. This may seem like an impossible expectation, but, we do it all the time in everyday discourse. We participate in meetings and conversations with the confidence that we can understand one another's reasoning and that we can communicate our own thinking effectively. We enjoy humor, irony, and wit. We hear stories and know what their point is, and we tell stories to explain ourselves and to guide others. We take for granted a myriad of things that those who do not share our experiences or who do not know our culture and our assumptions would only struggle to comprehend.

---

§§§§§ In Figure 18 the analysts have added an *evaluative* element as well. They have noted within each oval, diamond, and large arrow their understandings of the actual *truth, plausibility, implausibility, falsity,* or *uncertainty* each of the ideas serving as data, warrants, and intermediate claims.

In analyzing everyday discourse, we often consider literal interpretations naïve, uninformed, and unsophisticated. Were it otherwise, most popular culture, music, slang, drama, comedy, news, and public policy debates would be as inaccessible to our understandings as they are to preschoolers. It would be foolish to restrict our attention to word count or to focus only on grammar and the dictionary meanings of words. For example, we know that at times a sentence in the form of a question should be taken to be a statement. Why else do some TV news programs offer grammatically interrogative headlines which are not too subtly disguised political declaratives like "City prosecutor soft on crime?"

In drafting and redrafting decision maps, the analyst is responsible for making explicit a decision maker's communicative intentions. Certainly each analyst will be offering his or her interpretations. But interpretations can be compared and they can be evaluated. Some are better than others. The revised interpretation offered in Figure 16 is better than the first pass offered Figure 15, for example. The advantage of this, from the point of view of empirical research, is that other analysts can then check to see if they agree or disagree with the interpretations. They can correct and improve one another's work. Decision maps are interpretations that are open to scrutiny and correction by the community of scientific investigators. And maps can be presented to interviewers for validation when it is appropriate for the research design and the protection of human subjects. Doing collaborative research using the A&H Method, we have found that the amenability of data parsing and decision mapping to inter-subjective review, evaluation, and improvement enables A&H Analysis to result in more accurate and reliable findings.

An Extended Decision Map Example

Now let us consider a more complex example of decision mapping using a longer interview. We will include the complete interview in which a person describes his decision to withdraw as a candidate for a senior executive management position after completing one on-site interview. This analysis will use an authentic interview with the candidate. To understand the cultural context of this person's reasoning, it is helpful to know that the person had been a candidate for the position of Chief Operating Officer (COO) of a North American company with headquarters in New York. The person expected that the COO position would be, as it normally is, the clear second in command behind the CEO. In the United States, there are political realities at work in any management group. Divisional managers with significant areas of responsibility within the corporation are expected to maximize the profitability of their own divisions. At the same time, each of them must be responsive to the need of the corporation as a whole to maximize its profitability. This results in a classic "individual good vs. common good" nest of problems. The COO is responsible for sorting through these problems and resolving them in order to move the overall organization forward as indicated by its strategic plan. To do this, the COO must have the authority and the information necessary to provide direction to the divisional managers.

The Job Case

Interview question initially focusing on the decision: "I understand that you were a candidate for a COO position at a major company based in New York but you withdrew. Can you talk about how you made that decision?"

Responses to initial question and subsequent prompts for further clarifications: "It's flattering when they come and try to recruit you. That they would think that you would be the person who could come and solve the problems in the new organization [is flattering]...

"I am a problem solver. I was attracted because there were challenges here...Size, scope, and prestige. The company sold a good product. And was socially responsible. And it was a stepping stone to a CEO job. An exciting metropolitan area. This is a good job opportunity.

"But the organization had trouble..... And the trouble was at a level at which the job I was interviewing for couldn't fix. The CEO's leadership style was a problem. I knew this by what I knew about the current CEO. He had a reputation for letting the VPs hash out problems like an emperor watching gladiators. There was no team approach. He's close to retirement. And I think he doesn't want any major change. I heard from my CEO that this guy was extremely conservative. He wants the COO to just mind the store and affirm the decisions he made in the past. He's been CEO there a long time. It's like a family business, if you know what I mean. Family businesses are problematic in some ways for those outside the family. The CEO didn't bother to meet me when I went for my interview. That's the person I'd work for. And you never get to meet that person! If he respected my decision in the matter he would have met with me. The message was that the candidate's choice doesn't matter.....only if they want to choose you. [Their only concern is whether they want you.] And then I'm meeting with this interview committee; and one of the managers, a guy who would be reporting to me, tells me he has special contact with the CEO. He actually said that they get together at dinner and talk over key decisions. He made it clear that I wasn't invited. That was a signal!

"I was interviewing to be the COO. There were problems in the organizational structure. The VP for information, the CIO, should have reported to me, but she reported to the president. If the COO is the number two in the company, then everyone else should report to the CEO through the COO. Their priorities were strange. The same for the VP of marketing. They had redundant manufacturing functions. They had redundant sales forces serving overlapping regions. An incapacity to override autonomy of individual managers. Redundancies of this kind are evidence that the regional managers are too independent. Redundancies are financially costly. Efforts to eliminate these are politically divisive -- which they needed to do to advance the company. They had an anachronistic notion of inventory control... These challenges I would have relished, but only with the backing of the CEO. And the mandate to make change.

"I've always taken management jobs that were full of problems. Organizations others might well not have wanted to risk becoming the leader of [I've taken jobs here]. I'm 55. I'm going to work another 15 years at most. A person should commit about 7 years to a big job. And [I] probably have two more big jobs in me. And my ambition was always to be CEO of a major company. If I didn't do this, then would I ever attain that goal? The timing was right for me for a move.

"But there were also family things. My wife said she couldn't see herself moving from her job right away. My wife won't move. She has a very good job. And one that is not easily replicated. It would have been a bi-coastal marriage... Not much prospect for being mutually satisfactory... Not likely to resolve itself in a reasonable time. If I went I couldn't come back for several years. When you take a new job you should stay at least a few years. We timed out the trip -- the travel for one of us to visit the other. And tried to figure out if it [the commuter marriage] could work. [If we made this decision it would mean] transcontinental flights for conjugal visits. Neither of us was sure we could handle that. There was also stress on family relationships. Children and grandchildren, and good weather all on the west coast. A lot of friends lost. I would have had a monkish existence in some little apartment. And not even in Manhattan because the company headquarters was way out in the suburbs. I wouldn't be living in Manhattan. You shouldn't live too far from headquarters...Queens, I think. So I wouldn't have gotten the benefits of the city.

"The way they tried to tell me I would like the job was to stress the challenges. The interview committee was excited about the kind of leadership I could provide. Some said I'd 'wake the place up... Others said ... 'take it to the next level.' The headhunter argued that I could be CEO at another company if I did this for a couple three years. They got me to call a woman who did this same job in the past. She was now a CEO. She tried to tell me that this CEO was a great guy. She (the CEO I called who used to be COO) described his office as a long room and you kind of approached him, in his regalness. Her current company was no big deal. Not even as interesting as my current job. I wasn't impressed [with the argument that I would be a CEO]. I would be a CEO like her. But this started me thinking that taking this job would later cause me to inherit a new set of problems in a new location where I wouldn't necessarily like living. My next job might be at an undesirable location.

"This would be a promotion -- greater responsibility and opportunity for leadership, a definite advance in the career.

"Salary was not a factor. I'm making an excellent salary now. Although this would have been a substantial increase. But at some point, it's not about more money.

"I've been in my current role a very long time, and my peers all wonder why I haven't moved ahead to a COO or CEO job. But this wasn't the company for me. This company had too much decentralization. It had over extended itself financially. No vision...Maybe they did have a vision, but they had no strategic plan. They were just going along; and a very strong sense of resistance to change. This was how their descriptions came across."

We will analyze this decision using the techniques presented thus far. In the next sections we refine the analytical strategies presented earlier by illustrating and discussing the processes of capturing the chronology, identifying the components of the various arguments being made (data, claims, and warrants), determining the relationships between the components, and developing iterative drafts of the interpretative decision map.

Chronology of "The Job Case" Argument Components

We begin to analyze the chronology of the voiced assertions that are the component data, claims, and warrants of the decision maker's claims and reasons by parsing and numbering those data segments as described earlier. If one happens to know whether a given statement is true or false, that can be indicated at this point. While not critical to the interpretation and mapping *per se*, it will be relevant in the evaluation phase of A&H Analysis.

After parsing the narrative, we identify the main claim and, following the speaker's reasoning backward from there, some of the most significant intermediate claims. In "The Job Case" example, the sentence in the last paragraph, "But this isn't the company," comes closest to being an explicit declaration of what is implicit in the person's response to the interviewer. The speaker never actually utters the words, "And so I decided that the best thing to do was to withdraw my candidacy." That is the main claim, the point of the whole explanation. It might have been phrased somewhat differently, but this is what was decided. In the context of the interview it follows directly from the person's inference that "this isn't the company."

In anticipation of the first draft of the decision map, note in the list of data segments the main claim (line 93-C) marked in bold and underlined. It is helpful as well to note most significant intermediary claims (underlined). Implicit but unspoken data, claims, and warrants can be identified and inserted later into the text where appropriate and needed for the analysis.

After the initial parsing of the data, in a second or third pass, when one is confirming and refining the parsing, it can be useful to anticipate the evaluative work to be done later by making some preliminary judgments about the truth or falsity of the various warrants, claims, and data statements. Components can be marked true (T) or false (F) when this can be determined, otherwise uncertainty can noted using (?). Or, if more gradations are preferred, Plausible (P+) or Implausible (P-) can be added. The component's role can be noted along with the apparent truth value using 'd' for datum, 'c' for claim, and 'w' for warrant. This gives combinations like '(cT)' for "claim thought to be true," '(wP+)' for "plausible warrant," and '(d?)' "uncertain datum." Brackets are used to add needed clarifications. Here are the data segments parsed from "The Job Case" with indications of the analyst's interpretation of their role in the reasoning as datum, warrant, or claim, and the truth values the analyst attributed to each.

> 1). It's flattering when they come and try to recruit you. (cT)
> 2). That they would think that you would be the person who could come and solve the problems in the new organization [is flattering]. (dT)
> 2-D). I am a problem solver. (dT)
> 3). I was attracted because there were challenges here. (cT)
> 4). ...Size, scope, and prestige. (dT)

5). The company sold a good product. (dT)

6). and was socially responsible. (dT)

7). and it was a stepping stone to a CEO job. (dT)

8). an exciting metropolitan area. (dT)

8-C). <u>This is a good job opportunity</u>. (cT)

9). But the organization had trouble. [rhetorical force of "but" signals a change in the course of the reasoning]. (cT)

10). <u>and the trouble was at a level at which the job I was interviewing for couldn't fix</u>. (cF)

10-C). <u>The CEO's leadership style was a problem</u>. (c?)

11). I knew this by what I knew about the current CEO. (w?)

12). He had a reputation for letting the VPs hash out problems like an emperor watching gladiators. (dT)

13). There was no team approach. (d?)

14). He's close to retirement. (dT)

15). and I think he doesn't want any major change. (c?)

16). I heard from my CEO that this guy was extremely conservative. (dT)

17). He wants the COO to just mind the store and affirm the decisions he made in the past. (c?)

18). He's been CEO there a long time. (dT)

19). <u>It's like a family business, if you know what I mean</u>. (cT)

19-C). Family businesses are problematic in some ways for those outside the family. (cT)

20). The CEO didn't bother to meet me when I went for my interview. (dT)

21). that's the person I'd work for. (dT)

22). and you never get to meet that person! (dT)

22-W). If he respected my decision in the matter he would have met with me. (wT)

23). The message was that the candidate's choice doesn't matter. (cT)

24) only if they want to choose you [Their only concern is whether they want you]. (dT)

25). and then I'm meeting with this interview committee. (dT)

26). and one of the managers, a guy who would be reporting to me, tells me he has special contact with the CEO. (dT)

27). He actually said that they get together at dinner and talk over key decisions. (dT)

28). He made it clear that I wasn't invited. (dT)

29). That was a signal! (cT)

30). I was interviewing to be the COO. (dT)

31). <u>There were problems in the organizational structure</u>. (cT)

32). The VP for information, the CIO, should have reported to me. (cT)

33). but she reported to the president. (dT)

33-W) If the COO is the number 2 in the company, then everyone else should report to the CEO through the COO. (wT)

34). their priorities were strange. (d?)

35). The same for the VP of marketing. (dT)

36). They had redundant manufacturing functions. (cT)

37). redundant sales forces serving overlapping regions. (dT)

38). an incapacity to override autonomy of individual managers. (cT)

38-W) Redundancies of this kind are evidence that the regional managers are too independent. (w?)

38-W). Redundancies are financially costly. (dT)

38-D). Efforts to eliminate these are politically divisive. (dT)

39). which they needed to do to advance the company. (cT)

40). They had an anachronistic notion of inventory control… (dT)

41). These challenges I would have relished. (cT)

42). but only with the backing of the CEO. (dT) {Speaker expresses qualifying condition}

43). and [only if I had] the mandate to make change. (dT) {Speaker expresses qualifying condition}

44). I've always taken management jobs that were full of problems. (dT)

45). [For] organizations [that] others might well not have wanted to risk becoming the leader of [I've taken the job]. (dT)

46). I'm 55. (dT)

46-D). I'm going to work another 15 years at most. (dT)

46-W). A person should commit about 7 years to a big job. (wT).

47). and [I would] probably have two more big jobs in me. (cT)

48). and my ambition was always to be CEO of a major company. (dT)

49). If I didn't do this then would I ever attain that goal? (cF)

50). The timing was right for me for a move. (cT)

51). But there were also family things [that counted against taking the job]. (cT)

52). My wife said she couldn't see herself moving from her job right away. (dT)

52-C). My wife won't move. (cT)

53). She has a very good job. (dT)

54). and one that is not easily replicated. (dT)

55). It would have been a bi-coastal marriage. (dT)

56). …Not much prospect for being mutually satisfactory. (cT)

57). …Not likely to resolve itself in a reasonable time. (c?)

58). If I went I couldn't come back for several years. (dT)

58-W). When you take a new job you should stay at least a few years. (wT)

59). We timed out the trip -- the travel for one to visit the other. (dT)

60). and tried to figure out if it [the commuter marriage] could work. (dT)

61). [If we made this decision it would mean] transcontinental flights for conjugal visits. (cT)

62). Neither of us was sure we could handle that. (cT)

62-W). Intimacy is very important. (wT)

63). There was also stress on family relationships. (cT)

64). Children and grandchildren, and good weather all on the west coast. (dT)

65). A lot of friends lost. (d?) {Loss Aversion Heuristic}

66). I would have had a monkish existence in some little apartment. (cT) {Simulation and Affect Heuristics}

67). and not even in Manhattan because the company headquarters was way out in the suburbs. (dT)

67-C) I wouldn't be living in Manhattan. (c?)

67-W). You shouldn't live too far from headquarters. (w?)

68). ...Queens, I think. (dT)

69). So I wouldn't have gotten the benefits of the city. (cF)

70). The way they tried to tell me I would like the job was to stress the challenges. (dT)

71). The interview committee was excited about the kind of leadership I could provide. (cT)

72). Some said I'd 'wake the place up.' (dT)

73). or for others, … 'take it to the next level.' (dT)

74). The headhunter argued that I could be CEO at another company, if I did this for couple three years. (dT)

75). They got me to call a woman who did this same job in the past. (dT)

76). She was now a CEO. (dT)

77). She tried to tell me that this CEO was a great guy. (dT)

78). She (the CEO I called who used to be COO) described his office as a long room and you kind of approached him, in his regalness. (dT)

79). Her current company was no big deal. (dT)

80). Not even as interesting as my current job. (dT)

81). I wasn't impressed [with the argument that I would be a CEO]. (cT)

81-C). I would be a CEO like her. (cF)

82). But this started me thinking that taking this job would later cause me to inherit a new set of problems in a new location where I wouldn't necessarily like living. (c?)

82-D). My next job might be at an undesirable location. (c?)

83). This [job] would be a promotion, (dT)

84). greater responsibility, (dT)

85). and opportunity for leadership, (dT)

86). [This job would be] a definite advance in the career. (cT)

87). Salary was not a factor. (cT)

88). I'm making an excellent salary now. (dT)

89). Although this would have been a substantial increase. (dT)

90). But at some point, it's not about more money. (dT)

91). I've been in my current role a very long time. (dT)

92). and my peers all wonder why I haven't moved ahead to a COO or CEO job. (dT)

93. But this wasn't the company for me. (c?)

(93-C). So I decided that the best thing to do was to withdraw my candidacy. (cT)

94). This company had too much decentralization. (dT)

95). it had over extended itself financially, (cT)

96). [it had] no vision, ... (c?) {Claim with unvoiced data}

97). maybe they did have a vision. (cT) {Pause. Speaker mentally reconsidering whether the organization had vision or not.}

98). But they had no strategic plan, (cT)

99). they were just going along, (dT)

100). and a very strong sense of resistance to change, (dT)

101). this was how their descriptions came across. (dT)

Identify the Argument Strands by Reasoning Backward

We have suggested that the analyst begin the actual graphic mapping by reasoning backward along the pro and con paths to discover the argument maker's intermediary claims. These can be found by asking questions like, "What reasons does the speaker give for doing/believing X and for not doing/believing X?" where X is the main claim. In complex decisions, reasons will cluster, like the branches of a river – the more preliminary claims acting as reasons that feed into subsequent more major ones. There might be several major reasons pro and con, and each of these may or may not be explicitly supported by groups of more preliminary reasons. To discover these, one must patiently continue to ask "Why?" Working backward, explore along each of the argument maker's strands of reasoning, always seeking the person's starting point data and warrants. In this step and in the next step the analyst is likely to have to add statements that make explicit what the argument maker obviously intended and understood to be taken as necessary and relevant intermediary claims. Like the tributaries of a powerful river, the intermediary claims typically represent the intermediate or interim conclusions of arguments pro and con that constitute the decision process as a whole.

Redrafting one's map and revising one's interpretation is to be expected. Assertions that may first appear to be claims can, on reflection, be better understood as data or warrants, for example. Expect the process to be iterative, with more and more refined analyses being achieved as one examines the data segments and considers what roles the speaker intended them to play in conveying the person's decision making. Again, the goal at this point is to analyze and to interpret, but not to improve upon, amend, repair or reform. The working assumption, therefore, must be that the decision maker would not have made the assertion if he or she had not deemed the information somehow relevant to deciding what to believe or what to do. Analysts should operate with the presumption that anything expressed by the decision maker as part of the explanation of his or her reasoning was presented with a purpose in mind and should find its place in the decision map.

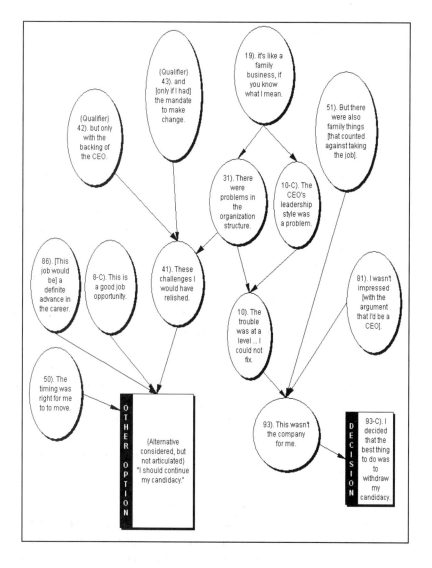

FIGURE 19: "DECISION TO WITHDRAW CANDIDACY"

Figure 19, "Decision to Withdraw Candidacy," reflects the linkages of the major intermediary claims to the decision to withdraw as a candidate. Three flow toward the penultimate claim (93) "This wasn't the company for me." Four intermediary claims flow toward the unspoken alternative, "I should continue my candidacy." It is interesting that an earlier intermediary claim, other than the seven mentioned, namely, (31) "There were problems in the organization structure," flows toward both the pro and the con sides of the final decision. This often happens. Reasoners can and do interpret data and intermediary claims as having implications for both sides of the final decision. Statement (19) "It's like a family business, if you know what I mean," is open to both positive and negative consequences. The speaker sees the CEO's leadership style as a negative, but the problems that emerge from the family business approach as at least a potential positive.

Figure 19 demonstrates that providing larger numbers of arguments in support of one alternative is not necessarily predictive of choosing that alternative. Behavioral theorists have long argued that it is the weighting of the pros and cons – not the raw number of pros or cons – which more often determines the eventual choice or decision.[58,59] Others argue that decisions are ultimately made using only one most prominent consideration.[60] A&H Analysis will help us test these opposing theories.

"The Job Case" –

Detailed Maps of Each Major Argument Strand

The interpretive analysis in Figure 20, "There Were Family Things," illustrates the cluster of arguments which support just one of the major intermediary claims, namely (51) "There were also family things [that counted against taking the job]." And these things were not likely to resolve themselves soon (57). These considerations were stress on family relationships (63), loss of intimacy from living apart (62), loss of friends (65), and something the speaker imagines and appears to regard negatively which he calls a "monkish existence" (66).****** Note that the speaker describes the future in terms of losses, rather than gains or opportunities. We describe the potentially powerful impact of such heuristics as "Loss Aversion" in Chapter 6. This particular decision map does not show

---

****** The monkish existence could relate to the loss of intimacy, which is how we have mapped it in Figure 20. Or the speaker may have intended that it refers to not being able to live in Manhattan, which is the topic that follows in lines 67-69. In either case, the speaker is averse to that prospect.

underlying assumptions as they are not needed to understand the reasoning process.

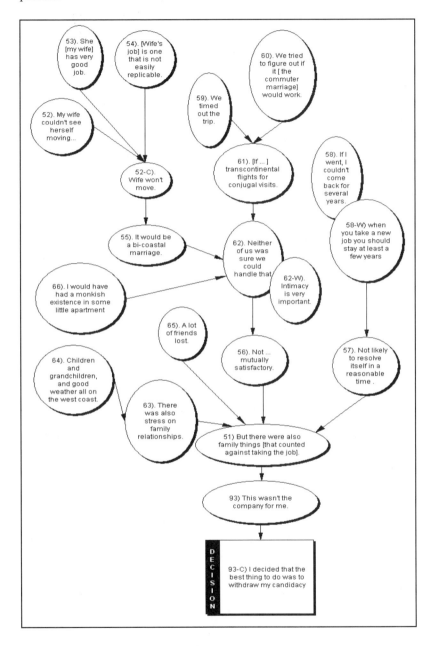

FIGURE 20: "THERE WERE FAMILY THINGS"

In mapping large complex decisions, it often is helpful first to map the intermediate claims leading directly to the major alternatives which were given serious consideration. Figure 19 gives this overview. Once the overall is reasonably clear, the analyst can then begin to excavate the arguments strands which support each of those intermediate claims. This process yields a set of more detailed argument maps, each illustrating how the decision maker arrived at one or more of the intermediate claims. The main map would supply a synoptic overview showing the reasoning pattern leading from those intermediate claims to the decision. It is this work that provides the analysis of the overall reasoning process. Errors in the overview are likely to be uncovered by the more detailed analyses, and revisions of the overview map may be necessary as a result. Figure 20 is only one of the subordinate maps for "The Job Case."

For purposes of publications and poster presentations the synoptic overview map is often preferred. However, to conduct a thorough evaluation of the reasoning using the A&H Method, the details manifested in the set of subordinate maps are needed.

From Analysis and Interpretation to Evaluation

In "The Job Case," our decision maker, having at one point conceived of the opportunity as providing definite career advancement toward the goal of becoming a CEO, later finds the headhunter's argument to the same effect entirely unpersuasive, if not counter-productive. Our decision maker appears to take as true the headhunter's claim that he would turn out to be a CEO not unlike the woman on the phone. Why the speaker saw that as the future, and not something else, and why that portion of the reasoning process weakened the persuasive strength of the argument that the job was a definite step closer to becoming a CEO, are not questions that logical analysis will answer. Sound reasoning is a necessary condition for being a good decision maker on a consistent basis, but it is not a sufficient condition. We must consider also the heuristic thinking evident in the interview and how it appears to have influenced the decision maker.

Given that the family issues were well known far in advance of exploring the job prospect on the other coast, what were all the little decisions along the way that put the person in a position to have to struggle with the possibility of withdrawing as a candidate? It should have been easy for the job seeker to have foreseen those family problems when the headhunter first contacted him about becoming a candidate for that particular job. We will have to consider this missing data, but clearly the decision back at that point to explore the possibility was the first step down the path to the larger dilemma. Was it that the person always envisioned someday becoming a CEO? Was the person overly optimistic about his chances of maintaining a happy family life or about his capability of controlling events and emotions? Was it that many of his professional peers had become COOs, thus making available a number of examples with which the person could identify? More data might have been uncovered had the interviewer prompted the speaker to "say more" about these issues. (See: "Think Aloud Interviewing Technique" in Chapter 3.)

Having completed the analytical and interpretive aspects of the A&H Method, the next steps call forth its evaluative strategies. Each level of evaluation can enrich the research findings. Chapters 5, 6, and 7 describe the A&H Method's evaluation processes.

Chapter 5:
Evaluating Argument Making

The A&H Method requires both a precise analysis of human reasoning and a careful evaluation of that reasoning. As Chapter 2 indicated, that reasoning is modeled as the interaction of argument making and heuristic thinking. This chapter presents a strategy for evaluating the quality of the arguments humans advance to explain their decisions or beliefs. This strategy relies on the application of four criteria: *logical strength, soundness, relevance,* and *non-circularity.* [††††††] These four criteria apply to all three of the major kinds of logical structures used in human argument making: (1) *Analogical*, which is reasoning from one idea to another based on similarities or associations perceived to be relevant points of comparison; (2) *Axiomatic*, which is reasoning from assumptions and deeply held values and principles to their specific implications about what should be done or what should be believed; and, (3) *Empirical*, which is reasoning from experiences and observations to more abstract hypotheses and general theories meant to explain those events. A full discussion of these forms of human reasoning and the more specialized evaluative considerations appropriate to each is presented in Appendices C, D and E. The aim of this chapter, along with the ancillary material in Appendix B, is to supply a systematic, integrated, and reasonably complete set of tools for the logical analysis of human arguments. Using these tools, the researcher can evaluate the quality and the credibility of the widest possible variety of arguments humans use to explain, sustain, and defend their decisions about what to believe and what to do.

Four Presumptions of the Human Practice of Argument Making

At times people apply questionable or faulty warrants. Even if the warrants are true, at times people apply them in circumstances that are not relevant or not sufficiently similar to the intended use of the warrant.[61,62,63] For more than 2500, years the field of study known as Logic, with its historical roots in rhetoric and argumentation, has explored the question of how to evaluate various kinds of arguments in order to decide whether or not the claims

---

[††††††] For a more detailed treatments of Logic, one might review any of number of standard textbooks on the subject, including those referenced in the endnotes to this volumn.[62, 63, 66, 67]

based on those kinds of arguments should be accepted.[64] The wisdom and intellectual treasures of many of the world's great cultures and civilizations are evident in the rich history of logic, as are any number of approaches and ideas that, over the course of time, turned out to be incomplete or impractical.

Fortunately, there are many important and enduring lessons that we can mine in regard to such fundamentally important things as testing the logical strength of different kinds of arguments, interpreting expressions that qualify various warrants, evaluating reasoning based on analogies, recognizing common fallacies, and appreciating the intricacies of inferential statistics, mathematical reasoning, and scientific investigation. The A&H Method draws on these lessons in proposing an approach to the evaluation of the explanations and arguments humans make to support their decisions about what to believe or what to do.

Throughout the world, wherever and whenever people engage in a sincere effort to make arguments to one another pro or con regarding a decision about something of serious mutual concern, a key set of argument making presumptions are at play in their conversation. These presumptions provide the basis for a series of tests which, applied in a certain order, define a broadly applicable procedure for evaluating the logical merit of arguments humans make.

The first presumption is: *The truth of a person's claim derives to some degree from the assumed truth of the reasons provided.* In other words, accepting the truth of the data and the warrant justifies belief in the truth of the claim. The second presumption, related to the first, is: *The statements offered as data and warrants are, in fact, true.* As a rule, people collaborating with one another do not intentionally use erroneous information or lie to each other. If a disagreement about the truth of any statement arises, then the people make a reasonable effort to review the evidence for that statement or they qualify the force with which they wish to assert and maintain any claims based on that statement.

The third presumption of the practice of reasoning together is: *The data and the warrants are judged by the argument maker to be relevant to the truth of the claim.* The idea is that we should come to accept the truth of the claim because of the truth of the datum and the warrant, and not for other independent or extraneous reasons. The fourth presumption is that the reasoning in argument making is essentially a one way street: *The various reasons flow toward establishing the acceptability of the claims, not vice versa*. The direction of the flow of reasoning is from datum and warrant toward claim, not the other way around. Data might support more than one claim, and an intermediary claim might support a further claim downstream, but the basic presumption is that the reasoning goes in one direction only, from the reasons toward the claims.

The Four Tests of the Acceptability of an Argument

The four presumptions above argument making as an interpersonal human activity form the bases for the four evaluative criteria applicable to all arguments. In other words, *it would be unreasonable not to accept a person's argument if it met all four of the conditions* implied by those presumptions. Recalling that an "argument" as we understand it is the "reason-claim" combination, for all practical purposes then, we can specify the set of conditions which are individually necessary and jointly sufficient for an argument to be considered worthy of acceptance. We can specify those conditions by reference to characteristics of the reason as a set of statements (including, at a minimum, an explicit or implicit datum and warrant) and in terms of the features of that reason-claim relationship. The four conditions for an argument's acceptability are these:

1. The logical relationship between the reason and the claim is such that the claim must be true or very probably true if the reason is taken to be true.

2. The facts as they are known are such that the reason is deemed indeed to be true.

3. The relevance of the reason to the claim is such that the truth of the claim actually depends on the truth of the reason.

4. The truth of the claim is not part of the basis for believing any of the reasons.

These four, taken together, define a strategy for evaluating the logical adequacy or, as we shall use the term, ___acceptability___ of human arguments. The four suggest the four simple tests used in the A&H Method to evaluate the human argument making dimension of decision making: the Test of Logical Strength, the Test of Soundness, the Test of Relevance, and the Test of Non-Circularity. Let us consider each in turn.

Logical Strength

The Test of Logical Strength requires imagination. To apply this test you challenge yourself to identify or devise a scenario, if possible, in which both the datum and the warrant are true but the claim is false. Logicians call statements expressing the datum and the warrant the premises of the argument. The claim statement is the argument's conclusion. According to logicians, an argument's premises work together to form a reason.[65] If there is no possible scenario in which all the premises of an argument can be true while at the same time its conclusion is false, or if such a scenario is extremely improbable, then the argument passes the Test of Logical Strength. However, to the extent that such a scenario is possible, plausible, likely, or actually true, the argument fails this test.[66]

If under <u>no possible scenario</u> the datum and warrant could be both true and the claim false, then logicians would call the argument deductively valid. If there is a possible scenario, but it is <u>remote and implausible</u>, perhaps as unlikely as one chance in twenty or one chance in a thousand, then we can have a comparable degree of confidence in the argument's logical strength. From the logical point of view, the more remote the possibility is, the stronger the argument or the more confident we can be in the truth of the conclusion given those premises. These arguments logicians refer to as inductively strong, meaning that the reason given makes the truth of the claim highly probable. In science we use this insight to establish appropriate confidence levels in the statistically calculated results.

A "reason," as we are using that term, is different than a premise, as logicians use the word "premise." By "reason" we mean the combination of two premises (a datum and a warrant). So, to argue to claim 'c' by giving reason #1 and reason #2 is not the same as making an argument to claim 'c' based on two premises. Consider the argument

> Right now our website is down. (d)
> When its website is down a business cannot receive Internet orders. (w)
> So, right now we cannot receive Internet orders. (c)

The example uses two premises to support its claim. Contrast that example with this one that gives two separate reasons for the same claim:

> Right now our website is down. (d-1)
> And our local in-house computer network is down too. (d-2)
> So, right now we cannot receive Internet orders. (c)

To see that there are two reasons at work in this case, even though neither warrant is made explicit, notice that to begin receiving Internet orders the technicians will have to fix two problems: the website and the in-house network. To evaluate the logical strength of this claim relative to the two reasons given, one would apply the Test of Logical Strength to both of the arguments. When there are two or more reasons for a claim, then there really are multiple arguments being made and the merits of each require separate evaluation.

Soundness

If an argument passes the Test of Logical Strength, we continue evaluating its merits by applying the second test, the **Test of Soundness**. The Test of Soundness requires inquiry. We are challenged to determine whether either the datum or the warrant is in fact false. Logicians call an argument with true premises that passes the Test of Logical Strength a sound argument.[67] The idea behind the Test of Soundness makes good sense, for we would not find the argument below to be a sound basis for believing that cows can fly since, obviously, the first premise is false.

> Every animal with a tail and four legs can fly.
> Cows have four legs and a tail.
> So, cows can fly.

Consider the case of a claim supported by two reasons.

> "I'm not an alcoholic. Look, I only drink beer. Actually, I've never been drunk in my life."

Suppose we learn that our speaker is speaking truthfully when he says that he only drinks beer. Even so, the warrant he seems to be relying on, "If a person only drinks beer the person can't be an alcoholic," is false. So that argument fails the Test of Soundness. In fact, we find out that he's speaking the truth when he says that he's never been drunk in his life. This, along with the generally accepted truth of the implicit warrant "A person who has never been drunk cannot be an alcoholic," indicates that his second argument passes the Test of Soundness. The argument also passes the first test, the Test of Logical Strength. So, it would seem reasonable to accept that our speaker is not an alcoholic, even though one of his reasons (that he only drinks beer) was poor. His argument, based on the other reason, which is independent of the first, was sound.

This is an important point for A&H Analysis. People often provide multiple reasons for a given claim and some of them may turn out to be false. One may be inclined to dismiss the claim itself, hearing a false reason being articulated. Yet if there is a true reason among the group, then the argument will pass the Test of Soundness. Dismissing an otherwise worthy claim simply because one or more of the arguments made on its behalf contain false reasons is one of the most common human reasoning errors. Each reason-claim combination is a separate argument. Thus, before determining that a claim should be rejected on the basis of being unsound, we would need first to find problems with the truth of all of the different reasons advanced.

One further consideration is helpful here, namely, the evaluation of consistency. Police dramas frequently include scenes where the detectives interrogate a suspect whose alibi turns out to be inconsistent with other facts. For example, suppose the suspect says that he was at a friend's house at the time the crime occurred and, so, he could not have committed it. The argument's soundness depends on the truth of the suspect's assertion. So the detectives check and find that the suspect was not at his friend's house when the crime occurred. Having learned that their suspect lied about his whereabouts, the detectives reject his alibi, which is, indeed, the reasonable thing to do. It is inconsistent to believe both that the suspect was at his friend's house at the time of the crime and that he was not at his friend's house at that time. The two ideas are inconsistent because they contradict each other. Only one of them can be true, not both. The suspect cannot have it both ways. Given all the facts that are known, his argument is no longer worthy of being accepted.[######]

Relevance

There are two somewhat more subtle tests needed in order to complete our set of the four tests to assess the quality of an argument. The **Test of Relevance** requires subject matter knowledge and experience appropriate to the context and issues under discussion. For example, United States laws against discriminating among promotion candidates based on their gender express American society's judgment that a person's gender is not a relevant consideration when deciding whether or not the person merits a

---

[######] Arguments with self-contradictory premises always fail the Test of Soundness.

promotion. In another country with a different set of cultural mores, gender-based promotion decisions might be considered both legal and reasonable.

The challenge in applying the Test of Relevance is to determine that datum and warrant are, in fact, relevant to the claim. If one or the other is not relevant, then the third fundamental presumption of argument making has been violated. It is not the case that accepting the truth of the claim <u>depends upon</u> accepting the reason being given (i.e. the datum and the warrant). Although the claim may be true for independent reasons, the argument for that claim from the reason being offered by the argument maker fails. From classical times up through the present, mistakes regarding relevance, (often called *__fallacies__*) were and are given special names to help people avoid being taken in by such erroneous reasoning. With just such a purpose in mind Milos Jenicek, MD, has authored an enjoyable and useful book on fallacies in the practice of medicine.[68] He lists over 100 kinds of fallacies, some being more likely to occur in relationship to medical research, some in the context of clinical diagnoses and treatment decisions, and some relationship to interactions with colleagues, students, patients, and the general public. The examples he gives can be readily translated or transferred to other professional fields.

Here are a few examples of obviously unacceptable arguments – not from medicine – offered here only to be quick illustrations of the fact that truth of a reason might not be relevant to the truth of the claim it is presented as supporting:

- John, a world famous violin virtuoso, endorses Brand XYZ motor oil. So Brand XYZ motor oil is an excellent product.

- Mary is the Master of Ceremonies for tonight's gala. So, Mary must be a man!

- Everyone I know down in the marketing department thinks the CEO is doing a great job. So, the CEO is doing a great job.

- Everyone surveyed said they were highly satisfied with the quality of the food sold at XYZ Markets. So, the food at XYZ Markets must be of high quality.

- I can't think of any practical alternatives to gasoline as a vehicle fuel. So, there is no practical alternative.

- At yesterday's meeting when I asked about strategic planning, you didn't say a word. So, you must not know anything about the topic.

- If we look around us, we see that people everywhere value human life. So, it is right that we should defend this value over all others.

- If we're going to Vegas I have to bring my blue socks. They're my lucky socks. I've never won at slots without these socks. So, I won't win a dime from the slots if I don't wear those socks!

In each case the questions of relevance come to mind: "What does the reason have to do with the claim?" What about being a great violinist qualifies one as an expert on motor oil? Apart from the ambiguity of the term, what about being a "Master" of ceremonies leads one to think that we are talking about a person's gender? Can we not say with near certitude quality of the CEO's job performance is independent of whatever everyone I know in the marketing department might think? When did the Food and Drug Administration replace product testing with customer satisfaction as the measure of the quality of food? Are the limits of the possibilities, when it comes to alternative energy sources, to be equated with the limits of my imagination? Could there not have been many reasons, other than ignorance of the topic, why you did not speak up at yesterday's meeting when the issue of strategic planning was raised? Why does the fact that many people value something make it imperative that it be regarded as the highest of all possible values? Would we say the same for other things people everywhere value, such as a true friend, a respectful and appreciative supervisor, or satisfying dinner followed by delightful entertainment and a good night's sleep? What is the causal relevance of the color of one's hosiery to an increase or decrease in the probabilities of success at games of chance in Las Vegas?

This last fallacious example, often called the "Gambler's Fallacy" in logic text books, is interesting in that, scientific proof notwithstanding, the speaker is still apt to make something in his mind of the coincidence he truly observed. He has never won at slots except the time or times when he was wearing blue socks. The Test for Relevance is the more intuitive test to run in a case like this. Unless we have at least some explanatory theory working in our minds, an argument like the blue socks example lacks a warrant that is true and applicable. In fact, the argument would fail the Test of Logical Strength. The argument maker in a case like this believes in luck and believes that things within his control can influence his luck. His belief in luck is held as a metaphysical theory, meaning that it does not require scientific testing, nor is it in principle open to scientific testing. We will look at the power and influence of metaphysical reasoning later in this chapter. In the next chapter we will see its connections to cognitive heuristics.

The progression from coincidence to correlation to explanation is very important. For example, scientists first observed that there were a number of cases of heart disease where, coincidentally, the person was a smoker. With further, more systematic research, it was learned that there was a strong positive correlation between smoking and heart disease. At this point we came to believe that smoking might have some relevance to heart disease; perhaps smoking was a contributing factor of some kind? However, before making a defensible argument that quitting smoking would reduce a person's chances of heart disease, researchers had to explain scientifically how smoking caused heart disease. In fact, scientists later learned that nicotine constricts blood vessels in the heart. Heart attacks result when the blood supply to the heart muscle is reduced. Being able to explain this relationship scientifically gave scientists considerable confidence in predicting that smoking would cause heart attacks in the future, and further observations have continued to support this argument.

It is not as possible to move all the way from coincidence to correlation to explanation in some other contexts. For example, predicting the behavior of the stock market remains a hazardous and uncertain adventure. As the divergent prognostications of economic experts indicate, we do not really know how all the factors that influence the market interact. We are not able to predict with certainty what will happen in the market. Some analysts turn out to be right, others wrong. Often it seems as though the analysts are saying things that are true (e.g. citing changes in the jobless rate, the prime interest rate, the consumer confidence level, etc.) as *ex post facto* explanations of what the market did after it closed. But those same analysts are not able to use those same factors to predict accurately what the market will do in the future. If their explanations of the past behavior of the market were correct, one would expect that they would be able to make reliable predictions about the market's future behavior. That we are not able, yet, to make good predictions about the future leads us to suspect that we do not yet know, beyond the level of coincidences, what factors in what combinations are relevant to explaining the behavior of the stock market. The prognostications of market analysts frequently fail the Test of Relevance because their arguments fail to explain how the reasons they give for why the market went up or down are actually connected to those market fluctuations.

Non-Circularity

The fourth and final test of logical acceptability is the **Test of Non-Circularity.** This test requires perspicacity, for one must assure oneself that a claim is not being relied upon either implicitly or explicitly as part of a chain of reasoning used to support its own reason. If such a chain looping back on itself is found, then the argument maker is reasoning in a circle. Recall the idea of an argument as a river that flows in one direction. A river cannot feed itself and still be described as a river; rather, it becomes a stagnant moat. So it is with good arguments in the context of decision making: Claims cannot be the bases for their own reasons. If they were, then the reasoning would simply be stagnant and self-justifying in the most unflattering sense.

The problem of reasoning in a circle results most frequently from the use of multiple arguments in combination with each other. At times a person loses track of the reasons for their beliefs, forgetting, for example, that their basis for believing one idea, 'A', was because they accepted another idea, 'B', and that their reason for accepting 'B' had been their belief in 'A'. The result is that the person has high confidence, although misplaced, in both ideas. However, because their support for 'A' is 'B' and their support for 'B' is 'A', the reasonable thing would be to have no confidence in either. For example, consider the pair of arguments in this passage:

> I'm sure we can make this marriage work. That's why we're talking through our problems. Which shows that we still care for each other. And that's why I'm sure we can make this marriage work.

The speaker's reason for the claim that the marriage is salvageable is the belief that she and her husband still care for each other. And the basis for believing that goes back to the idea that the marriage can be saved. This pair of arguments is as fragile as a house of cards; touch it in the least with an analytic finger and it collapses upon itself.

False Assumptions and Common Mistakes

Aristotle (384-322 B.C.E.) and many other logicians down through the centuries have supplied lists of the kinds of deceptive arguments that people nevertheless tended to find persuasive.[69,70,71] When it comes to being deceived by the rhetoric of gifted speakers and eloquent writers, we are no wiser or more sophisticated than people were in Aristotle's millennium. At times we can be misled, or mislead ourselves, because of how subtle and seductive these erroneous assumptions can be. The kinds of fallacies which misled the ancient Greeks retain their powers even today. A fallacy is simply a mistaken argument, one that should not be accepted as a demonstration of the truth of its conclusion. But, because some of the mistakes are so prevalent, persistent and pervasive, they have earned themselves a specific name. Table 7 offers a short list of common fallacies to be alert for when evaluating arguments in decision making contexts.[§§§§§§]

TABLE 7 -- COMMON HUMAN ARGUMENT ERRORS AND FALLACIES[72]

Appeal to Ignorance: Relying on the false warrant that the mere absence of a reason for (or against) something counts as a reason against (or for) it. "I like the President's approach to trade with China and I haven't heard anyone give any evidence that it is not effective. So it must be the right thing to do at this time."

Appeal to the Mob: Relying on the false warrant that because everyone believes something (or is doing something) that it must be the correct thing to believe (or to do). "All the kids at school are smoking, how can you say that I shouldn't?"

***Ad Hominem* Attacks:** Relying on the false warrant that because the person making the argument is deficient in some real or imagined way, the person's argument, work product, or views should not be accepted on their own merits. "I'm sorry, but I don't find his income and expenses projections credible. I don't see how he could have done those numbers correctly. After all, we know he's on the market. He has no company loyalty."

Equivocation: Relying on the vagueness, ambiguity, or a skewed definition of words or phrases in attempting to support a claim. "Even one who is in prison can still be free, for true freedom is the knowledge of one's situation. The more one knows about one's self, the more one is truly free."

[§§§§§§] In addition to the approach taken in this chapter, there are other good taxonomies for classifying fallacies and for establishing the acceptability of arguments. Appendix B offers a succinct refresher on Logic emphasizing ways to make strong arguments.

False Cause: Any of a group of fallacies based on false assumptions regarding causality. Most commonly assuming that because event B happened after event A, that event A must be a cause of event B if not the singular cause of event B. "Look, I put the CD into the player and the windshield wipers wouldn't turn on. It has to be that the problem with the wipers is somehow connected to the CD player."

Misuse of Authority: Relying on the false warrant that when influential or powerful people make claims outside of their areas of competence or expertise that these claims must be true. "When asked why the curriculum had been changed, the superintendent replied that the city's Chamber of Commerce had advised that the students in the Junior High School would be educationally better served if all teachers spent more class time preparing the students to take standardized math tests and less time on American History, Creative Writing, Social Studies, and Health Education."

The Gambler's Fallacy: Any of a group of fallacies that rely on false warrants regarding probability, such as that random events are causally connected. "Hey, Baby, blow on the dice and you'll roll a seven every time."

Composition: Relying on the false warrant that a characteristic of each part of a thing is necessarily a characteristic of the whole thing. "It is in each person's financial interest to cheat a little on their income tax return. So it is finacially good for the nation If people cheat on their taxes."

Division: Relying on the false warrant that a characteristic of the whole thing is necessarily a characteristic of each of its parts. "Fetal stem cell research should be banned because every single human cell is a human being and human beings should not be used for medical research without their informed consent."

Straw Man Fallacy: Relying on the false warant that by refuting the weakest of a series of reasons for a given claim, one has successfully refuted the claim. "Look, we can't approve your request for additional advertising funds. You said that one of the four marketing options you were reviewing was web page design. But we have a policy not to support any further web-based development."

Playing with Numbers: Any of a group of fallacies that relies on false warrants regarding the uses of numbers, especially percentages and raw numbers in order to exaggerate or diminish the apparent significance of the conclusion. "It's January tenth and already six people have ordered new glasses with plastic frames. Last year only four people had ordered plastic frames by this date. That's an increase of 50%. We had better stock up."

False Dilemma: Wrongly claiming that there are no more options to consider when there are options, or that a choice must be made between the options at hand when such a choice is not required, or that all of the options at hand are unacceptable when one or more of them is acceptable. "You say that the President had no other choice but to build the anti-missal defense system in violation of international treaties. And your reason is that if he hadn't we would be vulnerable to terrorist attack. That's a false dilemma. For surely the billions we are spending on hardware of questionable utility could have been used in other ways to combat international terrorism, for example, by improving our foreign relations, by beefing up the CIA, and by economic development investments in the countries that currently harbor terrorists."

Affirming the Consequent: Mistakenly reasoning from "If A, then B" and "B is true" to the faulty conclusion that therefore "A must be true." For example, suppose it is the case that "If the river continues to rise, then the carpet will be wet." And suppose that we observe that the carpet is wet. It does not follow that the flooded room necessarily resulted from the river rising, for it may have resulted from an entirely different set of events (for example, the dishwasher overflowing).

Denying the Antecedent: Mistakenly reasoning from "If A, then B" and "A is not the case" to the faulty conclusion that "B must not be the case." For example, "If we see a light in the window, we know that there is someone at home. But we do not see a light in the window. So there can't be anyone at home."

Our hypothesis is that part of the persuasive and pervasive character of these common fallacies is due to the influence of heuristic reasoning. Humans commonly use heuristic shortcuts, so we are accustomed to reasoning without fully thinking through all of the logical relationships implied by the warrants we rely upon or by the descriptions of the data we accept as accurate. In a way it would be comforting to know that part of why we are deceived by common fallacies, like those identified here, has to do with how our species evolved and developed. Yet, even so, this reinforces the significance of meta-cognition to examine and correct our own reasoning, lest we continue to be misled so naturally.

Argument Contexts and Evaluative Terms

There is nothing about argument making for purposes of coming to a decision that requires the format to be a debate or in any way an adversarial confrontation. In fact, it does a great disservice to decision making as well as to education to imagine continually the process as a confrontation of opponents pro and con. In such an adversarial frame, it is too easy to forgo truth-seeking in the false belief that argument making is simply the search for facts that support one's preconceptions. The courageous desire for best knowledge is trumped by the competitive need to vanquish the opposition. The honest pursuit of reasons and evidence wherever they may lead, even if the reasons and evidence go against one's preconceptions or interests, is abandoned because intellectual honesty and integrity are not always suitable virtues for warriors who must bring home the victory for their side.

Good arguments – subtle and yet effective as solid proofs that their claims are warranted – occur within a variety of linguistic behaviors and activities. In natural language contexts, argument making takes many forms. It can be a personable and friendly conversation exploring options and considering ideas. It can be embedded in warnings, recommendations, preambles to policy statements, public addresses, conversations, group meetings, negotiations, monologues, reflections, and even the lyrics of songs.[73] The sixties folksong group Peter, Paul, and Mary gave us this example in a gentle piece of music which begins by setting up an analogy.[74]

> If I had wings, no one would ask me should I fly.
> The bird sings. No one asks why.
> I can see in myself wings as I feel them.
> If you see something else keep your thoughts to yourself.
> I'll fly free then.

The argument claims that freedom is as natural to human beings as flying is to birds. It is just that people can see the wings on birds more easily than they might be able to perceive that all persons are free. The lyricist asserts that he can feel his own freedom just as strongly, however, as if he were a winged creature. As a result, even if others are not able, for whatever reason, to overcome their inability to recognize his freedom, they should not be asking him to justify his exercise of his rights as a free person.

The vocabulary we use to evaluate arguments needs to be as flexible as our understanding of the contexts of argument making. A conversation with a colleague about an impending decision can be helpful, even if we would not wish to apply words like "valid," or even "persuasive." Natural language offers such richness in its evaluative repertoire that it seems wise, at least at this early point, not to close our options by prematurely stipulating a set of evaluative categories. Thus, with the understanding that these terms are not meant to be interpreted rigidly or in some special technical way, let us simply go forward with our evaluation of arguments using common language. Table 8 offers some suggestions regarding the range of evaluative adjectives that might reasonably be applied when evaluating the different elements of major concern, data, warrants, claims, and arguments.

TABLE 8 -- EVALUATIVE ADJECTIVES FOR ARGUMENTS AND THEIR ELEMENTS

DATA	POSITIVE: True, Possible, Probable, Verifiable, Believable, Valid, Cleaned, Accurate, Factual, etc.
	NEGATIVE: False, Improbable, Self-Contradictory, Fanciful, Fabricated, Unknowable, etc.
WARRANTS	POSITIVE: Certain, True, Probable, Verifiable, Relevant, Wise, Sensible, Well-Applied, Possible, Believable, etc.
	NEGATIVE: False, Improbable, Self-Contradictory, Poorly–applied, Irrelevant, Foolish, Irrational, Fanciful, Unknowable, Vague, Equivocal, Ill-Conceived, Circular, etc.
CLAIMS	POSITIVE: Well-Documented, Strongly-Supported, Well-Argued, Certain, True, Reasonable, Possible, Probable, etc.
	NEGATIVE: Improbable, Poorly-Supported, Unfounded, Self-Contradictory, Uncertain, False, Biased, Preposterous, etc.
ARGUMENTS	POSITIVE: Acceptable, Sound, Valid, Logical, Strong, Persuasive, Reasonable, etc.
	NEGATIVE: Unacceptable, Unsound, Fallacious, Illogical, Incomplete, Unreasonable, Trivial, etc.

To appreciate some of the richness of the evaluative language available, consider this argument. Imagine a person looking into a mirror and seeing something on their skin which they may not have noticed before.

I've got this brown spot. (dT)
It's nothing to worry about. (c?)
As far as I know, brown spots like these are nothing to worry about. (w?)

If we accept the warrant without challenge, then there is no sense in which the reasoning does not seem sound. But, suppose that we are uncertain whether the warrant correctly applies to the relationship between the data and claim. That is, we are not sure if the brown spot on the skin is the kind of brown spot that is not worrisome. If the warrant does not apply, then the validity of the argument is questionable. And if the warrant is mistaken, the argument should not be accepted either. With these doubts in mind, the claim will be uncertain and perhaps false. A decision to ignore the newly discovered brown spot based on this argument, with its attendant uncertainties, would seem in this case unwise. If we add (make explicit) the datum, "Some brown spots are signs of significant illness," a statement implied by the warrant itself, then the potential danger of the decision to ignore the spot is more obvious. It is this potential, inherent in a complete A&H Analysis, which offers new tools to those who help others think through high stakes decisions. Seeing the explicit assumptions often lays bare the weaknesses of poor arguments.

The Inadequacy of Logical Analysis Alone

Consider a passage excerpted from narrative data provided by a forty-five year old female. She was asked whether she would see her health care provider if she were to discover a change in her body that caused her to worry about the possibility of breast cancer. The interviewer and the woman are talking about her possible self-discovery of a worrisome sign of breast cancer, such as a lump she might find when doing a breast self-examination.

> Interviewer: "You're very religious. Could you see yourself waiting awhile before going to the doctor and praying instead?"
> Respondent: "Oh, no. For one thing, God is a wonderful God; he made doctors. You know, my mother in law – I'm divorced, I was married then – she had had a heart attack. And, she definitely [would pray instead of go to the doctor]. She loved the Lord and she remained in God's will. But at times people have to understand that God doesn't make things [as] complicated as people kind of want to make it. And it's not about religion; it's about God, your personal relationship with Him. And God, He made some [people] become doctors to want to help. You know that's how I feel. You know, I'll say this until the day I die and go back to the Lord. I'm a practicing Christian; I love the Lord. I just know God works within common sense. That's why He gave us a brain, you know. And I would definitely go to the doctor."

This piece of text is a verbatim transcription taken from an interview discussing the decision to seek a provider evaluation for a breast symptom. Figure 21 is our map of this speaker's decision.

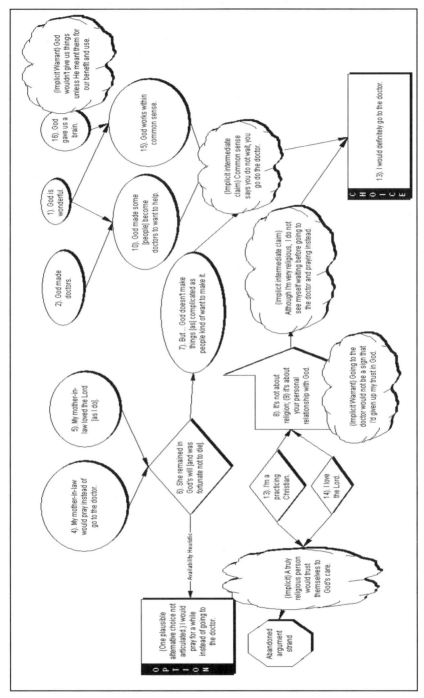

FIGURE 21 – "I WOULD DEFINITELY GO TO THE DOCTOR"

Although she is actually talking about her own decision, the woman's analogical reference to her mother-in-law is important. Notice first that the woman knows that her mother-in-law's medical problem is different, although the mother-in-law did have to confront the same choice, either to seek or not to seek an evaluation. The key similarity for this speaker is not the potential illness, but rather that both women are deeply religious. Yet, while the mother-in-law chose to pray and to delay seeking medical care, the speaker makes a different choice. For her, upon reflection, the meaning of "being religious" has to do with a "personal relationship with God." For her, going to the doctor would not be a demonstration that she has lost her faith in God. And so she decides not to regard being religious as an impediment to seeking an evaluation.

We observe also that the mother-in-law's case is immediately available to mind. It is someone in her own family, someone she knows well, a woman, like herself in many ways, someone with whom she can identify. Thus it would have been easy for the speaker to simulate herself being as fortunate as her mother-in-law and deciding to delay."""""" Because the analogy is strong, she could infer that delay would not be fatal in her own case, for it was not fatal in the case of the mother-in-law. But, she does not.

Notice that one of her key beliefs, "God doesn't make things [as] complicated as people kind of want to make it," is metaphysical. It is impossible to know how complicated God intends things to be. Aside from knowing the mind of God, humans can neither confirm nor disconfirm the generalization. The speaker then appeals to common sense saying, "I just know God works within common sense." Without doubt, people at different times and places have ascribed wildly inconsistent ideas to common sense. This highly unreliable source has been advanced as the basis for a wide variety of true and false assertions about virtually everything. Arguments that appeal to common sense are slightly disguised versions of the classic "Appeal to the Mob" fallacy described above.

The speaker's confidence in the benevolence of the Lord is the other basis for her conviction. God has provided us with doctors for our care and given us brains to realize that we should use what He has provided. The warrant "God wouldn't give us things unless He meant them for our benefit and use," is another metaphysical statement which defies confirmation and disconfirmation. In the event of difficulties, the benefits persons of faith

---

"""""" Both of these reasoning maneuvers involve heuristic thinking, discussed in detail in the next chapter.

perceive are that we are being tested and purified by the suffering and trials life brings. And good things, of course, are blessings the Lord has sent. It is difficult, if not impossible, to imagine a counter-example to these generalizations. One cannot evaluate arguments of this kind as logically sound. Certainly they can be consistent and logical in the way that reasoning in mathematics or the reasoning inside the structure of a complex game can be consistent and logical. We can tell when one belief statement contradicts another, and we can tell when one belief statement is implied logically by another. But there is not, in principle, any way to confirm or to disconfirm the factual truth of the beliefs in such systems. And, without knowing that the data and warrant statements are true, we cannot be sure that the arguments based on them are sound.

When analyzed from the point of view of logic, the speaker's argument resulting in the firm decision that she would definitely go to the doctor is rife with problems. The analogy seems at least partially misapplied, the argument relies on a classic fallacy, and a central warrant is a metaphysical statement which cannot be substantiated. There is hardly a test of the logical quality of arguments identified in this chapter that her reasoning would pass. And yet, there is absolutely no disputing that the woman's argument has great persuasive force for her and for many men and women like her.

The fact is argument making alone simply does not determine human decisions. As a result, logical analysis alone cannot supply an arsenal of sufficient power for us to understand human decision making. To comprehend human decision making we must supplement the traditional forms of logical analysis, often conceived of as indicating how humans "ought to" reason, with findings derived from empirical studies of human decision making, often conceived of as describing how humans "do" reason. The reasoning heuristics described in Chapter 6 will reveal a large part of the story. Chapter 7 will then describe how humans use both logical reasoning and heuristic thinking to make choices with sufficient conviction to sustain acting on the basis of those decisions.

Chapter 6:
Evaluating Heuristic Thinking

Shakespeare called humans the "paragon of animals." Aristotle observed that we are a species of bipeds which reasons. Not too respectful of human intelligence, yet an honest examination of how we generally think would have to admit that we humans make reasoning mistakes quite regularly. At our best we make vitally important decisions for ourselves, our families, our communities, and our planet by endeavoring to take into consideration all the relevant evidence, conceptualizations, methodologies, contexts, and standards. At our worst we allow our judgments to be based on unfounded assumptions and fallacious reasoning. The list of argument making fallacies in Chapter 4 is hardly complete. It does not include all the ways that our decision making can be led astray by biases and errors associated with the misapplication of cognitive heuristics. Fifty years ago, Herbert Simon described human reasoning as "bounded rationality." He said, "Full rationality implied by the rational choice model was an unrealistic standard."[75]

Heuristic thinking strategies are ordinarily reliable maneuvers to guide decision making, particularly in familiar contexts. They play larger roles under conditions of uncertainty and in unfamiliar contexts or where the evidence which would support sound arguments and claims is lacking. Errors in heuristic thinking can result in serious problems when the risks are great and the stakes are high.

The first step toward evaluating the influences of heuristic thinking is being able to recognize where and how these strategies are used in human reasoning. So we shall begin this chapter with descriptions of individual heuristics and then discuss examples of how and where they occur in the human decision making process. As we shall see, two or more heuristics can occur occasionally in combinations which can improve or diminish the quality of human decisions. Once the potential risks associated with a given heuristic maneuver are clear, it is an easy matter to evaluate a given decision making experience. The chapter concludes with an illustrative extended case study.

Specific Heuristic Maneuvers – Descriptions, Benefits, and Risks

The names and descriptions below are intended to assist in identifying and differentiating various human reasoning heuristic maneuvers.[††††††] There are potentially beneficial consequences associated with relying on the maneuver in each case, but a misapplication of the maneuver can yield harmful results as well. We will describe fourteen heuristics individually and then summarize all of them in Table 9.[‡‡‡‡‡‡]

1. Satisficing

Cognitive maneuver: Given an option that is good enough, decide in favor of that option. We humans typically do only what must be done to achieve our purposes. When faced with choices, instead of expending the resources necessary to attain the maximally optimal alternative, we decide in favor of an alternative we deem satisfactory.[76,77,78] We tend to divide the world into "good enough" and "not good enough," and search for a solution until a solution is found which is good enough to attain the desired outcome. System-1: Reacting to a falling object, how far would we move? Far enough to get out of the way. System-2: Seeing a new job, how hard would we look? Hard enough to find one that meets whatever are our basic criteria for pay, proximity to home, nature of the work, etc. Truisms like "If it ain't broke, don't fix it," and "'Perfect' is the enemy of 'good'" reflect the satisficing cognitive maneuver.

The running mate of satisficing is temporizing, deciding that a given option is "good enough for now." We often move through life satisficing and temporizing. At times we look back on our situations and wonder why it is that we have settled for far less than we might have. If we had only studied harder, worked out a little more, taken better care of ourselves and our relationships, perhaps we would not be living as we are now. But at the time, each of the decisions along the way was "good enough for the time being."

[††††††] Some refer to heuristic "shortcuts," but we prefer "maneuvers." True, heuristic thinking does save time and effort, so it is a mental shortcut. But "shortcut" suggests that one had the destination in mind all along, whereas "maneuver" suggests a shift in tactics and a movement in a new and perhaps unexpected direction. And, if a heuristic maneuver results in a poor decision, as may happen at times, and the decision needs to be revisited and revised, then it was hardly a useful shortcut.

[‡‡‡‡‡‡] If you are familiar with this literature and comfortable with identifying heuristic thinking and its misuses, skip ahead to Table 9.

There are important potential advantages to satisficing. These include conserving time, money, and energy.[79] If you have to put in 10% more effort and time to gain only 1% more value, your return on investment may not be worth the cost. The main disadvantage of satisficing is that the best option/outcome may be lost to us while we rely on an approach mistakenly judged to be "good enough." Why did the better team lose the game? Because, underestimating its opponent, the team failed to play up to its own potential.

The use of satisficing in particular situations is no doubt a reflection of beliefs and values about what can be achieved roughly versus with precision and what can be sacrificed in the absence of careful effort to achieve the maximal fit of solution to problem. There is also information about expectations in the use of satisficing, for the "good enough" solution meets the decision maker's expectations, but may not meet others' expectations of what is good enough. Finally we learn something about the decision maker. Perhaps we learn that the decision maker is does not desire the outcome strongly enough to do all that would be needed to assure that the outcome was reached. Or we may learn that decision maker does not appreciate what is necessary to attain the level of success others expect. These are only examples. You will likely find more when you apply this method to your own study of other decision making contexts and situations.

2. Affect

Cognitive maneuver: Take an initial stance in support of, or in opposition to, a given choice consistent with one's initial affective response to that choice.[80,81] There is no question that many different kinds of experiences can cause us to respond with joy or sorrow, with desire or revulsion, with enthusiasm or dread. A "gut reaction," that is, an affective response, can orient us positively or negatively toward the object.

Human thinking processes entail the making and testing of mental representations of the problem and its solution in order to select one that has a preferred outcome.[82,83] Facing the need to make a judgment, we review either consciously or unconsciously the emotional markers which have been included in the mental representations of the elements involved in that judgment. Those emotional markers become parts of the valances we attach to our possible choices.[84] The result is that we feel more positively disposed toward choices that coincide with our positive emotional markers. This can have obvious advantages and disadvantages. Research on the relationship between facial symmetry, perceived attractiveness, and health suggest that first affective impressions have ecological value. Affective response can influence us toward embracing a choice that "just feels right." Affect can steer us away from an option we see as frightening or repugnant. But, what if that option is actually the best and most reasonable? For example, what if our fear of the anticipated consequences of radiation or chemotherapy influenced us to reject those options when one or both of them were are best possible treatment options? It may take significant amounts of reflective System-2 reasoning to overcome a powerful System-1 affective response to an idea, but it can be done. And at times it should be, because there is no guarantee that our affective responses are necessarily always veridical.

At times, the affect heuristic influences us to make judgments and decisions based on our initial impulsive and subliminal responses to things. Marketing experts know this propensity and have coined the expression, "The package is the product," to indicate how important the wrapping, the container, and the initial appearance of a product are to making the sale.[85] Certainly a broken dorm window and an unkempt campus lawn are not necessarily indicative of an academically substandard college. But college recruiters know that these things had better be fixed before prospective students and their parents show up for the campus tour. And on reflection, no one would argue that a cabernet in an attractively designed bottle with a classy label is necessarily superior to a cabernet in a common looking bottle with a plain looking label. But first impressions count when choosing a college, choosing a wine, and when choosing in many other contexts.

The heuristic determination of "good" might lead to argument strands claiming that some possible problem solution brings pleasure, avoids pain, or provides fulfillment through compassion. In contrast, a "bad" gut reaction will likely invite the making of one or more arguments for why one must or should avoid, diminish, or extinguish the issue in question. Use of the affect heuristic, and subsequent related arguments, reveal information about the beliefs and values of the decision maker. One habit of mind that might accompany this type of heuristic reasoning is the disposition to cognitive integrity. If one has a negative heuristic reaction to an issue or choice, it will require a measure of cognitive integrity to go forward and think about things that are frightening or highly unpleasant. Someone without this habit of mind might fail to ask the "hard" questions in their consideration of an issue or problem, and we should see supporting evidence of this failure in the overall argument map analyzing their decision process.[86]

3. Simulation

Cognitive maneuver: Estimate the likelihood of a given outcome based on one's ease in imagining that outcome.[87,88] Simulation is a mental process of construction wherein humans estimate their propensity for taking a given action and their probability of achieving desired states. If we experience ease in processing a simulation, this influences us to believe that achieving the anticipated outcome is more likely.[89,90] A person choosing among several options might simulate taking each option, making a movie in their mind about how each will play out for them. The person will be influenced by their imaginings to select the option which plays out in their mind as resulting in the most desirable outcome, heedless of the actual probability of that result actually occurring.

Bandura's research demonstrates the value and power of simulation to increase attitudes of self-efficacy.[91,92] Mentors and coaches use simulation as a technique to improve performance and to help people anticipate being able to succeed at challenging things. Successful advertising often depends on stimulating simulation. Car ads, for example, often show someone with demographics just like the intended buyers taking great pleasure in driving the model of car the ad is promoting. The idea is that if you match those demographics you would then be led to see yourself in that car and then want to buy it. The process of simulation is quick, easy, and need not be reflective. In fact, it might be better for the advertiser if you do not reflect too much on the actual costs and benefits of buying that new car.

In focus group research and in interview data, subjects can appear to employ the simulation heuristic while continuing to speak. One might observe a short pause, a verbalization such as "oh" or "um," a repeated word or phrase, or some other vocalization which does not advance the content of the statement being made. With a prompt like "What were you thinking just then," the subject may reveal the simulation, as in, "I was imagining myself driving to Los Angeles alone." The advantages of improving self-efficacy have been noted. The obvious disadvantage of this cognitive maneuver is the potential to err in estimating the likelihood of the imagined outcomes. This can result in misplaced confidence and unwarranted optimism. "I don't know what happened!" said the sales representative after the failed meeting. "Yesterday I could see myself closing that deal."

An analysis of the use of simulation provides a window into the subject's expectancies and beliefs regarding achievable outcomes as a result of behaving in a given way. Take for instance the example of hang-gliding from the cliffs above the Pacific Ocean. This simulation will be unique to each of us. I might play the movie that shows myself sailing in the silent clear blue sky … among the gulls … wearing my glistening black wetsuit … and my sail sporting all the colors of the rainbow. The water below is a glorious expanse of greens and blues. There are waves and beach below me, and I will land on that beach when I have tired of this wonderful past time. I would be more likely to argue for the value of a decision to take up hang-gliding if this is my simulation than if I play the movie where the glider is heavy, my arms are aching, and I am fearful … or I actually see myself crashing on the rocks below. The point here is that you will know something of my beliefs and expectancies by analyzing the content of my use of simulation to make a judgment.

4. Availability

Cognitive maneuver: Base the estimate of the likelihood of a future event on the vividness or ease of recalling a similar past event.[93,94] This heuristic influences us to attach a higher subjective probability to outcomes which more readily bring to mind vivid or personally salient prior events. When a story or vivid memory comes easily to mind of something that happened to us or to someone close to us, or was presented vividly through the media, we are influenced to overestimate the likelihood of future events unfolding in the same way. People tell stories of things that happened to themselves or their friends all the time as a way of explaining their own decisions and warning or advising their friends and family about the future. In the retelling, the actual events may be mistakenly remembered, misunderstood, or misinterpreted. Accuracy aside, such stories can have an unwarranted amount of influence on decisions about what to expect, what to believe, and what to do.

A motion picture vividly dramatizing the tragic story of one young woman's death as the victim of savage religiously-based discrimination can be more powerful than an abstract report which may accurately make the same point. The stories teachers, mentors, parents, and friends tell are often intended to guide us toward one decision rather than another. But, objectively speaking, the actual probabilities of our experience being exactly like those in the story may be rather different than our subjective estimates. The disadvantage of availability based judgments is their tendency to wrongly estimate the actual probabilities that a given outcome will occur.[95,96] In the aftermath of the horrendous killings of over 30 people at Virginia Tech University in April of 2007, parents, students, faculty, and staff at the nation's more than 4200 colleges and universities suddenly revised sharply upward their estimates of the probabilities of their becoming victims of a similarly deranged killer's assault on their own campuses. Campus security was increased, counseling centers were given more funding, legislative hearings were held at the state and national levels, campus emergency plans were updated, and readiness drills were conducted.

The use of this heuristic usually occurs when an individual does not have a more objective estimate of the prevalence of an event or its likelihood of recurrence. But we've observed individuals who use this heuristic in order to manipulate a situation. As a result, they can feel confident in what they might otherwise see as an overestimation of either positive or negative outcomes. When they have predetermined a desired outcome, they call up a particularly vivid memory of a past event of similar character. Rather than taking a more deliberative approach when they wish to argue emphatically against a given side of argument, they use this remembered event, perhaps even embellishing it a bit to make it more impressive to others, to argue against an undesired choice and in favor of their own position. This use of availability is not necessarily reflective and appears to be a habit of mind, even though at times the thinker seems to know that they are exaggerating or even thinking poorly.

For example, suppose it must be decided by a group whether a significant amount of money should be spent to obtain new software package for a business. While clearly one might take an organized approach to evaluating the quality of the software in question, it is not rare to observe someone arguing that the software purchase is ill-advised before any research on the software is undertaken. They might use a vignette of a past experience where software was purchased and it resulted in unexpected costs, struggles to train staff, loss of sales, and missed deadlines. This person is arguing against the software purchase, expecting the group to overestimate the likelihood of negative sequellae as a result of the software purchase. If the others use the availability heuristic (as the story teller expects) they may collectively decide not to purchase the software. But, we can hope that some in the group will take a more reflective approach to the problem. If so, some may surface other examples and infer that this story is neither typical nor likely to occur in their company's case. Others may argue that even if all of these problems are typical, there will be other positive benefits to the software purchase that should first also be considered before making a decision about the purchase.

5. Representativeness – Analogical

Cognitive maneuver: Infer that because X is like Y in some way or other, X is like Y in relevant ways. A perceived similarity becomes the basis for assuming that there is an analogical relationship between two things, an analogy which may or may not be warranted.[97,98] [§§§§§§] For example, someone might say, "My father and I were alike in so many ways … in our life styles and how we thought about things. Dad died last year of lymphoma at 82. You know … as much as I don't like the idea, I probably have about 20 years until cancer gets me." The speaker in this example appears to be overestimating the probability of contracting a fatal lymphoma or other cancer, or even of dying at age 82. This thinking is disconnected from any analytical reflection on the scientific evidence regarding the genetic and environmental factors which estimate a person's cancer risks. When we take the time to examine reflectively whether an analogy is warranted, we are doing System-2 thinking. But otherwise we are at risk of unreflectively permitting the analogical representativeness heuristic maneuver to unduly influence our beliefs and choices.[********]

But the more fundamental and relevant the similarity, the more reliable will be the analogy based on it. For example, suppose your boss fired your coworker for missing sales targets and you draw the reasonable conclusion that you are no different in relevant respects from your coworker, so if you miss your sales targets you'll be fired too. Good thinking.

Or the similarity might be superficial or not connected with the outcome, which would make the analogical inference unwarranted. For example, you see a TV commercial showing trim-figured young people enjoying fattening fast foods and infer that because you're young too, you can indulge your cravings for fast foods without gaining excess unsightly poundage. This is another example showing that heuristic thought needs to be monitored when it is used to make important decisions. Usually this heuristic operates below the level of reflective thought, but if one has the habit of mind to examine how one is making a particularly important decision, it is possible to notice

---

[§§§§§§] In the early heuristics literature "Representativeness" covered a wide range of things. Here we use "Analogical" as the name for some and "Associational" as the name for others. At times, these heuristics are found in the literature under the title "Similarity."

[********] Appendix C discusses analogical reasoning. Along with the discussions of axiological and empirical reasoning in Appendix D and Appendix E, criteria for evaluating each of these important modes of human inference are presented.

that an important decision may be hinging on whether or not a comparison made using the analogical representativeness heuristic is really appropriate. Self-monitoring and self-correcting one's thinking can help assure that conclusions are warranted.

6. Representativeness – Associational

Cognitive maneuver: Connect ideas on the basis of word association and the memories, meanings, or impressions they might trigger. We all have experienced conversations where one comment seems connected to another by nothing more than word association. Someone might suggest, "Let's take our drinks outside to the picnic table." To which someone else might respond, "Remember the picnic three years ago when Grandpa had his heart attack? I'm never going to that park again." The representativeness – associational heuristic is operating when a word or idea reminds us of something else. Typically this is System-1 thinking – reactive, associational, and not critically reflective. For example, one person might associate sunshine with happiness and another person might associate sunshine with skin cancer. Or, as in the example above, picnic with Grandpa's heart attack. The salient negative experience brought to mind by the mere use of the word 'picnic' influenced the speaker to assert the decision never to return to the park where the sad event occurred. This was not what the group had been talking about; but it was the System-1 reaction triggered by the association in this person's mind.

The observation of associational reasoning, particularly if it is frequent, is informative of a person's habits of mind. We all use associational reasoning quite often when we use memory and conceptual knowledge to inform and enrich our thinking processes. Evidence of this in spoken or written data provides evidence of memory recall, and can be informative about beliefs and values. Occasionally, associational reasoning results in a change in train of thought or perhaps even a loss of one's direction when making a judgment. Recall hearing someone say, "I'm not sure why I got off on this, but let me get back to the issue at hand." This individual is monitoring their thinking meta-cognitively to evaluate their thinking process. Someone who does not do this and often changes the direction of their thought as a result of associational reasoning will appear to have rambling thought processes. Associational thinking, unmonitored, is of little value, logically speaking. But it can be creative, frustrating, and entertaining all at the same time.

7. Generalizing from One to All

Cognitive maneuver: From a single salient instance, draw a generalization about an entire group. Although an anecdote is not data, we have all heard people draw conclusions about whole groups of people based on their experience with only one or two people who are members of that group. We call this stereotyping or profiling. The Tom Hanks film, *Band of Brothers,* illustrated what it was like to be a combat infantryman during WWII by telling the story of one company. The generalizations may not have been perfect, but few veterans took issue with the movie; most found it true to their lived experience. The advantages of stereotyping and profiling are many, and the risks are high as well: bigotry, prejudice, misunderstanding, and mistrust, to name only a few.

The tendency to think that our personal experience of a single instance is predictive of what we would find were we to sample more systematically a whole class of individuals can undermine decision making in almost any context. We drive a rental car made by a given automaker and then generalize our evaluation of that car to all cars made by that automaker. Not entirely a bad inference, given that cars are mass produced. Does this work for paintings by a given artist, songs by a given songwriter, and novels by a given author? What about courses taught by a given professor, patient problems treated by a given health care provider, or decisions by a given manager? We do not have the time to make systematic scientific surveys of everything we may need to know. So we take the shortcut of basing decisions on relatively few instances. This is what we are doing when we ask a friend if she or he knows a good dentist, doctor, real estate broker, or lawyer. Or if we ask an alumna to tell us how good her college experience was when we are trying to decide where to go to school. The trade-off between effort expended and the reliability of the information derived makes this approach risky. Here again, monitoring one's habits of mind is a good idea.

8. The "Us vs. Them" Dynamic

Cognitive maneuver: Reduce problems to a simple choice between two opposing forces. Battle lines are drawn with phrases like: "Those who are not with me are against me," "There can be no middle ground;" and "There can be no negotiations." ††††††† Once we have used this heuristic many other

---

††††††† Dualistic thinking divides the world into black and white with not shades of gray. For dualistic thinkers all problems have right answers or wrong answers only. But psychological dualism is a broader construct. It is better understood in the context of cognitive development. The

decisions are simplified. Toward "them" we have no obligations, but if you are one of "us" we will stand by you to through thick and thin.[99] In its most extreme manifestations, the "Us-vs.-Them" Dynamic can set up the tendency to regard "Them" as non-persons, objects off the ethical radar screen, "Others" who can be manipulated or removed without ethical concern. Called the *false polarization effect,*[100] it can be a very dangerous approach to problem solving, and a potentially explosive and negative strategy for a society or a leader to take. Let us not be naïve about this. If humans are strongly influenced by Us-vs.-Them thinking, then it would be foolish of us not to take that into consideration when approaching others for the first time. Generosity of spirit and openness are wonderful virtues, but venturing into potentially hostile territory with caution thrown to the wind is seldom likely to be the optimal choice.

Journalists, politicians, zealots, and evangelists of all stripes know how easily people can be manipulated by playing on the natural tendency to mistrust "Those Other People" – the ones who are not part of "Us" – the ones who are different, the ones with whom we disagree. Manipulative leaders know how easy it is to make an enemy out of the opposition; to ascribe evil intentions rather than to take their point of view seriously; to demonize them; to engender fear in "Us" lest "They" should "get what they want," "come to power," or "take what is rightfully ours." During a recent trip to Washington DC, we visited a congressional office. We urged support of a bill and gave a good reason. The response was that the congressperson could not support the bill with that reason. Why? Because that was a reason being used by the opposition to support the same bill! Did we not understand? If the other party wanted the bill passed for that reason, then the congressperson's party should oppose the bill on those grounds. The risks associated with dualistic thinking are serious enough. These risks are only compounded when fear and mistrust are set in opposition to loyalty and group identity. We do not see much hope for redemption in relying on Us-vs.-Them thinking, but we see abundant examples of it everyday. Held beliefs and values are shown clearly when this heuristic is in play.

9. "Master – Slave" Power Differential

Cognitive maneuver: Accept without question a problem as presented by, or a solution as proposed by, a superior authority. Social hierarchies abound at home, at work, in government, in religion, and even in recreation. Many

---

"Us vs. Them" Dynamic, as cognitive heuristic, can influence decisions made by people whose cognitive development has progressed beyond dualistic thinking in many domains.

are benevolent and respectful. But even in these cases, and certainly in those which are manipulative and abusive, there is a tendency to defer to the individual or group in charge. It may be something as benign as agreeing on when to eat dinner or which TV show to watch. The decision to defer, that is, not to dispute or challenge, the decisions of others higher in the food chain, manifests itself in accepting not only what they may decide to have us do, but also to how they see the world and how they frame the problems we are being asked to help solve. Middle managers are susceptible to similar pressure from senior executives, as are second children from their elder sibling, or junior officers relative to their superiors. In a gang, for example, the power differential between the gang leader and his or her followers, when combined with the "Us vs. Them" heuristic for viewing the world, can strongly influence gang members to internalize gang rivalries and to agree with violent responses to perceived threats.

There may be some advantages to recognizing the realities of power differentials and not bucking the system. Not only can this save cognitive resources, it might save your job and your domestic happiness as well. After all, if the boss wants the client list updated, why not update it? And if your partner wants to go to a movie that might not have been your first choice, why not go anyway? Having people see things your way may not be the highest of all values, even if you are smarter than they are about some things. We have all heard the saying, "You've got to go along to get along." Harmony is a value, too.

On the other hand, how many times have we seen clearly that the boss was heading the department in the wrong direction, or that the team captain was employing an ineffective strategy, or that our elder sibling was wrong, or that our leaders were motivated more by self-interest than the common good? Any full evaluation by mature adults of the reasoning presented by those in power over us – religious, political, managerial, or otherwise – should include consideration of whether the benefits derived from the current power structure relationship warrant continuing that relationship or whether it is time to consider seriously other options.

Observation of this heuristic influence in a decision process is informative of expectations that frame the problem before it is engaged. We may feel there is no need to even consider options outside our reach. Misjudgments here are observable as expectations of failure, as perceived lack of opportunities, and as forced undesirable social role behaviors. One service a good consultant can provide is to listen to the framing of problems by clients, hearing the arguments for what is unchangeable and what alternatives are perceived as the only ones available. The job of the consultant then is to disabuse the client of the misuse of this heuristic, helping them to discover power were they have not been able to see it.

10. Anchoring with Adjustment

Cognitive maneuver: Having made an evaluation, adjust as little as needed in light of new evidence.[101,102] When we are making evaluative judgments, it is natural to locate or anchor our evaluation at some point along whatever scale we are using. If we are being more reflective, we may have established some criteria and we may be working to apply them as fair-mindedly as possible. As other information comes our way, we may adjust our evaluation. The interesting thing about this cognitive maneuver is that we do not normally start over with a fresh evaluation. We have dropped anchor and we may drag it upward or downward a bit, but we do not pull it off the bottom of the sea to relocate our evaluation. First impressions, as the saying goes, cannot easily be undone. For example, a professor applies a grading rubric and assigns one of the first student papers in the batch being graded a C-. Then later, after having read several more papers in the batch, the professor recalls that early paper and that thinks that by comparison to the others it deserves a better grade than a C-. So the professor adjusts the grade upward a bit, maybe to C or a C+. But the professor probably will not decide that the paper rates a B+ or higher. Having anchored initially on the C-, the professor feels compelled to adjust the grade upward, but not by much.

One advantage of this heuristic is that it permits us to move on. We have done the evaluation; there are other papers to grade, other things in life that need attention. We could not long endure if we were to constantly re-evaluate every thing anew. Part of developing expertise is learning to calibrate and nuance one's judgments, refine one's criteria, and adjust the criteria to fit the complexities of the circumstances of judgment. Anchoring with adjustment can reflect a progression toward greater precision, a way to refine not only judgments about particular things, but the criteria applied when making those judgments. The unfortunate thing about this heuristic, however, is that we sometimes drop anchor in the wrong place; we have a hard time giving people a second chance at making a good first impression. How often have we seen it happen that a coworker's performance is initially evaluated as sub-par (outstanding) and almost nothing that happens subsequently can move that initial evaluation marker very far from where it started? Subsequent outstanding work (poor work) is regarded as a fluke or an anomaly, not as genuine counter evidence which should result in a thorough re-evaluation.

The comment about the need to monitor heuristic reasoning when the stakes are high is probably getting a bit old by now, but never is it more important to examine one's assumptions than when one has anchored inappropriately in a high stakes situation. The need to figure this out alone is rare, because usually we are being urged by others repeatedly to reconsider and "think things through again." The literature on critical thinking dispositions is rich in this area, emphasizing the need to value a full reconsideration of problems once new evidence is available and to pursue a better judgment while actively working to overcome bias due to preconceptions.[103,104]

11. (Illusion of) Control

Cognitive maneuver: Estimate the level of control you have over the actual outcome of events upon the amount of desire or energy you put into trying to shape those events. When used correctly, this heuristic helps calibrate estimates of our effectiveness when working at solving problems or being influential to a situation. Thompson and her colleagues[105] have proposed that humans frequently overestimate their actual ability to control the outcomes of events. Human reasoning frequently fails to account for the actual contingencies involved in the control of events and distorts one's actual control of assuring a given outcome. We generally do not carry out the demanding task of calculating actual contingencies when estimating our control of events.[106] Rather, we tend to overestimate the actual connection between our actions and attaining the desired outcome. Wanting a given outcome strongly, we tend to think that decisions we make or actions we take are genuinely instrumental in bringing about or failing to bring about that outcome regardless of the actual contingencies, forces, and factors at work. Some have described the misuse of this heuristic as the "illusion of control."

One example of the tendency to misestimate control is hindsight bias. **Hindsight bias** occurs because successful events are more often remembered and reconstructed as being the result of the acts of the agent.[107] Past failures are more often forgotten or reconstructed as having resulted from chance or someone else's doing. Our human need for accuracy, predictability, and self-justification is believed to motivate this hindsight biasing behavior.[108] The result is illusory control – a condition which can occur even when the event itself is actually controlled only by chance, for instance picking lottery numbers.[109,110] The tendency to take undeserved credit for good outcomes or to shift responsibility to others for undesirable outcomes in certainly not limited to supervisors or those in positions of power.

A second example of misuse of the control heuristic is the tendency toward an *optimistic bias*. Cognitive scientists have documented optimistic bias in human estimates of their personal risk.[111,112,113,114,115] When asked to estimate personal risk for a wide variety of hazards, humans typically (~75% of the population) estimate their own risk as less than that of peers with identical characteristics as themselves. The use of this heuristic is believed to be advantageous, since the constant dread of serious hazards would be detrimental to mental health. However, since their risk of hazard is actually no better and no worse than others', all things being equal, this built-in bias results in poorer and perhaps more risky judgments in some situations. Regardless of the psychological effects on mood of incurable optimism, demonstrating this cognitive habit of mind can often result in predictably poorer judgments.

Hindsight bias and optimistic bias can work together to threaten sound judgment. Optimistic bias involves failing to take into account the actual risks of an undesirable outcome, and this leads us to approach decisions with the view that *whereas others might fail, we are going to be successful.* Hindsight bias adds fuel to the fire of our confidence, for it disposes us to believe that actions we have taken actually did have a strong impact on the outcome of events. For example, managers, failing to take into account the threat to market share posed by a competitor's introduction of a new product, may approach decisions about the redesign of their own product with the view that the competitor's new product will indeed take market share away, but it will be taken from other competitors and not from them. Or, the managers may recall that in the past they have offered product discounts hoping to boost slipping sales numbers. So they do so again. And when sales do not fall as far as had been feared, hindsight bias might lead the managers to infer that it was their decision to offer discounts, rather than other factors, such as weak competition, new tax incentives, or general improvements in the overall economy, which led to those sales numbers. The inference here, stripped to its core, goes something like this: "I wanted to impact X and so I did Y. X came about as I had hoped. So my having done Y is explains this result." And from this it is an easy, albeit illogical, step to "Aha! When I want to impact X, I should do Y."

The illusion of control, an unwarranted belief in one's control of events, can be difficult to override with reflective thought, perhaps because it is so influenced by emotional state. Here is a hypothesis we would put real money on: the likelihood of using the illusion of control heuristic to make a judgment goes up exponentially in relationship to our desire to achieve a given outcome, particularly when other people perceive the outcome to be possibly unwise or risky. Analyzing a decision process to see exactly where an individual misused the control heuristic and exhibits an illusion of control when they have little or no control informs us of beliefs and values, and probably false expectancies.

12. Elimination by Aspect

Cognitive maneuver: Eliminate an option or group of options from consideration upon the discovery of an undesirable feature. There are simply too many choices! The Excalibur Hotel in Las Vegas boasts a 500-dish smorgasbord. DirecTV offers hundreds of channels, as does XM radio. Want to buy a car, a downtown condo, a fancy watch, or an MBA program? There are thousands from which to pick. How do we move efficiently through this maze of opportunities? Certainly not by giving our full attention and due consideration to every option. Rather, we hack through the choices individually or in whole bunches at a time, pushing the clutter out of our cognitive path as quickly and efficiently as possible. Elimination by aspect is our strategy. As soon as we identify a "reason why not," we dump that option and options like it. The reason does not have to be monumental either. I don't like brown cars or used cars. That's it. For me the car buying choices have just been reduced by tens of thousands. Don't like cream sauces? Great, that cuts the smorgasbord problem down by a huge percentage. Don't like to wait behind other folks grazing through the food line? Fine, step around them to an open spot along the smorgasbord and never worry about looking back at the dozens of culinary delights you may have skipped.

In situations where we enjoy a plethora of acceptable choices, the cognitive utility of elimination by aspect cannot be overestimated. However, the price we pay for conserving all that energy and time is clear too. Applying this heuristic may result in a final selection that does not reflect the best holistic choice we might have made. The used car I refused to consider may have been just as good in every way as a new car of the same make and model, but thousands of dollars less expensive. I will never give that car its due consideration having eliminated it entirely from view when I rejected it along with all others that were labeled "used." In situations where our choices are limited and where no option is perfect, which is often the case when evaluating candidates for hire or for political office or when thinking about how to solve one of life's many human problems involving relationships, this heuristic can be a liability. One-issue politics and political litmus tests, for example, could paralyze a pluralistic democracy. If we try to solve our human relationship problems, or if we set out to select our employees, our friends, and our leaders on the principle that any flaw is a fatal flaw, we might as well become hermits. This habit of mind risks lost opportunities, and if it becomes a major part of one's decision making style, it is likely to dampen one's capacity for making optimal choices in most situations.

13. Loss Aversion and Risk Aversion

Cognitive maneuver: Avoid the foreseeable risk of sustaining a loss by not changing the status quo. Not losing anything, not going backward, at least staying where we are, for most humans, is the preferred default outcome, particularly under conditions of uncertainty. Research demonstrates that most humans are more likely to pass up an opportunity to make a gain rather than risk a loss.[116,117,118,119,120,121] Humans psychologically privilege the status quo. Rather than opting for more dramatic change, whenever possible, humans take an incremental approach, seeking to avoid uncertainty and the difficult cognitive tasks of weighing and combining information or trading-off conflicting values. Muddling through personal decisions, attempting to avoid any loss, is the norm rather than the exception. This heuristic is implicit in the adage, "A bird in the hand is worth two in the bush."

Making decisions on the basis of what we do not want to risk losing can be a rather serviceable approach in many circumstances. People do not want to lose control, they do not want to lose their freedom, and they do not want to lose their lives, their families, their jobs, their possessions. And so, in real life, we take precautions. Why take unnecessary risks? The odds may not be stacked against us, but the consequences of losing at times are so great that we would prefer to forego the possibilities of gain in order not to lose what we have.

We are more apt to endure the status quo, even as it slowly deteriorates, than we are to engage in "radical" change. Loss and risk aversion can lead to paralysis or delay precisely when action should be taken. Having missed that opportunity, however, when the crisis builds and the calls for change are louder, it often requires a far greater upheaval to make the necessary transformations. Worse, on occasion, the situation has deteriorated beyond the point of no return. In those situations we find ourselves wondering why we waited so long before doing something about the problem back when it might have been possible to salvage the situation. History has shown time and time again that businesses which avoid risks often are unable to compete successfully with those willing to move more boldly into new markets or into new product lines.

14. Zero-out tendency

Cognitive maneuver: Simplify decision contexts by treating remote probabilities as if they not even possibilities. By and large when making decisions we do not calculate Bayesian probabilities. Computers might, but humans do not. Rather, we have done reasonably well for ourselves over the millennia in contexts of uncertainty by operating as if the exact probabilities did not really matter. Instead of thinking that there is precisely a 92.4% chance of this occurring or a 17.3% chance of that occurring, we tend to simplify our estimations and move them toward the extremes, as in "very likely" or "highly improbable." If the chances are 1 in 100, or 1 in 10,000, do we really think about the mathematical differences in those situations? No. Instead we tend to treat both of them as if the odds were the same, and, in fact, as if they were both zero. The zero-out tendency treats remote possibilities as if they were, for all practical purposes, "impossible." That is, as if the actual odds were 0 in 100 or 0 in 10,000.

When we stop and really think about things, there are all kinds of risky situations. A person could be hit by a car walking across the street. But, really, what are the chances? They are in fact not equal to zero. But if even the smallest risk of such a great loss as the loss of one's life were perceived, that could influence one to never venture out into the world. So, we push that decimal point out further and further in our minds, nullifying the risk, treating it as if it were not present at all. I've gone ice skating hundreds of times, so what are the chances that tonight I'll fall and crack my skull? There are thousands of commercial flights each day, so what are the chances of a near miss involving my flight? Sadly if one of those remote and unfortunate possibilities were to occur, we often think, "I never thought that would happen." A main advantage to the zero-out tendency would seem to be that it helps balance the paralyzing influences of loss and risk aversion.

TABLE 9 – HEURISTIC MANEUVERS AND THEIR REASONING DISADVANTAGES

NAME	COGNITIVE MANEUVER	DISADVANTAGE / RISK
Satisficing and temporizing	Given an option that is good enough, decide in favor of that option	Good enough may not be best
Affect	Take an initial stance in support of or in opposition to a given choice consistent with one's initial affective response to that choice	Feelings may mislead
Simulation	Estimate the likelihood of a given outcome based on one's ease in imagining that outcome	Over-estimation of one's chance of success or likelihood of failure
Availability	Base the estimate of the likelihood of a future event on the vividness or ease of recalling a similar past event	Mistaken estimations of the chances of events turning out in the future as they are remembered to have turned out in the past
Representativeness – Analogical	Infer that because this is like that in some way or other, it is like that in relevant ways	The analogy may not hold
Representativeness – Associational	Connect ideas on the basis of word association and the memories, meanings, or impressions they might trigger	Jumping from one idea to the next absent any genuine logical connection and drawing inacurate inferences from the combined thought process
Generalizing from One to All	From a single salient instance draw a generalization about an entire group	The one may not be representative of the many
"Us vs. Them" Dynamic	Reduce problems to a simple choice between two opposing forces	Conflict which excludes reasonable compromise

"Master – Slave" Power differential	Accept without question a problem as presented by or a solution as proposed by a superior authority	Working on the wrong problems, applying a mistaken solution
Anchoring with Adjustment	Having made an evaluation, adjust as little as needed in light of new evidence	Failure to reconsider thoroughly
(Illusion of) Control	Estimate the level of control you have over the actual outcome of events upon the amount of desire or energy you put into trying to shape those events	Over-estimation of one's power to control events or under-estimation of one's actual responsibility for what happened
Elimination by Aspect	Eliminate an option or group of options from consideration upon the discovery of an undesirable feature	Failure to give full holistic consideration to viable options
Risk and Loss Aversion	Avoid the foreseeable risk of sustaining a loss by not changing the status quo.	paralysis of decision making stuck in the deteriorating status quo
Zero-out Tendency	Simplify decision contexts by treating remote probabilities as if they are not even possibilities.	failure to appreciate the possibilities that events could actually turn out differently than expected

Heuristics Occurring in Combination

We have observed many more examples of how particular heuristics often occur together, and we believe that this insight has only begun to be apparent to those examining heuristic thinking. As an example, consider how elimination by aspect might provide the basis for someone with the propensity of over using the loss aversion heuristic to reject proposals for change.

Here is another example of three heuristics working back to back, creating a strong sense of confidence in the judgment being made:

"I know some businesses fail, particularly those based on technological innovation. But there were only three failed ventures last year, so I decided that the risk of failure was actually pretty small **[Zero out]**, and I decided to go for broke and invest, and ... you know... I'm pretty good at what I do, and I am really watching things closely now so that nothing happens that will threaten my investment. **[Illusion of Control]** I just don't think I can miss on this one. **[Optimistic Bias]**

True, it is wise to consider the percentage of businesses that fail, and to do all that one can to run a business well. And the business may not fail, but even the speaker himself would not be likely to invest with confidence were it not for the misuse of heuristic reasoning, providing hope, a bit of confidence, and a sense of being in control of the investment.

There are other potential combinations of note: For example, satisficing can often be seen with anchoring with adjustment. How far do you have to drag the anchor when revising your opinion? Not very far – just far enough to account for all the key variables you have identified. Both of these can combine with loss aversion, leading us not to change the status quo where we are anchored, or leading us to adjust it only as much as we absolutely must to achieve the incremental change which brings about a situation that good enough for the moment.

In the following example, we find several heuristics in play including association, affect, and the tendency to generalize from one case to all cases.

Husband to wife: "I'm looking forward to retiring. I've worked for 35 years in offices without windows, and, now that I'm retired I want to be outside. I can see myself on the 5th tee right now!

Wife replies: "Same as my Dad; he used to say how much he hated the winter especially -- going to work when it was dark outside, working in a windowless office all day, and then coming home when it was dark."

Mother-in-law: "That seniors' apartment you showed me was terrible. Only one window! I need more light. I'm never moving to an apartment! You're going to have to drag me out of my house."

In the first paragraph, availability and simulation influence the husband to link the idea of being outside immediately to his vivid and happily remembered hobby [availability]. He sees himself golfing [simulation]. projecting how much easier it will be to play golf when retired. As is common with the availability heuristic, he may be over estimating his opportunities to be on the 5th tee. Meanwhile, his wife is still thinking about the original topic, namely retirement. However, she associates her husband's expressed distaste for his windowless office with her father's similar expressions of distaste for the same work environment [representativeness – analogical]. At that point the mother-in-law introduces a new topic, her mind having jumped from "windowless" to an association with darkness [representativeness – associational] and from there to her vividly recalled [availability] negative [affect heuristic] experience of recently seeing one dark apartment. Clearly she is overestimating the likelihood that all apartments will be dark. And, given that she has introduced this new topic rather than join the conversation, this comment has the ring of a bolstering argument for a long term debate about whether she will agree to move to an apartment. The option of moving to an apartment is off the table as far as she is concerned. And more, not wanting to lose control of her own lifestyle, she expresses her decision to her children – regardless of their obvious age in this context – as a decision she will not permit them to override. Our point here is that while these verbalizations are entirely rational, they are better understood in light of a heuristic analysis.

There are other cognitive strategies of great interest that are commonly used in or influence our everyday arguments. They can be identified and analyzed in text transcriptions of authentic arguments.[122,123] Complex and high stakes decisions entail consideration of a larger number of contextual details, have serious consequences, require a more specialized knowledge base, are often time constrained, or present conditions that are novel to the decision maker.[124,125,126,127] Neurological research on how the mind remembers and recalls things, how it maps new knowledge using semantic networks and mental representations, and how it uses episodic memory can shed additional light on the functioning of cognitive heuristics.[128,129,130,131] Readers are directed to the research and writings of Kahneman, Slovic, Tversky, Montgomery, Fischhoff, and Janis and Mann for seminal work in this area.[132,133,134,135,136,137,138]

The Settlement Case – A Study in Heuristic Thinking

To summarize this discussion of the analysis of heuristic reasoning, here is a case example where heuristic reasoning appears to have had a strong influence on a public, high stakes decision. The example begins with a summary which provides information needed to understand the reasoning process of the characters in the case. The decision makers conceive of themselves as thoughtful people making a well reasoned determination about what action to take. Although fully rational in every relevant sense of the term, they move forward with their decision making unaware of the influences the heuristic maneuvers have on their reasoning.

The Settlement Case

Delladex employs 110 people in its bulk mail distribution division. Three years ago the division's director, Angela Austin, in one of her first acts as a newly appointed director, fired a high salaried employee, Frederick Verdi. Verdi, who was 61 years old at the time, had been with Delladex for 25 years. Verdi lost his company retirement and health benefits because of being fired. Austin cited sub-standard performance as her reason for firing Verdi.

Frederick Verdi sued Delladex for $2,500,000, alleging unlawful termination due to age discrimination and negligence for its failure to train and supervise the manager, Austin. Verdi's lawyer secured copies of Delladex e-mail and other documents showing that Verdi had received positive annual evaluations from all the division's managers during his entire period of employment with Delladex, with the exception of the period when Austin was put in charge. At that point, although Austin had only been manager for three weeks, she gave Verdi a thoroughly negative annual evaluation. Austin's letter of evaluation did not propose steps whereby Verdi might remedy the perceived deficiencies. Six weeks later, Director Austin fired Verdi for failing to show satisfactory improvement. The Delladex documents recovered by Verdi's lawyer include a memo from Austin to her management supervisor in which Austin indicates that she is seeking ways to terminate "higher paid older workers" in order to hire replacement staff at lower salaries.

Three years ago, when the suit was first brought, Delladex's legal department offered Verdi $250,000 to drop his suit. Delladex regarded the offer as a "generous gesture to a long term employee." Delladex believed its $250,000 settlement offer was a low risk proposal, because the company carries liability insurance that covers legal fees and settlement costs up to $1,000,000 per incident. Over these three years, worried Delladex executives often raised the question of being forced to reinstate Verdi. However, the Chief Counsel always dismissed the idea, saying that except in the most egregious cases the court is most unwilling to impose such a severe penalty on any employer.

Delladex has always felt confident that it had a strong defense against Verdi's legal challenges. Austin has maintained that her negative evaluation was correct, in that Verdi's performance had in fact fallen below acceptable standards. She was prepared to cite examples. Further, Delladex's Chief Counsel argued that, whether or not the evaluation was correct, the evaluation, and all actions based on it, are legal because evaluation of management is a supervisor's prerogative. Thus in issuing the evaluation, Austin acted within her authority.

However, throughout the intervening three years, Verdi has steadfastly rejected the $250,000 offer. His case is finally scheduled to go to court, except that the trial judge has insisted that one final attempt be made to reach a settlement, this time with the assistance of a professional mediator. Lawyers for Verdi and Delladex agreed on a professional mediation firm, and the date for the settlement negotiation was set. Delladex has sent three people to the mediator's offices: Director Austin, Mr. Donald Badger, who is the Chief Counsel for Delladex, and Dr. Claudia Carole, who is Vice President of Operations for Delladex. Vice President Carole has full authority to agree to any settlement terms that make reasonable sense. Badger and Austin are participating in order to advise and consult with Carole.

As the settlement meeting begins, Austin, Badger, and Carole are in a small conference room where they can deliberate privately about the terms and conditions of possible settlement options. The mediator, who has read all the relevant background depositions, has visited them, listened to their arguments, and offered an opinion on the merits of their company's position. The mediator tells them that Delladex has, at best, a 20% chance of winning the legal case if Verdi's case goes all the way to trial. In response to this legal opinion, hopes of wining in court are virtually extinguished. **[Zero Out]** The Delladex team decides to increase their settlement offer to $500,000, arguing that this larger amount will be attractive enough to persuade Frederick Verdi to settle, but not more than they have to spend on this situation. **[Satisficing]**

Next they wait, reiterating the soundness of this move as the mediator presents this new offer to Mr. Verdi and his attorney. Here is some of what transpires while they wait:

Carole looks at her two Delladex colleagues, Austin and Badger, and says, "I'm thinking we should cut our losses. Am I correct, we've already spent $200,000 so far defending ourselves? Donald, what do you project as the additional dollar costs of a trial in the event that we lose?" **[Loss Aversion]**

Badger confirms the $200,000 figure, and then, with predictable vagueness, Badger cites the many possible expenses of a trial, such as expert witnesses, additional depositions, and legal fees if Delladex decides to employ outside counsel. Delladex would incur these expenses even if it should win. "The minimum additional cost if we go to trial will be $200,000," says Badger, "and the final number could easily be double that much."

"In other words," says Austin. "If we go to trial and win, it will definitely cost us less than if Verdi accepts our $500,000 offer.

"If we win, then yes. But there are the costs associated with losing to consider," says Badger. "Verdi is asking for $2,500,000 in compensatory damages. If we go to court, the jury could award all of the requested compensatory damages and even hit us with several million more in punitive damages. There was a case like this last year in New York and the jury did just that. They gave away the farm." **[Availability]**

Austin asks, "Remind me. Does our liability insurance cover us?"

"Our insurance will cover all our legal costs if we win, since those expenses will be less than $1,000,000. And, given what we have spent so far, our insurance will cover us fully if we can settle this thing today for less than $800,000. But, if we go to trial and lose, the most our insurance will cover is $1,000,000 in legal expenses and compensatory damages combined. It will not cover any punitive damages." **[Loss Aversion]**

"In other words," says Austin, "we can go up to $800,000 at no additional cost to Delladex, because the insurance will cover us."

"Wait one minute," says Carole. "$800,000 may be our ceiling, but let's not rush there. The mediator is presenting our $500,000 offer to Verdi right now. Let's wait to see if Verdi accepts that or comes back with a reasonable counter-proposal. Maybe we will not have to go much higher." **[Satisficing]**

"You know," says Badger, "I'm just sitting here thinking of a case like this one I litigated before joining Delladex. The decision went against us and we were looking at a $7,500,000 judgment. We filed so many appeals over so many years that the other side ended up cutting that figure in half just to get something from us." **[Availability]**

"What are you saying?" asks Austin.

"Well ... **[Simulation: Likely results of using the appeals process to delay or diminish the cost of a loss in the case]** ... I'm just looking at how we might do something like that in this case. How old is Verdi now? 62?"

"No, he's 64," replies Austin.

"Right. So, if the jury rules for him and if we appeal first on the merits of the case, then on the size of the award, and then on technical constitutional grounds, we could litigate this for at least another four years. These kinds of delays would cost Verdi's lawyers a small fortune in expenses that they know they might never recover. This could easily motivate them to recommend to their client that he should accept some amount significantly lower than what the court might have initially awarded.

"Sounds like an interesting possibility to me," said Austin.

Up until this point Carole had been quiet, but before Badger could say anything else, she cut him off, saying, "The Delladex family still owns most of the stock in our company and, don't forget, there are seven Delladex family members on our Board of Directors. I can't see old Grandma Delladex ever agreeing with that approach." **[Simulation: The likely impact on the company of a protracted battle of appeals]**

Badger responded, "She's only one vote. All we have to do is explain to the others that we might save half a million or more by delaying, and they'll go along. …" **[Illusion of Control]**

"Forget it," said Carole. "We're not going to risk crossing that tough old lady. That option is off the table." **[Elimination by Aspect]**

Everyone sat quietly for a few minutes and then Austin said, "The more I think about this, it's the trial itself that I don't like. It will mean that every member of my personal staff is going to have to give a deposition and probably testify. **[Simulation of the experience of the trial process]** That's not only going to waste a heck of a lot of time, it's going to result in lots of stress."

"Serious divisions of opinion too, I dare say," suggested Carole. "I've heard off the record that some of your key people think you were hard on Verdi."

Austin was taken aback by the vice president's unexpected lack of support. This comment from Carole can only be bad, she thought. **[Affect Heuristic]** Austin replied, "My people are loyal. They'll say whatever I … we need them to say." **[Illusion of Control]**

"You're not suggesting that you have asked them to lie under oath?" inquired Counselor Badger.

"By no means," said Austin, her anger at the insinuation hardly contained. "I mean that my staff agrees with my judgment about Verdi. He may have been a good worker in some prior time, but he did not pull his weight on my watch. We're all very happy now that he's gone."

"Might it be that they are reluctant to say otherwise?" said Badger. **[This inference is possibly true. To facilitate better thinking is one reason people hire good consultants. Unfortunately, this nice piece of truth-seeking is greeted with the customary enthusiasm.]**

"I resent that comment," snapped Austin.

"Enough," said Carole, "we have more important things to discuss."

"Indeed," said Badger. 'Well actually, my intention was to support Austin's main point. A trial would be highly divisive and dysfunctional for her area of responsibility and probably for all of Delladex. The kinds of innuendoes and accusations I've just voiced are going to be made by Verdi and his lawyer. The results will be mistrust and destroyed morale no matter what."

Austin turned toward Badger with a look first of surprise and then of realization. "Thank you." she finally said. "Obviously, I didn't understand where you were going with your question. Yes, and let me say again that a trial would be a very bad thing to have to endure."

Just then the mediator returned to the conference room. The mediator informed the Delladex team that Verdi was not at all interested in a cash settlement. He was fully prepared to go to trial, more confident than ever that he would win. Yes, the mediator had shared with Verdi the same opinion he had shared with Delladex, namely that Delladex has a weak case. "But," said the mediator, "Verdi does have a counter offer for you to consider."

"Well, what is it?" demanded the vice president.

"He says he will drop his lawsuit if he is reinstated to his former position, his benefits and retirement programs are fully restored, his salary is commensurate with what it would have been had he maintained continuous employment, and if Delladex covers his legal fees."

"No way!" said Austin, shaking her head. **[Affective heuristic: there is nothing good about this option]** "It's never going to happen."

Carole, on the other hand, paused for several seconds. **[Simulation: the reinstatement of Verdi].** Then, much to the surprise, if not shock, of the others, she said, "Well, this is an interesting idea. How much would you estimate the legal fees piece to be?"

"You're not seriously considering reinstating him?" said Austin.

The mediator, responding to Carole, said, "I'm sure we could reach an accord where the legal fees element was no higher than $200,000."

"And we could have a signed confidentiality agreement in which it was stipulated that Delladex does not admit to age-discrimination or any other illegal acts?" asked Counsel Badger.

"Mr. Verdi would be very receptive to those additional conditions," said the mediator, "if Delladex is willing to reinstate him to his former position as I've indicated."

The vice president looked at her two colleagues and said, "I think we have a serious option that we need to discuss privately.

As soon as the mediator had left the small conference room, Austin said, "We can't do this! Verdi's incompetent. You can't stick him back in my department."

Badger could already see which way the vice president was headed. This was her call, after all. And Badger, a survivor in the corporate jungle, knew better than to take issue with someone as powerful as Claudia Carole over something that was, in the final analysis, unlikely to affect Delladex's bottom line very much one way or the other. **[Power Differential]**

"If I may," said Badger, "there aren't may choices. We can go to trial, maybe we'd win, but probably we'd lose. If we lose we will end up paying a lot of money sooner, or, as I suggested, later. Or, we could try offering Verdi a much bigger cash settlement than we have discussed so far.[‡‡‡‡‡‡‡‡] If Delladex has the resources, we could …"

"No!" said Carole, "As far as I'm concerned our limit is the same as the limit of our liability insurance." **[Anchoring with Adjustment, Loss Aversion]**

"But," said Austin, "if we reinstate him, it will undermine our whole system of evaluation.[§§§§§§§§] None of our employees will take a negative

---

[‡‡‡‡‡‡‡‡] Logical argument for the to-be-chosen decision.

[§§§§§§§§] Logical argument against the to-be-chosen decision.

evaluation seriously again." **[Representativeness: If we back down, every other employee who receives a negative evaluation will sue].**

"Perhaps not one you give," said Badger. "But, really, I think you are exaggerating the impact of this one settlement on a company the size of Delladex."

Ignoring Austin's objection, Carole asked Badger. "Our costs to reinstate Verdi would be negligible. Isn't that so?"

"Yes. Verdi's salary line has been held vacant by Human Resources," said Badger. "That is our policy in the case of litigation."

Austin could sense that a decision was imminent, and one that she did not want to accept. It looked as if the vice president might be ready to agree to Verdi's proposal. Austin thought that she had one trump card still to play. **[Illusion of Control]** Yes, it was a risk, but not a big one. Nothing really bad could actually happen, she imagined. **[Optimistic Bias]**

So, Austin said, "I'm Verdi's supervisor and I worked with the man. In my judgment he did not fulfill to our standards of performance. I said so in my evaluation and then I fired him. If Delladex cannot back me up in this, then I'll have to seek other employment."

There was a long pause while the vice president considered what Austin was saying. Then, she replied, "Don't overreact. The settlement of this legal matter has no direct bearing on how Delladex evaluates your work as a manager. On the other hand, if I saw no future for myself with a given company, I would most probably get my resume in order."

Austin was stunned. So, that's how it was. She thought of her predecessor who had been fired and Austin saw her own career at Delladex wither in just the same way. **[Availability and Simulations: her own possible firing or marginalization by Carole]** But, in spite of these envisioned consequences, she still hoped to stop Carole from taking Verdi back. "What a mess that will be for my division if we have to take him back!" she asserted.

Badger, who was rather pleased with the vice president's response from a legal perspective, said, "Can we get back to Verdi's counter-proposal? I've done a rough cut at the numbers and they look good for us. The salary is already in the budget as a vacant line. Total cash cost for reinstating the benefits, and the retirement, and covering his legal fees is going to be no more than $400,000. He's offering us a better deal than the one we offered him."

"If the only thing we think about is money," said Austin.

"I admire your spunk," said Carole to Austin. "You know, this mess with Verdi reminds me of a situation twelve years ago. I had to reinstate some screw up who was working in the purchasing department. Turned out to be one of our worst Delladex employees ever ... **[Availability: suboptimal experiences with this first reinstated employee]** ... I hate to do business like this!" **[Representativeness -- analogical: Verdi will be just as bad]** Then she turned to Badger and said, "I think we may have to accept Verdi's proposal. What am I missing?"

"Nothing significant, as far as I can tell," replied Badger.

"And so you're telling me we're stuck?" said Austin. "We have to reinstate Verdi into my department and I have to watch him be unproductive and drag my division down until he finally retires. What kind of message does that send to all our other employees?"

"I don't see that we really have any other choices," said Carole.

The three sat silently for a few moments. The Chief Counsel, Badger, thought about how it would play with Verdi and his lawyer when he communicated Delladex's acceptance of the reinstatement proposal. **[Simulation]** Vice President Carole thought briefly about the budget adjustments that she would need to make to cover the salary and benefits costs, and then her mind moved on to envisioning a needed training program for company managers on employee evaluation policies and procedures. Something that would prevent this from happening again. **[Simulation]** Director Austin imagined how her staff was going to react when she broke the news that Verdi would be rejoining them after being away for three years. **[Simulation]** Her thoughts kept being interrupted by visions of her own resignation and departure from Delladex. **[Simulation]** She couldn't see herself continuing at Delladex after this humiliating loss.

Notice that never once does anyone in the group point out or evaluate the influence of the heuristic thinking embedded in the reasoning process they are collaboratively pursuing. Rather, they would likely describe their thinking only in terms of analysis, inference, and evaluation. In the final moments of this negotiation, one can sense the inevitability and the relative irrevocability of the stance the vice president is taking on the final decision to accept the reinstatement proposal. In the next chapter we discuss factoring this phenomenon into the analysis of human decision.

Chapter 7:
Holistic Evaluation of the Decision Process

To understand fully and to be able to influence individual and group decision making in contexts of risk and uncertainty, we must explore how humans acquire sufficient confidence in a given option such that they discard other possibilities and form the firm intention to act on that option. Whenever presented with a problem, our cognitive heuristics and our capacity for logical reasoning play critical roles in the natural human quest to find some resolution that we can assert with plausible confidence to be our best available option. We call this option the dominant or superior option in any given context. In decision making we move, more or less quickly, through a process that includes sorting through options, discarding the implausible ones, identifying one or more promising options, evaluating it or them on the basis of decision critical criteria, and selecting the option we come to judge to be superior.[139] Psychological research by Henry Montgomery and others is, as we shall see below, consistent with the idea that both argument making and cognitive heuristics are central factors in our search for a dominant option on the basis of which we move from cognition to action. But there is something more. We come to feel confident in our choice, at least confident enough to act on that choice. It is the confidence which sustains action that is the chief focus of this chapter. After first characterizing the phenomenon known as "Dominance Structuring," we suggest ways to enhance group and individual decision making processes which are affected by this pervasive aspect of human decision making.

Dominance Structuring: Moving from Decision to Action

Henry Montgomery's "Search For Dominance" theory of human decision making resonates with the experiences we have all had when making decisions involving risk or uncertainty. As an empirical model of decision making it has the virtues of relative simplicity, familiarity, and completeness. Although even Montgomery agrees that, as a theory, it would be difficult to falsify[140] and that there are situations in which we appear to make decisions without building a completed dominance structure[141] in support of our designated option. As cognitive psychologists, Montgomery and others engaged in this research are not proposing how human decision making ought to proceed; rather they are describing scientifically how it naturally does proceed. Let us put aside the "ought" in order first to understand the "is."

Dominance structuring is a necessary strategy for deciding between alternative options when the conditions of the situation are unclear and uncertain and action is needed. This strategy can go awry when there is no meta-cognitive monitoring of the thinking process. Montgomery describes the human search for a single dominant option among the many possible choices we might make in any given decision making context as having four phases:

Pre-editing,
Finding one promising option,
Testing that option for dominance, and
Structuring the dominance of the option selected.[142]

In **pre-editing**, we start out by selecting a group of possible options and a number of attributes that we think are going to be important as we decide which option to finally pick. Take, for example, the problem of hiring one new employee from a large applicant pool. We want to interview only a small group of highly qualified candidates. We want them to have relevant work experience, academic training, letters of reference, and the like. We may also have in mind that the final choice will be a person who has strong communication skills, enthusiasm for the position, and a schedule that permits them to work the kinds of hours we might require. We see evidence of reasoning in the selection of criteria which are designed to hire the person whom we judge will best satisfy the demands of the job. And we expect further evidence of reasoning in the systematic approach taken to identify potential candidates by advertising the position and screening the applicants to cull down the list to a group of interviewees. But we simply do not exhaustively rate every candidate on every critical attribute. Rather, at this stage we are looking for ways to make the decision easier by eliminating as many alternatives as possible with as minimal an expenditure of effort as must be committed to the task.

Typically we use the *satisficing* heuristic to make our work go more quickly, judging whether each candidate is good enough, later we would probably group them into broad categories such as "well-qualified," "qualified," and "marginal." During this pre-editing phase, some candidates can also be eliminated if they fail to satisfy the minimum threshold we have set on any of our critical attributes. For example, if we have said that a college education is a prerequisite for the job, then every candidate who has not completed college will be eliminated on that basis, regardless of how highly they might rate on the other critical attributes, such as work experience. In this process we use the cognitive heuristic *elimination by aspect*.

The second phase of the search for dominance is **the identification of a promising alternative**. We do this by finding *one* alternative that is more attractive than the others on at least one critically important attribute. There are many reasons why one choice may become more attractive and be judged more and more optimal. Perhaps this choice is most in tune with our values or current desires, or it is least threatening or most economical. Whatever the source of the attraction, once this choice is identified, it becomes our superior or dominant option. Using our hiring example above, suppose there are four finalists who have passed through our initial screening process, and we plan that a committee will interview them all. And suppose that candidate number one has the most job experience, number two is most energetic, number three is most analytical and cautious, and number four is the most congenial and articulate. It is possible everyone on the committee will discover a consensus candidate from the onset. It is also quite likely that different members of the committee will find varying candidates to be optimal for varying reasons, thus setting the stage for a difference of opinion as to which candidate should be the one hired.

Phase three of the search for dominance is to **test our promising alternative for dominance** against the other options. Essentially this involves comparing our promising alternative to the other options in terms of the set of decision critical attributes. But typically we are not seeking here to show that our currently favored alternative is superior to the others on those decision critical attributes. Rather our cognitive attention is focused more on testing whether our promising option has any salient disadvantages as compared to other options or as compared to some specific external criterion. Returning to our hiring example, if five years of relevant work experience is decision critical as a hiring criterion, then we will not be seeking to show that our favored candidate must be hired because he or she has seven years of experience, rather only that our candidate's seven years is not a relevant disadvantage as compared to some other candidate's eight years. In fact, if we are attracted to candidate four because of his or her congeniality, we are likely to argue that this candidate's two years of experience is more than enough. In practice, the line between phase two and phase three is not as well defined as some might like it to be. If our promising alternative is "comparable to the others," or "about as good as the others," or "neither better nor worse than the others," or "good enough" on the other decision critical attributes, the promising alternative becomes the chosen alternative. Then, our initial preference for that candidate, who was the first one we found whom we liked, wins out and we become more and more firm in our choice. Even when we find that our promising alternative appears to have a salient disadvantage as compared to some other option, we do not abandon our "to-be-chosen" alternative easily. Once we begin to appraise and anchor on a given promising alternate, we seek to establish a rationale for selecting this promising or "to-be-chosen" alternative over the others.[143]

At this point in the decision making process we enter the fourth phase, known as **dominance structuring** – we humans restructure our appraisals of the alternatives so as to achieve the *dominance of one option over the others*.[144] As Montgomery indicates, this restructuring as we search for dominance can be more or less rational, more or less in touch with reality, and, hence, more or less likely to lead to the intended and desirable results.[145] One strategy is to review the decision critical attributes, putting them into categories such as "more important" and "less important," and, thus, de-emphasizing attributes that our promising candidate may be weaker on (caution) or bolstering our candidate by increasing the significance of an attribute on which our candidate is stronger (energy). Another strategy is to collapse attributes into larger groupings; for example, we could combine educational training and job experience into the single attribute, "background experience." Now we can hire someone with more education and little job experience, overriding our concern for job experience *per se*. Or, because we do not favor candidate number one who has the most job experience, we may need to diminish this apparent strength. We might argue that work experience is an advantage of candidate number one, but relative inflexibility of work hours is a disadvantage, so the one can be said to cancel the other. And, because of this, we might argue, candidate number one is not the person to hire.

The processes of *de-emphasizing, bolstering, trading-off, and collapsing* attributes continue until we find that one alternative stands above the others as the dominant choice. Good judgment and sharp reasoning skills are critical to this complex and dynamic process of making comparisons across attributes. Obviously one might be able to quantify within a given attribute, for example, by comparing two candidates on the basis of their years of relevant background experience. But it is not clear how one would compare, for the purposes of possible trade-offs, communication skills against energy with similar ease. And yet, the arguments will be made in support of the *to-be-chosen* alternative as the decision maker's search for a dominance structure to support this choice above all others continues.[146] When the decision is being made by committee, and the stakes are perceived as high, this process can at times be ruthless.

According to Montgomery, if dominance is not achieved by restructuring the decision critical attributes relative to the information given, the entire decision making process loops back to the beginning.[147] In our example about filling the position, if we could not agree with our colleague on a candidate to hire, we would either decide to hire nobody or decide to continue our search, perhaps by re-advertising the position and starting over with a fresh candidate pool responding to the original job description, or perhaps by modifying the job description first and then seeking applicants. The first approach, in effect, is to try to solve the original problem (filling the job with the best available candidate) a second time. The other approach is to try to solve a related but different problem (finding a candidate to hire for a job that has been redefined by the committee, but, if filled, may leave us with some residual hiring needs).

There are a number of manifestations which suggest that the search for dominance has been completed by the people engaged in the decision making. First, unless they are intentionally dissembling, the people describe themselves as having made a decision, rather than as being undecided or as still thinking about their options. Second, people tend to dismiss as unimportant, refute, or abandon strands of reasoning which appear to be leading to a decision other than the one they embrace. Third, if interview data are available, an A&H examination of the chronology of that data may reveal numerous, less well elaborated, bolstering arguments occurring later in the interview. Fourth, as illustrated by Figure 5 in Chapter 1, the A&H decision map often reveals visually a plurality of arguments supporting the chosen decision or a relative dearth of arguments supporting any of the other possible options.

Everything is Negotiable

Our last discussion may seem to some a harsh critique of human decision making. But there are countless examples that display this tendency toward dominance structuring. Apart from the obvious outliers, such as philosophers, politicians, and zealots, even sane groups engaged in decision making have been known to revisit, and, at times, modify or reinterpret, virtually every element involved in judging what to believe and what to do. Even if we assume that the decision makers are paragons of intellectual honesty, we should not underestimate the power of clever minds to extend dominance structuring. Certainly there is no implicit restriction which would limit attention simply to renegotiating the decision critical attributes. When it comes to our enthusiasm for our to-be-chosen option, objectivity requires cognitive discipline. Research demonstrates that humans desire to be successful in achieving solutions to their problems, and thus are willing to modulate their appraisal of the competing options in order to find solutions.[148]

Critical thinking theory identifies five elements that are essential: *evidence, methods, conceptualizations, standards,* and *contexts of judgment.*[149] Perhaps the O.J. Simpson jury demonstrated the power of the mind to redefine reality most dramatically. The DNA evidence was questioned and found wanting. The methods of the police investigation were attacked and found to be inadequate in the minds of the jurors. The context of concern was shifted from the violence done to the murdered people to the motives of potentially racist officers and to the character of those who were killed. The concepts that were used by the defense went beyond jurisprudence to include those ideas and theories some associate with the politics of race. The standard for a conviction, "beyond a reasonable doubt," appeared to be given a new meaning in which virtually every doubt might be conceived of as reasonable. In other words, for the jury members, the to-be-chosen alternative was that the accused was innocent and whatever needed to be done was done in order to restructure the relevant set of beliefs and standards of judgment in order to bring that option to dominance. It took not simply the will to find the accused innocent to achieve this, it took considerable creativity and reasoning prowess to provide the jurors with the language and the conceptualizations that would permit them to go in the direction of the to-be-chosen alternative – "innocent." Arguments had to be made, data presented, warrants advanced, claims supported, and counter-arguments refuted. Simulations had to be invited, affective responses created, options eliminated by aspect, and countless other opportunities for heuristic thinking made available.

In fact, it could be argued that Mr. Simpson's defense team demonstrated outstanding rhetorical and logical skills by being able to reframe the entire problem in the mind of the jury. Instead of trying to decide the question of the accused guilt or innocence, the jury appeared to become engaged in the problem of how to make a political statement about the systematic oppression of African-Americans in a society that tacitly condones a criminal justice system rife with racism, incompetence, brutality, and evidence tampering. Reasonable or not, one of the strongest moves one can make in group decision making is to be able to focus the problem solving efforts of the group on the problem you want solved using the terms and concepts that tend to advantage the outcome you most prefer.

In the human search for a dominant option, the heuristics of anchoring with adjustment, elimination by aspect, and satisficing are at work. In this mix one also finds argument making being used to judge what to believe about the different options as one builds and evaluates the arguments for and against competing alternatives. As we have seen, once a solution is judged good enough, and even before officially making a choice, we may recalibrate our evaluation of any given alternative, raising the relative value of the to-be-chosen alternative and lowering that of all other not-to-be-chosen alternatives. We may renegotiate what we view as an acceptable solution to the problem in order to increase dominance of the choice being made. We may even redefine the problem, reinterpret the evidence, alter the methods, and reconsider the context of judgment. In ways like these, the decisions which human beings make are fundamentally unlike those made by computers, algorithms, or functionaries who are compelled to follow rigid protocols.

Evaluating the Human Element

When evaluating the decision making process holistically, we must take into consideration concerns about intellectual integrity, objectivity, and the openness of the decision makers to give due and fair-minded consideration to any of the not-to-be-chosen options.

The result of dominance structuring is confidence, whether reasonable or unreasonable, in the option we have decided upon. That is, from the dominance structuring process we humans derive a level of confidence sufficient to motivate and to sustain action based on that decision. Obviously, the more unreasonable, biased, irrational, and unrealistic we have been in our dominance structure or problem restructuring, the greater the risks of a poor decision. On the other hand, if we have made the effort to be reasonable, truth-seeking, informed, open-minded, and neither too hasty nor too tardy in coming to our decision, then there is a greater chance that the decision will be a wise one. It would be a mistake to think of this human process as intentional self-deception or as a conscious attempt at being unethical or unfair. Rather, what cognitive psychologists, like Montgomery, are offering is a description of how humans bolster confidence in their judgments under conditions of uncertainty. Humans seek to establish a strong and enduring rationale for the belief that one alternative dominates over others to such an extent that we can act and continue to act on the basis of that belief in the enduring superiority of that option. We surround our choice with a rationale for its being superior to the others, and this strategy allows us then to move forward to act on that decision.

This helps explain why reconsideration after the choice is made is extremely difficult, why the criticisms of our choices seem unpersuasive, why the virtues of other options are less compelling, and why their vices appear larger than they may in fact be. When the dominance structure has been created, it is not uncommon to hear people describe the results of their deliberations with phrases like "In the end we really didn't have any other choice." This mantra is *prima facie* evidence that the search for dominance has resulted in one option having been elevated to the top position and all other options having been discredited or discounted to the extent that, at this point, it is unclear to the decision makers why other options were ever imagined as viable in the first place.

Searching for dominance in conjunction with elimination by aspect, satisficing, and anchoring with adjustment involves certain cognitive risks. First is the risk of making poor decisions due to a lack of due consideration of all reasonable alternatives. Second is the risk that decision makers find it very hard to appreciate that their decisions might be seriously flawed and in need of revision. At some level we recognize these potential problems in human decision making. Our judicial system, for example, generally provides for appeals to be made to some person or judicial panel other than the one which rendered the initial decision. We know that once people have fixed their mind on a given result, it is very difficult for them to change their judgment.

This process is largely unreflective, but were we to ask, "Should we dominance structure or not?" the answer can only be the affirmative. We often need to make decisions about what to believe and what to do in contexts of risk or uncertainty, and thus we need some method for arriving at a dominant choice. The development of superior decision making skills demands that we understand this about ourselves as individuals and as groups, and that we take reasonable precautions. We can use our meta-cognitive skills to self-monitor and self-correct our decision making as it is unfolding. Using these skills, we can be cautious about how we frame the problem, how we describe the most viable options, and how enthusiastic we allow ourselves to become about specific options during the early going. We can take precautions to assure that we are following due process, that we are diligent and systematic about gathering relevant information, that we are remaining open to new possibilities. We can courageously follow the reasons and the evidence wherever they lead, being unafraid to consider any possibility and unafraid of asking difficult questions. And we can be tolerant, if not encouraging of our colleagues, friends, and family members who ask those tough questions and caution us to be reflective, reasonable, and thorough in how we approach problems and make decisions.

After we have made our choice we can seek to remain open to reasonable criticisms and to the signs that our choice may not be turning out to be optimal. Instead of sustaining our decision after the arguments for it have been exposed as inadequate, we can strive for the intellectual courage needed to reconsider and perhaps revise our choice. Too often, weak decision makers change their rationales but not their decisions. They flit from one reason to another, seeking any that might seem to work, rather than having the strength of mind to realize that the decision itself may have been mistaken and may now need to be revised. They surround their choice with a plethora of reasons, many of which are flawed, and in this way they sustain their defensive wall around a faltering and unfortunate prior choice.

Once one is aware of the phenomenon, it is relatively easy to spot the unwise use of dominance structuring when it is occurring in group decision making. Even when the members of the group do not resort to modifying their description of the problem, one can see certain decision critical criteria begin emphasized over others and one can see the to-be-chosen option gaining credence while the others begin to decline. Group-think plays a role in this. It is not often that a person seeks to revive a dying option, nor do people risk displeasing the leader or leaders of the group by defending options which those individuals appear to have abandoned. The group-think phenomenon, as described by Irving Janis, includes close-mindedness, bolstering decisions by making up reasons for them after the fact, the illusion of control, optimistic bias, the "Us-vs.-Them" dynamic, over-estimation of the group's moral superiority, and pressures toward uniformity generated by self-censorship, social exclusion of those who disagree, and a tendency to minimize the significance of one's own misgivings.[150]

Dominance structuring in one's own individual decision making is somewhat more difficult to detect, but the precautions suggested above can be useful disciplines as one seeks to maintain an open mind during the evaluation of competing options.

Chapter 8:
Displaying the Results of A&H Analyses

Regardless of which argument mapping software you use, it will become obvious quite early in the process that producing a complete decision map often requires a considerable area of two-dimensional space. Plotting decision maps for use in poster presentations offers no unusual problems, but arriving at figures suitably sized for publication in a standard sized book or journal requires some planning. As we have worked with the outputs of A&H Analyses, we have found various ways to display their differing components. Many of them have been used in the figures and tables in this book, and thus can serve as examples. This chapter addresses the issue of displaying the outputs of A&H Analyses in part by reference to those earlier examples and in part by providing additional examples.

Tabling the Results of a Content Analysis

Presenting the content of the arguments made is a familiar mode of data display. Tables which report the various arguments made by subjects in regard to a given decision are frequently included in published papers. Tables 2 and 3 in Chapter 1 are examples. The left column in each identifies the argument strand leading toward a specific major option, and the next column summarizes in a thematic way the content of each argument strand.

When the data display seeks to summarize the arguments made by a group of individuals, the table can be expanded to include frequency statistics reporting how commonly a given argument was made by the sample subjects. The table might also distinguish differences in these frequencies by sample groups. For example, Table 10 below displays frequency differences between two groups of persons who offer the same subset of arguments for whether the drinking age should be lowered to age 18. We can examine this table and see at a glance what the most frequently offered arguments were for and against lowering the drinking age to 18 years old, and we can see that these reasons differed by age in this sample.

TABLE 10: THE TEN MOST FREQUENTLY MADE ARGUMENTS REGARDING LEGALIZING DRINKING IN THIS STATE AT AGE 18.

(Data collected shopping mall.)	Frequency in full sample N=100	Frequency in persons < 21 n=50	Frequency in persons 21 and older n = 50
ARGUMENTS FOR ALLOWING DRINKING AT 18 YEARS OF AGE			
An 18 year old can vote for the president so they should be able to buy and drink a glass of beer.	22 22%	17 of 50 34%	5 of 50 10%
If you treat someone like a responsible adult then they will live up to your expectations.	6 of 100 6%	2 of 50 4%	4 of 50 8%
Adults over 21 are just as irresponsible as the person 18-21 years of age when it comes to over indulging in alcohol.	19 of 100 19%	4 of 50 8%	15 of 50 30%
An 18 year old can enlist and die in a foreign war so they should be old enough to drink.	52 of 100 52%	42 of 50, 84%	10 of 50 20%
Most alcohol abuse problems in this age group occur in spite of the legal prohibition.	36 of 100 36%	13 of 50 26%	23 of 50 46%
ARGUMENTS FOR NOT ALLOWING DRINKING AT 18 YEARS OF AGE			
There will be more motor vehicle accidents due to driving drunk in teen drivers.	56 of 100 56%	15 of 50 30%	41 of 50 82%
Alcohol abuse in this age group is already extremely high and it will get worse if we legalize drinking.	20 of 100 20%	3 of 50 6%	17 of 50 34%
Street violence and sexual violence will increase if this age group has more exposure to alcohol.	16 of 100 16%	10 of 50 20%	6 of 50 12%

More people will become alcoholics at a very early age.	5 of 100 5%	2 of 50 4%	3 of 50 6%
This is going in the wrong direction, and we should discourage alcohol consumption for everyone.	50 of 100 50%	36 of 50 72%	14 of 50 28%

Reporting the Results of a Logical Analysis

In addition to a content analysis, the A&H Method also produces an analysis of the logical and heuristic components of the argument map. A display of the results of a logical analysis includes the summary of how sound the logic is that supports the judgment. Of course, to get an impression of the soundness of the reasoning process, one could count the logical errors and simply report in a table how many of the argument strands were based on sound and unsound reasoning. A flow chart display, illustrated in Figure 22 below, offers an alternative to a simple table. A flow chart display can be more helpful because its hierarchical visual organization shows the distributions of arguments by logical quality for a decision with more than a single "Yes-No" option.

Figure 22 shows a possible array of arguments made by two groups of persons who have just purchased a new car. One group of 20 people (left side of figure) purchased new hybrid vehicles making 192 total arguments (almost 10 per person) about why they made their decision. The other group of 20 people (right side of figure) purchased sports utility vehicles (SUVs), making 328 arguments in total for why they had made their decision. An examination of the frequencies, means, and standard deviations reported in the boxes indicates that sound and unsound arguments were not evenly distributed in these two groups. The thicker arrows indicate where the preponderance of arguments occurs. Figure 22 displays the proportion of sound and unsound arguments in each group, and also indicates whether the unsound arguments were due to poor reasoning, false factual information or both.

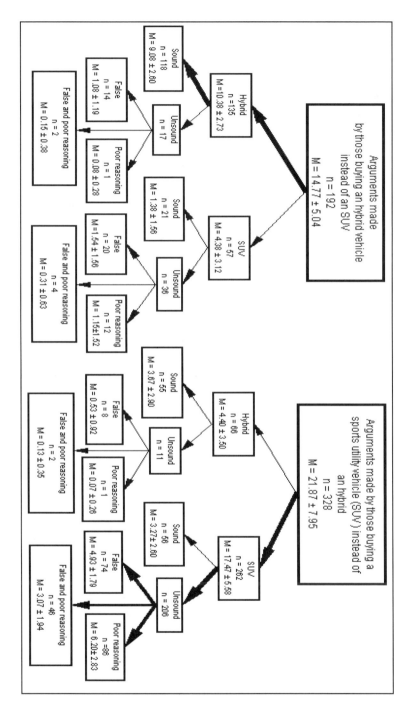

FIGURE 22: BUYERS' REASONS FOR PURCHASING HYBRIDS & SUVS

Tabling the Results of a Heuristic Analysis

Because we know that the use of heuristics is a normal part of human reasoning, when we report the use of heuristic reasoning in a decision process we should be very clear about how the heuristic was used or misused and the consequences for the decision process as a result. Table 11 below is an example of displaying findings in regards to the use of heuristic reasoning is one woman's decision about whether to take a new job.

TABLE 11: HEURISTIC REASONING STRATEGIES IDENTIFIED IN THIS ANALYSIS

Heuristic strategy	Description of the use of this cognitive maneuver in this decision	Potential consequences of this use/misuse
Affect Allows the thinker to take a stance for further examination of the issue.	"The minute I heard the job offer was in New York I was excited." New York: Good	Having taken the stance that the offer is somehow good, she must now evaluate it in detail to be sure that there are no compelling reasons to be wary of the new job offer.
Availability Vivid or personally salient past event is used as a basis to (over) estimate the likelihood of the event's reoccurrence.	"The last time I was in New York, we were having some key negotiations with a client on one of those great Spring afternoons...a beautiful day ... the negotiations really went well."	This episodic memory retrieved as a part of the use of the availability heuristic will need to be examined as to its predictive capacity for how the new job in New York will actually be experienced.
Representativeness (Analogical) Similarities, whether superficial or fundamental, are relied upon as sufficiently representational for purposes of expecting	"My cousin took a job in Dayton and after only four weeks he learned that the company was restructuring and he would be laid off."	This narrative has come to mind because of the similarity of the cousin being offered a new job in a new city. The caution that is felt about the risk of switching companies is only as valuable as the real similarity between

similar outcomes or categorizations.		new job situations.
Loss Aversion Negative association of change with loss and risk.	"I'll never find an apartment with a view like the one I have now" "I wonder what the office is like ... here at least I'm getting along."	If the job is turned down simply because it entails risk of loss due to change, then this heuristic has overridden all other possible opportunities evident in the new job opportunity.

Displaying a Complete Decision Map

For the purpose of this discussion, think of a complete decision map as a figure displaying all the alternatively considered conclusions and the argument strands supporting each of them. Figure 23 below is a complete map of an explanation given by one woman about why she had not yet quit smoking. Many complete decision maps are far larger, however. A complete decision map, even one containing several possible conclusions and 30 to 50 total argument strands, can be displayed on a computer screen in a digital mode or as a very large figure on a poster presentation. But in most presentations, paper and font size limitations require that information in decision maps be presented in stages. We illustrated this with "The Job Case" in Chapter 4. There, Figure 19 displayed only the final expressions of each argument strand leading to the two fundamental options, either to take the job or not. Figure 20: "There were Family Things," displays in greater detail the development of only one of those arguments strands.

The map in Figure 23 derives the oval containing "line 51" from the presentation of a number of family issues this decision maker brought forward. Simpler examples of single argument strand figures can be seen in Chapter 1. There, Figures 1 and 8 display only a single argument strand. Figures 2 and 3 display watershed ideas with two arguments strands diverging from those watershed ideas, and each strand flowing toward different conclusions. In Figure 2 we see that the decision maker (Howard) stops short of one of these conclusions (the not chosen solution: I shouldn't donate my kidney), and instead uses a counter-argument to reverse course and thus reach his chosen conclusion (Count me in as a donor). Table 3 in

Chapter 1 offers an example of how one might display watershed ideas only. The choice of what to include in a partial mapping depends on what must be communicated by the decision analyst.

Displaying the Overall Structure of a Decision

We believe that if a decision maker is shown their argument map and led to think again about each of the watershed ideas, the subject's decision process might become more reflective and complete. Whether the ultimate decision or conclusion of the thinking process is changed as a result of this process is a matter for research exploration. But the figures, tables, and maps have the benefit of externalizing the thinking and thus objectifying it. In the context of a thinking-based intervention strategy, this permits the decision maker to see, reflect, evaluate, and reconsider matters, perhaps with the assistance of another person.

Figure 23 displays the complete decision map of an interview with a woman who is explaining that she cannot quit smoking now. In this argument map, there are two possible conclusions and three watershed ideas. One argument strand leading from one of the watershed ideas is abandoned. The full decision map is rich with data for interpretation. For example, inspection of the figure reveals that she offered more arguments supporting quitting smoking now (5) than quitting later (4). This suggests that her dominance structuring around the continuing decision to continue to smoke may not be impervious. Relying on the numbers in the shapes to preserve the chronology of the interview, we can see that the subject first argues to quit smoking. (Phrase #2: smoking is dangerous to life). And although she never declares that she must stop smoking, it is an implicit statement in four of the five arguments strands for quitting now. But as the interview progresses her defenses build; she begins rather early in the interview to explain why she will decide not to try quitting right now (phrase #5), and her arguments can easily be seen to admit to the effects of the nicotine addiction ("it takes energy," "I need to function").

Figures like Figure 23 appear to have considerable value as visual aids to help the decision maker to see how she is using her argument making to delay her smoking cessation plan. Once the map has been drawn, the logical strengths and weaknesses of the argument strands can be assessed. Arguments and beliefs can be challenged. For example, one might question her basis for thinking that the quitting smoking is not compatible with having the energy needed to raise a teenage son. Her abandoned argument about being a responsible parent would also be an obvious omission inviting her further consideration. It might even be the case that she senses already that being a responsible parent entails not modeling behavior that one would not want one's children to emulate.

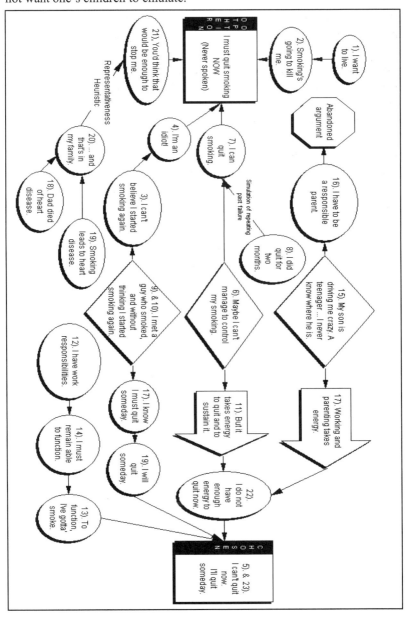

FIGURE 23: THE DECISION NOT TO QUIT SMOKING

Consider the map below, one that excludes the content in the argument strands and simply indicates how each argument strand relates to the three possible choices about which college to attend next year. The map uses the convention of indicating each argument strand with a single circle. Inside each circle, the argument strand is assessed as one that either supports attendance at the school (Pro) or one that argues against attendance (Con). Looking first only at these circles, one can see that most of the arguments, pro and con, are made in relationship to Michigan State (9 arguments overall, 7 of them in favor of attending Michigan State). If you were the parent of this prospective first year student, working with your son or daughter to help them think through their choice of college, you could observe that perhaps more thought might be needed to evaluate the other two schools. You might wonder whether your son or daughter has already chosen to attend Michigan State next year, and whether the figure is capturing the beginning of a dominance structure around this to-be-chosen option.

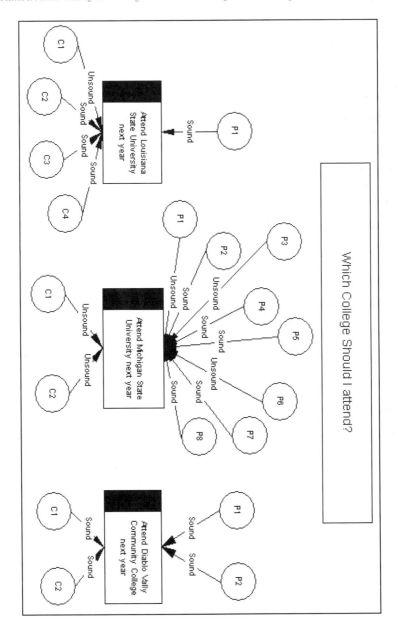

FIGURE 24: LOGICAL SOUNDNESS AND DEGREE OF ELABORATION OF A DECISION PROCESS

Figure 24 also shows that every argument strand for all three schools has been evaluated for its logical soundness. Although the process of evaluation is not shown here, the result of this evaluation has been added on each of the arrows connecting the strand to the prospective school. One might conclude that overall this appears to be a fairly sound reasoning process. The reasoning about Louisiana State University and Diablo Valley Community College is largely sound, although perhaps incomplete. Many potentially relevant considerations have not yet been examined. Most of the unsound arguments are being made in favor of attending Michigan State, and a careful examination of these argument strands offers the opportunity to correct misperceptions before the final choice is made.

Another example of this type of map can be seen in Figure 5 of Chapter 1. That map reveals the dominance structuring around a given option. This type of map can also be used to indicate at a glance the soundness of the overall reasoning process.

Analyzing Documents

There are many kinds of documents, some of which purport to explain decisions or make arguments.[*] Letters to the editor, such as the one about fixing the voting machines analyzed in Chapter 4, are an example. Legal briefs are another, for these are intended to present all the arguments in favor of a given opinion and all the counterarguments explaining why other opinions on the matter would be of lesser quality. Of particular interest are those documents which seek to explain important decisions made by those in leadership positions. In 2006, Arnold Schwarzenegger, then Governor of California, was faced with a decision of whether or not to grant clemency to a high profile inmate on death row, Mr. Stanley "Tookie" Williams. There had for some time been much criticism of the death penalty, and many well known Californians were joining the debate calling

---

[*] Some public documents serve only to record decisions, but not necessarily to explain them. For example, contracts written to commemorate agreements after negotiations have been completed often record only the final decision. The reason giving and argument making which were integral to the negotiations need not be reprised in the contract itself. Verdicts rendered by juries have a similar relationship to the reasoning which led to them. Arguments were made during the trial and during the jury's deliberations, but the verdict need not explicitly reference any of them. Other public documents are designed to communicate decisions, and yet at the same time often intended to obscure all but the most socially acceptable explanations. Announcements, such as major appointments or resignations, often have this character. Political speeches and debates rhetorically follow the pattern of argument making documents, with claims asserted and reasons advanced. However, one would be naïve to think that they always disclosed the speaker's full and candid thoughts on the topic. It can be particularly interesting to analyze the written or spoken comments of candidates for political office, since these often combine argument making with the use of highly charged vocabulary which calls forth strong heuristic responses in the listeners. At least with commercials one can cynically assume that the reason giving and the emotional or heuristic appeals have been thoughtfully orchestrated and field tested with the unabashed anticipation that they will lead some people to make the decision to purchase the service or product being promoted. With politics, it is much more difficult to know the full truth of the matter.

for Governor Schwarzenegger to commute Mr. Williams' sentence to life without possibility of parole. Mr. Williams' case was being discussed as a paradigmatic challenge of the death penalty law, because Mr. Williams was seen by many as a "changed man" since the commission of his crimes years ago.

Governor Schwarzenegger decided against clemency, and Mr. Williams was executed. In addition to speaking with the press about his reasons for this decision, the governor posted a document on the Internet describing his decision process (Appendix A). The decision map in Figures 25A and 25B display the structure of that decision.

Considering the overall structure, we can see that there is much more elaboration of the final judgment, denial of clemency. There are two main claims supporting this judgment: that Mr. Williams is, in fact, guilty, and that there is no other basis for clemency given that he is guilty. There are also a few additional arguments that Mr. Williams should not be granted clemency: That the gangs he formed continue to do violence, that his attempted escape risked the lives of law enforcement officers, and that the murders themselves were brutal in nature.

We can see that there were five watershed ideas considered by the governor: 1) claimed innocence, 2) claimed redemption, 3) a lack of apology, 4) fairness of the trial, and 5) good works while in prison. Several of these were endorsed as important considerations in the public debate prior to the governor's decision. The governor's public statement does not elaborate on any of these, nor does it explicitly assess their value as arguments for clemency. One might argue that this is a function of the type of document that is being published, one intended to support and defend the governor's final judgment. But it seems likely that if the governor had seen the mapping (Figure 25) of his reported decision process, he might have been more aware of the need to elaborate his thinking in regard to the not-to-be-chosen alternative, to grant clemency. Were he to talk more spontaneously about his decision, we might observe evidence of the influences of heuristic thinking in his decision process. But public documents, such as this one, tend to focus on the logic of the decision. One cannot know if the logic, in some cases, is not invented after the decision is already supported by a dominance structure, or whether this dominance structure was derived heavily from well applied or mistakenly applied heuristics. Thus, while our analysis does not provide us with all of the considerations the governor may have actually entertained while coming to this judgment, it does display the arguments offered to Californians for his ultimate judgment to deny clemency. And, as such, it is amenable to A&H Analysis.

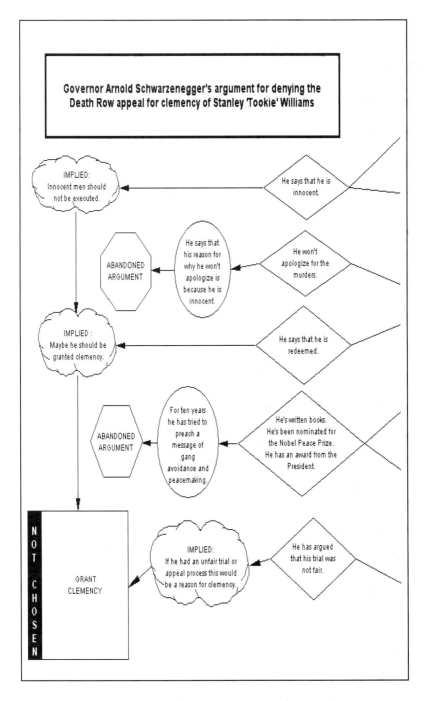

FIGURE 25A: GOVERNOR SCHWARZENEGGER'S REASONS FOR NOT COMMUTING THE DEATH PENALTY

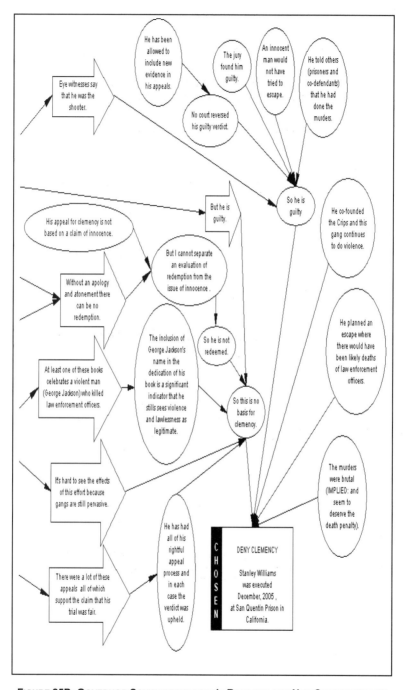

FIGURE 25B: GOVERNOR SCHWARZENEGGER'S REASONS FOR NOT COMMUTING THE DEATH PENALTY

Appendix A:
Governor Schwarzenegger's Statement on Clemency for Stanley Williams

Stanley Williams has been convicted of brutally murdering four people during two separate armed robberies in February and March of 1979. A California jury sentenced him to death, and he is scheduled for execution on December 13, 2005.

During the early morning hours of February 28, 1979, Williams and three others went on a robbery spree. Around 4 a.m., they entered a 7-Eleven store where Albert Owens was working by himself. Here, Williams, armed with his pump action shotgun, ordered Owens to a backroom and shot him twice in the back while he lay face down on the floor. Williams and his accomplices made off with about $120 from the store's cash register. After leaving the 7-Eleven store, Williams told the others that he killed Albert Owens because he did not want any witnesses. Later that morning, Williams recounted shooting Albert Owens, saying "You should have heard the way he sounded when I shot him." Williams then made a growling noise and laughed for five to six minutes.

On March 11, 1979, less than two weeks later, Williams, again armed with his shotgun, robbed a family-operated motel and shot and killed three members of the family: (1) the father, Yen-I Yang, who was shot once in the torso and once in the arm while he was laying on a sofa; (2) the mother, Tsai-Shai Lin, who was shot once in the abdomen and once in the back; and (3) the daughter, Yee-Chen Lin, who was shot once in her face. For these murders, Williams made away with approximately $100 in cash. Williams also told others about the details of these murders and referred to the victims as "Buddha-heads."

Now, his appeals exhausted, Williams seeks mercy in the form of a petition for clemency. He claims that he deserves clemency because he has undergone a personal transformation and is redeemed, and because there were problems with his trial that undermine the fairness of the jury's verdict.

Williams' case has been thoroughly reviewed in the 24 years since his convictions and death sentence. In addition to his direct appeal to the

California Supreme Court, Williams has filed five state habeas corpus petitions, each of which has been rejected. The federal courts have also reviewed his convictions and death sentence. Williams filed a federal habeas corpus petition, and the U.S. District Court denied it. The Ninth Circuit Court of Appeals confirmed this decision.

In all, Williams' case has been the subject of at least eight substantive judicial opinions.

The claim that Williams received an unfair trial was the subject of this extensive litigation in the state and federal courts. The courts considered the sufficiency of his counsel, the strategic nature of counsel's decisions during the penalty phase of Williams' trial, the adequacy and reliability of testimony from informants, whether Williams was prejudiced by security measures employed during his trial, whether he was competent to stand trial, whether the prosecutor impermissibly challenged potential jurors on the basis of race, and whether his jury was improperly influenced by Williams' threats made against them. There is no need to rehash or second guess the myriad findings of the courts over 24 years of litigation.

The possible irregularities in Williams' trial have been thoroughly and carefully reviewed by the courts, and there is no reason to disturb the judicial decisions that uphold the jury's decisions that he is guilty of these four murders and should pay with his life.

The basis of Williams' clemency request is not innocence. Rather, the basis of the request is the "personal redemption Stanley Williams has experienced and the positive impact of the message he sends." But Williams' claim of innocence remains a key factor to evaluating his claim of personal redemption. It is impossible to separate Williams' claim of innocence from his claim of redemption.

Cumulatively, the evidence demonstrating Williams is guilty of these murders is strong and compelling. It includes: (1) eyewitness testimony of Alfred Coward, who was one of Williams' accomplices in the 7-Eleven shooting; (2) ballistics evidence proving that the shotgun casing found at the scene of the motel murders was fired from Williams' shotgun; (3) testimony from Samuel Coleman that Williams confessed that he had robbed and killed some people on Vermont Street (where the motel was located); (4) testimony from James and Esther Garrett that Williams admitted to them that he committed both sets of murders; and (5) testimony from jailhouse informant George Oglesby that Williams confessed to the motel murders and conspired with Oglesby to escape from county jail. The trial evidence is bolstered by information from Tony Sims, who has admitted to being an accomplice in the 7-Eleven murder. Sims did not testify against Williams at trial, but he was later convicted of murder for his role in Albert Owens' death. During his trial and subsequent parole hearings, Sims has repeatedly stated under oath that Williams was the shooter.

Based on the cumulative weight of the evidence, there is no reason to second guess the jury's decision of guilt or raise significant doubts or serious reservations about Williams' convictions and death sentence. He murdered Albert Owens and Yen-I Yang, Yee-Chen Lin and Tsai-Shai Lin in cold blood in two separate incidents that were just weeks apart.

But Williams claims that he is particularly deserving of clemency because he has reformed and been redeemed for his violent past. Williams' claim of redemption triggers an inquiry into his atonement for all his transgressions. Williams protests that he has no reason to apologize for these murders because he did not commit them. But he is guilty and a close look at Williams' post-arrest and post-conviction conduct tells a story that is different from redemption.

After Williams was arrested for these crimes, and while he was awaiting trial, he conspired to escape from custody by blowing up a jail transportation bus and killing the deputies guarding the bus. There are detailed escape plans in Williams' own handwriting. Williams never executed this plan, but his co-conspirator implicated Williams in the scheme. The fact that Williams conspired to murder several others to effectuate his escape from jail while awaiting his murder trial is consistent with guilt, not innocence. And the timing of the motel murders--less than two weeks after the murder of Albert Owens--shows a callous disregard for human life.

Williams has written books that instruct readers to avoid the gang lifestyle and to stay out of prison. In 1996, a Tookie Speaks Out Against Gang Violence children's book series was published. In 1998, "Life in Prison" was published. In 2004, Williams published a memoir entitled "Blue Rage, Black Redemption." He has also recently (since 1995) tried to preach a message of gang avoidance and peacemaking, including a protocol for street peace to be used by opposing gangs.

It is hard to assess the effect of such efforts in concrete terms, but the continued pervasiveness of gang violence leads one to question the efficacy of Williams' message. Williams co-founded the Crips, a notorious street gang that has contributed and continues to contribute to predatory and exploitative violence.

The dedication of Williams' book "Life in Prison" casts significant doubt on his personal redemption. This book was published in 1998, several years after Williams' claimed redemptive experience. Specifically, the book is dedicated to "Nelson Mandela, Angela Davis, Malcolm X, Assata Shakur, Geronimo Ji Jaga Pratt, Ramona Africa, John Africa, Leonard Peltier, Dhoruba Al-Mujahid, George Jackson, Mumia Abu-Jamal, and the countless other men, women, and youths who have to endure the hellish oppression of living behind bars." The mix of individuals on this list is curious. Most have violent pasts and some have been convicted of committing heinous murders, including the killing of law enforcement.

But the inclusion of George Jackson on this list defies reason and is a significant indicator that Williams is not reformed and that he still sees violence and lawlessness as a legitimate means to address societal problems.

There is also little mention or atonement in his writings and his plea for clemency of the countless murders committed by the Crips following the lifestyle Williams once espoused. The senseless killing that has ruined many families, particularly in African-American communities, in the name of the Crips and gang warfare is a tragedy of our modern culture. One would expect more explicit and direct reference to this byproduct of his former lifestyle in Williams' writings and apology for this tragedy, but it exists only through innuendo and inference.

Is Williams' redemption complete and sincere, or is it just a hollow promise? Stanley Williams insists he is innocent, and that he will not and should not apologize or otherwise atone for the murders of the four victims in this case. Without an apology and atonement for these senseless and brutal killings there can be no redemption. In this case, the one thing that would be the clearest indication of complete remorse and full redemption is the one thing Williams will not do.

Clemency decisions are always difficult, and this one is no exception. After reviewing and weighing the showing Williams has made in support of his clemency request, there is nothing that compels me to nullify the jury's decision of guilt and sentence and the many court decisions during the last 24 years upholding the jury's decision with a grant of clemency.

Therefore, based on the totality of circumstances in this case, Williams' request for clemency is denied.

DATED: December 12, 2005
ARNOLD SCHWARZENEGGER,
Governor of the State of California

Appendix B:
Mapping Logic Elements, Heuristics, and Analyst's Notes

Showing Premises, Rules of Inference, and Heuristics

Several of the decision maps shown in this book have included a feature not described in the chapter on mapping conventions. This feature takes the form of a notation on the line arrow which connects one shape to another. Figure 1 in Chapter 1, for example, has one notation referencing the simulation heuristic and another note indicating the analyst's observation of a bolstering argument. There are other things an analyst might wish to note, for example, reliance on a specific rule of inference, statistical test, or heuristic in progressing from reason to claim.

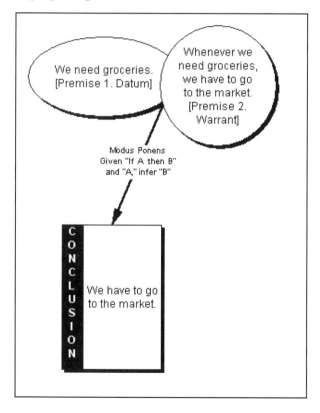

FIGURE 26: MAP SHOWING A RULE OF INFERENCE

Figure 26 illustrates a datum, a warrant, and the claim that reason supports. In the tradition of Logic, these elements would be named the argument's premises and conclusion. The argument map also notes that this inference is authorized by something which logicians have named "Modus Ponens." Human beings throughout the world regularly and naturally rely on this rule, although none need to know its name in order to apply it correctly.†††††††† Here is a second example, [151] this time illustrating a statistical inference.‡‡‡‡‡‡‡‡‡

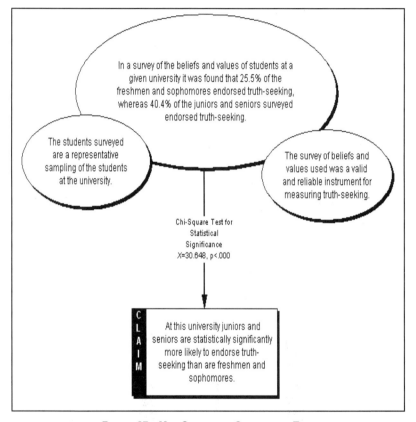

FIGURE 27 – MAP SHOWING A STATISTICAL TEST

---

†††††††† In addition to humans, computers rely on Modus Ponens, typically in the form of an "If-then, else" rule. If the "If-condition" is satisfied, the computer performs the task called by the "then" clause; otherwise the computer performs the task called by the "else" clause.

‡‡‡‡‡‡‡‡ Figure 27 indicates that the relationship being tested is a comparison of two groups of students in regard to their endorsement of the critical thinking disposition called "truth-seeking." The statistical test that is appropriate to make this comparison is the Chi-Square Test. The value of relevant statistic ("X") is calculated at 30.648. The probability that this calculation on these data could have happened by chance is less than one in a thousand, ($p < .000$).

Instead of the rule of logical or statistical inference, on the line between reason and claim we could insert the name of the heuristic that the person making the argument appears to be relying upon to justify the progression of thought from the reason given to the claim being made. Indicating the heuristic influence on the decision is the analytical precondition to evaluating the acceptability of that decision. The decision map in Figure 28 shows the influence of the heuristic Elimination by Aspect to be sufficient to override the considerations in favor of buying the car, namely that it met all of the specifications, except for its color, which the decision maker had initially set forth.

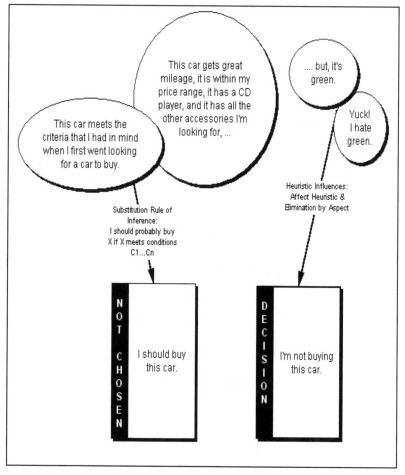

FIGURE 28: "BUT IT'S GREEN. YUCK! I HATE GREEN."

Formal and Informal Logic

From the time of Aristotle, logicians have used the strategy of replacing the specific content of arguments with symbols or letters so that they could expose the underlying syntactic and semantic structures of the various kinds of arguments. In the Nineteenth and Twentieth Centuries this approach, known as Formal Logic, eventually led to the development of the highly specialized languages used in computer programming. Algebraic geometry represents well the power of Formal Logic, for regardless of what the variables in the equation represent, we can calculate the dimensions, areas, and volumes of shapes and solids. The promising developments in computer applications aimed at language recognition and translation, artificial intelligence, and expert systems suggest that the potential for Formal Logic is far from exhausted.[152,153]

For all of its advantages in domains relating computationally and syntactically based inferences, the Formal Logic flounders when addressing the question of how best to interpret, and thus to translate into symbolic notation, the profoundly complex reasoning, often with key elements implied and contextually understood, which characterize the real world practice of human decision making.[154] It may be able to model that phenomenon, but it cannot replicate it.

The lessons most directly benefiting the A&H Method come from Logic's other focus, sometimes called Informal Logic. Informal Logic addresses the challenging nexus of problems associated with evaluating arguments presented in human to human communication using natural language conversation, with all its nuances, shading, subtlety, and malleability.[155,156] To appreciate the difference between formal and informal logic, consider the natural language argument made in the context of friends having a conversation about their weekends. One friend says, "John came for a visit Saturday and he watched television the whole time. I was really disappointed."

One interpretation of this argument using the techniques of Formal Logic would be to represent "John came for a visit" as 'p', "John watched TV" as 'q' and "I was disappointed" as 'r'. However, the structure thus revealed, [p and q, therefore r]" would not be valid by any Formal Logic test. Yet we sense that discounting the argument as invalid is a mistake, because in fact we understand very well on a social level what the argument is about. We could continue to wrestle the argument into other formal notation, but it would not be practical to do so.

The argument's logical strength derives from disconnection between what John did and what the argument maker had hoped or expected. To appreciate this, we must not discount the content of the statements spoken in this cultural context. In this case, reasoning that seems problematic at the level of syntax and semantics turns out to be neither obscure nor difficult to envision at the level of Informal Logic. As Figure 29 indicates, supplying the implicit but unspoken datum, claim, and warrant reveals more clearly the logical strength of the argument.

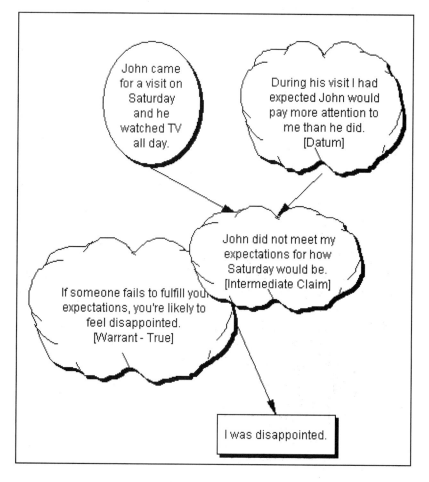

FIGURE 29: "I WAS DISAPPOINTED"

While acknowledging the tremendous achievements of the discipline of logic and its companion disciplines, mathematics and computer science, one must note that humans are able to generate and to evaluate the logical quality of a vast number of different kinds of arguments without ever having studied these disciplines. Why? Because, as indicated in Chapter 5, the practice of human argument making is governed by a series of shared understandings of how good arguments are to be made, presented, used, and evaluated.

Three Fundamental Modes of Human Inference

In Chapter 5, we suggested that one could valuably think of human inference processes as falling roughly into three categories, each with its particular modality and criteria of adequacy.

The first fundamental way we humans draw a reasoned inference is by moving from the more familiar to the less familiar. In parenting and mentoring, we give advice often by using a story that relates the current problem to a similar one we have experienced in the past. Legal reasoning uses this strategy in the appeal to precedent. Imaginative engineers and scientific investigators use this way of reasoning when they develop and apply theoretical models in the creative search for novel solutions to problems. The most fruitful explorations of this way of reasoning have come through Informal Logic. We will explore the creativity, complexities, and uncertainties of this mode of reasoning in Appendix C, "Models and Analogical Arguments."

The second fundamental mode of human reasoning is from broad principles to their applications or to other broad principles which they imply. In mathematics and in metaphysics we begin with a set of principles or assumptions and trace out their implications. This is what we are doing when we infer what is or is not permissible, or what is or is not possible, given a particular set of policies, rules, theories, or regulations. This way of reasoning is most closely associated with Formal Logic, for it is often possible to represent broad first principles in symbols that abstract from the content of their particular instantiations, and then to manipulate the symbolic representations in order to draw valid inferences regarding what these principles would entail. Appendix D, "Axiom Reasoning and Metaphysical Theories," examines the uses and potential abuses of this mode of reasoning.

The third mode of reasoning is from particulars to generalizations, which in its most refined development is the touchstone for the empirical sciences. We experience the frequency with which individuals who smoked tend to develop lung cancer and heart disease, and we form the generalization that there is a linkage, certainly a significant positive correlation, if not a causal relationship. The realization that our hypotheses about how the world works can be disconfirmed by appeal to observations, along with the power that statistical methods offer to assist us in estimating probabilities form the basis for modern scientific inquiry. We will explore the rigor, the power, and the limitations of this mode of reasoning Appendix E, "Scientific Investigation and Statistical Inference."

Appendix C:
Models and Analogical Arguments

One way humans draw inferences is by reasoning from the more familiar to the less familiar. We use powerful images, comparisons, models, metaphors, perceived similarities, and analogies to assist us in understanding things, and to shape our expectations, attitudes, and affective responses to toward those things. Here are some examples:

> President George W. Bush, Speech to the US Congress, September 20, 2001: "Al Qaeda is to terrorism what the mafia is to crime."[157]

> Animal rights activist: "We did not steal any animals from the lab. We rescued those monkeys because they were the helpless victims of torture."

> Cynic's observation: "Last year the CEO said we were all on the same team. Then the economy goes south and he wants everyone's suggestions for downsizing. Sort of reminds you of asking for volunteers to play Russian Roulette."

> Michael Douglas in the movie *Traffic*: "If there is a war on drugs, then some of the enemy are members of our own families. And I don't know how to wage war on my own family."[158]

> Evaluative comment: "You can hire John as the budget director if you want to, but if you ask me it would be like sky diving without a parachute."

> Theory development: "One fruitful way of exploring the nature of human cognition is using the computer model of list processing as suggested by Allen Newell."[159]

> Religion: "God said, 'Let us make man in our own image, in the likeness of ourselves'..."[160]

Because they communicate at the affective level as well as the intellectual level, analogies, comparisons, models, and metaphors are among the most persuasively powerful devices in our culture. Analogies help people understand less known things by relating them to more familiar things. Their fundamental mantra is "A is to B as C is to D." The most effective analogies rely on compelling images that trigger emotional as well as intellectual responses. In the first example, President Bush compared Osama Bin Laden's *al Qaeda* organization to the mafia in order to assert that it is responsible for terrorism on a very large and organized scale, in the same way that the mafia was responsible for large crime organizations. In addition, the President intended to evoke in the public the same loathing toward *al Qaeda* that is felt toward the ruthless Mafiosi. Stealing property is bad, but rescuing victims is good. The next two examples are carefully constructed contradictory comparisons: "Teammates" are supposed to protect and support each other, but Russian Roulette is an invitation to suicide.

Criteria for Evaluating Analogical Arguments

Analogies are like a fine set of carpentry tools: You have to know what a tool is for, or else it will be useless to you. To evaluate the merit of an analogy or model, one must assess the quality of the proposed comparison. The comparison is the warrant in an analogical argument. If the comparison is reasonable, then, claims the argument maker, a particular feature of the more familiar object is also a feature of the less familiar object. Usually there is not much doubt about the datum statement, which is simply that the more familiar object is aptly characterized as having a particular feature. So the emphasis for evaluation typically falls on the warrant with the question "Is the congruence between the two objects strong enough in critical respects to support inferring the ascription of features of the more familiar object to the less familiar one?" *The more pervasive the essential similarities are, the more relevant the comparison is and the more credibility a conclusion based on those similarities will have.* Analogical arguments draw their power from the perceived relevance and pervasiveness of the purported parallelism. In the best analogies, the comparison is familiar, simple, comprehensive, fecund, and falsifiable. Let us look at each feature in turn.

If the first object is not *familiar* to the listener, the analogy will not work. To appreciate why the argument maker claims that A is like B, the listener must have some familiarity with or understanding of the relationship of C to D. The relationship of C to D is known as the "model." The listener is expected to appreciate how A relates to B on the basis of the model of C's relationship to D. The more familiar the model (C to D) to which the comparison is being made, the more useful the analogy for projecting the possible relationship of A to B.§§§§§§§§§ Someone who either does not know what skydiving is or why skydivers need parachutes may not understand why hiring John to be your budget director would be suicidal. But, for most listeners it would be far less effective for the argument maker to have said, "You can hire John as the budget director if you want to, but if you ask me it would be like ingesting large quantities of sodium chloride." The point is the same, but this analogy is less effective because most people are not as familiar with consuming toxic amounts of salt as a means of self-destruction.

Simplicity is a virtue for analogies. The less complicated the model is, the more readily it will be understood and remembered. "Our nation is declaring war on drugs" is simpler, more familiar, easier to remember, and more emotionally charged than "Today I would like to announce a policy of concerted, long term, resource-intensive, multi-agency interdiction of illegal substances and the associated criminal prosecution of persons importing, manufacturing, distributing, or possessing those substances." Using a simple image, the argument maker can more easily capture the imagination of the listener.

The virtue of simplicity must be balanced by the importance of *comprehensiveness*. The more features an analogy helps us understand, the better. The question is, "Does the comparison capture enough of the critical elements?" Suppose, for example, you were trying to teach someone to swing an ax at the tree trunk. You could say, "Hold the handle like you would a tennis racket. Set your feet apart like you would if you were getting ready to push something heavy. And swing like you would if you were going to hit a nail with a heavy hammer." Three analogies were needed because none was comprehensive enough to apply to the whole effort. On the other hand, you might have said, "You swing an ax like you swing a baseball bat." In this example, that single analogy covers everything relevant including how to hold the ax, how to stand, and how to swing.

Some analogies are so rich that they allow us to reason correctly to additional aspects of the comparison. That is, they have greater *fecundity*, they suggest more implications that can be considered and explored. Comparing the swing of an ax into the trunk of a live tree with the swing of a baseball bat allows us to predict that the hips will rotate the same way in both cases. Comparing the government's policies on illegal drugs to a war

---

§§§§§§§§§ Good thinkers regard this projection as merely tentative, pending independent confirmation or disconfirmation by scientific investigation. Models suggest fruitful avenues for further investigation, in other words.

allows us to predict that there are "innocent victims" of the war on drugs who deserve all our compassion and that there are "mortal enemies" whom we must hate and destroy at all costs. Both seem to be reasonable predictions. The nation's children are often described as the innocent victims who are being targeted by the mortal enemy, the drug pushers.

At times, a fecund analogy suggests an unexpected and troubling prediction. In non-metaphorical wars our innocent victims are not our hated mortal enemies. But if one's child becomes a drug user and then, to support his or her habit, becomes a pusher, we have somehow eclipsed the power of the "war on drugs" analogy to help us understand what has happened. And, as Michael Douglas' character says, how can we wage war on our own family? No, we do not want the government waging war on our children. We want them helped if they have a drug problem, not incarcerated and punished. A model that is open to being refuted by an examination of the truth or falsity of the predictions it supports is superior to one that offers no opportunities for us to falsify what it is suggesting. Thus, *falsifiability* is another criterion for the evaluation of analogies.

One tactic for falsifying an analogy is to ask if there are crucial incongruities between the objects that the analogy proposes to compare. For example, suppose that in response to the notion that stealing experimental animals is really a kind of rescuing of innocent victims, a person replied, "No, under the law animals are property, not persons. Therefore, they cannot be considered victims in any sense that would excuse you from the legal consequences of your having taken property without authorization." Or, suppose that comparing the request for downsizing options to Russian Roulette were criticized in this way, "Not really, because in Russian Roulette you have to hold the pistol up to your own head, but what I plan to do is to recommend eliminating someone else's department, not my own."

The Utility and Liability of Analogical Reasoning

Analogical reasoning is widely used in policy development, operational planning, and jurisprudence through the familiar process of appealing to precedents. "We had a situation sort of like this before and that time we did such-and-so." Analogical reasoning is used in discussions of ethics, such as to compare cases and infer obligations.

> Making a promise to your help your sister rake the leaves is the same as when Daddy made the promise to take you to the zoo. Even though he was tired, Daddy had to keep his promises to you. He took you to the zoo.

Remember? So you have to keep your promise to your sister. You go outside now and help her rake the leaves.

Often analogies are used in public policy arguments. For example,

Because human stem cells can be cultivated and grown into human organs and cloned into whole persons, we should think of stem cells as potential human beings. We are never justified in taking the life of an innocent human being. So geneticists should not be allowed to experiment with human stem cells.

Analogies, termed "models," are relied upon in engineering to imagine possible solutions to structural puzzles. Models, not in a physical but in a conceptual sense, are used in science to suggest promising hypotheses for further testing.

The CEO's misuse of corporate funds was bad enough, but the way upper management lied to keep the Board from learning the truth was far worse. That deceit was a cancer that spread throughout upper management. And, like a cancer, it had to be mercilessly eradicated. Everyone had to go, even if it meant firing some people who never had any idea about what was going on. When you cut out a tumor you have to remove good cells too, because you can't risk leaving a single bad cell or the cancer will return.

In reasoning by analogy, the claim's persuasive power depends heavily on the suggested parallelism. For example, consider this argument for the claim, "Women should not insist on raising their children alone."

"Women, I know you *can* raise your children by yourselves. But children need fathers. And just because you can do something don't mean you should. You *can* drive a car only with your feet, but that don't mean you *should* drive a car only with your feet."[161]

The response to this argument that comedian Chris Rock received from the audience at the Apollo was loud and enthusiastic. Figure 30 diagrams his argument. The clever analogy brought home his point. It was an easy and humorous image for the audience to imagine. And, if raising children alone is like driving your car with your feet, you can see how awkward, clumsy, risky, and foolish that would be. And, in order to balance and complement the work done by the analogy on the negative side of the claim, the comedian bolstered the affirmative aspect of the claim with the observation, "Children need fathers." From the other remarks he had made in the same context, it was clear to that audience that Chris Rock was really speaking to both of a child's parents, calling for them to stay in a parental relationship with their child.

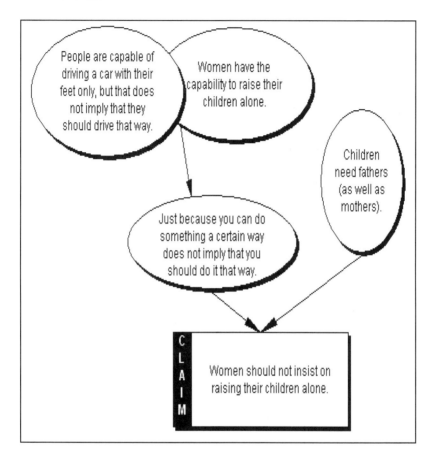

FIGURE 30:– "DON'T RAISE CHILDREN ALONE"

The persuasive power of comparisons, analogies, and models derives in part from our natural propensity to use heuristics like simulation and association. We imagine, for example, that AC electric current *flows* through the wiring in our homes and businesses. We know that if the wires are not connected to the sources, the electricity will not flow through them to our computers, lights, and appliances. The analogy is to water flowing through pipes. But, if that were true, then electric current should be gushing out of every open socket in the wall. Obviously, there is more to it than what the simple and familiar image of water flowing conveys. The application of simple and familiar images can be dangerously misleading for high-risk decisions.

Models with greater familiarity, simplicity, comprehensiveness, fecundity, and falsifiability are generally superior to those that lack one or more of these features.[162] Thus, analogies are useful for suggesting new directions of inquiry or pointing the way to possible solutions to problems, if the comparison of the current problem to the past one is sufficiently parallel in its essential elements. But, analogies are notoriously weak and unreliable, from the logical point of view.

Analogies often fail the Test of Logical Strength because, unless the comparison is essentially of one thing to itself, it is very easy to come up with points of dissimilarity from which one can generate plausible counter-examples. Also, it is easy for imaginative people to find reasons why the analogy is incongruent, thus indicating that the analogy fails the Test of Soundness. The relevance of the alleged similarities is easily disputed as well. For there may be similarities worth noting, but they may not be critical or essential, but rather superficial or even misleading.

There are so many ways that analogies can go awry that their logical merit is small. Yes, they are helpful ways of suggesting initially promising approaches. But it is not clear that anything can be established to a reasonable certainty by using analogies only. However, analogies can be memorable and persuasive, with the power to shape individual and group decisions. Analogies literally can take a nation to war. Their simplicity and familiarity often lead to a false sense of their relevance and applicability. The wise decision maker will be cautious when analogies and metaphors, rather than sound arguments, are used as a call to action.

Appendix D:
Axiomatic and *A Priori* Belief Systems

Beginning with broad and general beliefs about the world, relationships, values, and priorities, humans often reason to their general or specific implications. Here are some examples taken from the domains of law, physics and geometry, ethics and social policy, and politics.

The rules for claiming an income tax deduction on Schedule A of US Form 1040 for the interest on a real estate mortgage require that the mortgage be a loan on a dwelling held for the personal use of the taxpayer. So you cannot claim the deduction on Schedule A if the home is being used as rental property. That is a business use, not a personal use, as the Internal Revenue Code defines things.

Assume that time is a fourth dimension. Time extends forward and backward infinitely from the present moment. It follows that there can be no reality whatsoever other than the universe, for there can be no time beyond time, no heaven that comes at the end of time.

Our imaginations are bounded by the common sense geometrical assumption that through a point not on a straight line one and only one straight line can be drawn parallel to the given line. But if we suspend that unproven assumption, the possibility of curved space arises.

Taking the life of an innocent person is ethically wrong. An infant, for example, is an innocent person. Assume that personhood exists precisely so long as the soul enters into and remains within the body. So, if a fetus has a soul, abortion is ethically wrong.

Denying a competent adult the right to exercise autonomy over their own body is ethically wrong. Adults have the right to decide what medical procedures they will undergo. It is ethically wrong to deny persons the right to choose an abortion.

People are fundamentally good. I trust most to keep their word and to try to do what is right for their fellow human beings most of the time. This is why I support those who would maximize individual liberties and reduce the number of bureaucratic rules and regulations that legislators and administrators are constantly trying to impose on our personal and commercial interactions.

> People are fundamentally bad. If they can get away with something they will; they can be counted on to exploit every advantage in an effort to advance their own interests. This is why we need tougher laws and detailed regulation of commerce. More individual liberty will lead only to greater societal disintegration and the inevitable exploitation of the poor by those who have the means to do so.

These examples illustrate the power of reasoning from first principles. In the first example, a tax deduction worth several thousand dollars to a person is disallowed by the IRS code because the warrant that would have permitted the deduction does not apply if the datum is that the property is used for business purposes. In the second example, the argument maker claims that from the axiom that the universe is a four-dimensional reality that there can be no such place as heaven. On the other hand, the third example draws out the implications of making a different set of axiomatic assumptions about the universe. If we take a different set of warrants as our starting point, then we can infer different possibilities and open the door to a whole range of new investigations to determine if any of those possibilities might be real.

The fourth example makes two arguments. The first argument claims that a fetus is person. The argument maker's warrant for this claim is the metaphysical proposition that anything with a soul is a person, and their datum the assertion that a human fetus has a soul. The second argument in this example uses as its warrant the ethical principle that it is wrong to take the life of an innocent person. The second argument in this example claims that it is ethically wrong to take the life of a human fetus. And the datum is that the fetus (a "person" on the basis of the first argument) is innocent.

As is evident from the examples, axiomatic and metaphysical reasoning has a powerful impact on personal decisions. People are constrained or empowered, with life shaping consequences, because of their axiomatic beliefs about the world and about how one should live. Political orientations are applied with dramatically divergent visions of human society in mind. And, not surprisingly, persons deeply convinced that their way is the only right way seek to change or to destroy those institutions or those persons who threaten the "only right way" of living. The Christian Crusaders, the Taliban, the Nazis, the Stalinists, the Klan, racists, zealots, true-believers, and bigots of all stripes are likely to take rigidly axiomatic approaches in reasoning to their decisions about what is or is not the right thing to do or the proper way to live.

The chain of arguments in axiomatic and metaphysical reasoning flows from warrants that embody a core set of beliefs and values through which a person, or a community of persons, views and interprets reality. For example, in today's understanding of things, the burning of a woman alive at a stake could be interpreted as nothing but the most gruesome kind of torture. "Cruel and unusual punishment" seems hardly adequate to describe such a terrible thing. But centuries ago, many of European descent living in Salem, Massachusetts would have seen this horrific killing as an act of mercy. They interpreted the event as saving the woman's immortal soul from the clutches of Satan and the eternal fires of hell. Still, before we think of ourselves as "enlightened" relative to those of centuries past, let us remember that racism of the kind we know today in the United States was not a part of the culture of the Greek and Roman worlds, that virtually every advanced nation today, except the United States, outlaws capital punishment, and that much of the civilized world regards American culture as the world's greatest single source of decadence, injustice, waste, and corruption.**********

Evaluating Axiomatic *A Priori* Reasoning

Hundreds of years ago, the English statesman and philosopher, John Locke, described the habit of talking and listening only to those who agreed with the beliefs and opinions one already holds as a basic type of flawed thinking.[163] Today the critical thinking community refers to this disposition as a failure of courageous truth-seeking.

The persuasive and pervasive influences of our religious, ethical, political, or social belief systems and their attendant value structures and assumptions derive from three factors: First, typically these beliefs, values, and assumptions are widely shared by many of those with whom we live and work. Thus, accepting these beliefs, values, and assumptions is socially normative; those who disagree are seen as the persons who are mistaken, if not abnormal. Some might be classified by "normal people" as dangers to

---

********** Before the so-called "War on Terrorism" began a few years ago, it was difficult for many Americans to see this. Now the concern is that too many Americans might falsely comfort themselves with the thought that only extremists, radicals, and terrorists believe American culture is bad. That would be a mistake. There are a number of sensible and peaceful people in the United States and around the globe who have serious questions about American economic policy at the global level, about our consumerism, about our consumption of an inordinate share of the planet's natural resources, about our self-indulgent life style in the face of crushing poverty at home and abroad, and about our frequent support for brutal governments that others view as both illegal and immoral. Many seriously doubt that there is any rational justification for believing that the common good arises necessarily as each individual pursues their personal interests. Yet that idea is taken as axiomatic in American cultural and politics.

society. Socrates (470-399 B.C.E.), because he taught the people ancient Athens to reason for themselves and to question the unsubstantiated beliefs of the leaders of that city-state, was convicted of the capital offence of corrupting the youth.[164,165]

Second, beliefs, values, and assumptions of this kind are highly influential to decision making. They operate in the background of our consciousness as subtle but powerful influences on how we interpret reality. They set the limits of what we imagine to be possible and relevant. We do not often articulate these beliefs and values, rather they work like filters that color how we experience events and analyze particular situations.

And third, conceptually these beliefs, values, and assumptions are treated by many people as immune from scientific disconfirmation. This makes it very difficult for us to see them as mistaken. For example, we know of no scientific test to determine if the individual is more important than the social collective. We have not found a scientific way to verify or falsify the belief that knowledge is superior to ignorance, but most of us believe it is. There is no scientific way to investigate the claim that it is the will of God that America be destroyed. That axiomatically held beliefs, values, and assumptions are neither testable nor falsifiable is what leads us to call such beliefs, values, and assumptions " metaphysical."

The Axioms Determine the Facts

In our pragmatic American culture, we often observe that the facts of the matter appear to be irrelevant when people are arguing politics or religion. Consider the debate over gun control. Recent gun related tragedies have no influence on discussion of the right to bear arms. With metaphysical assumptions, as we are using the word, the facts do not determine the axioms, rather the axioms determine the facts. All of us see the world through our metaphysical constructs. It is like wearing a pair of glasses we can never remove. Thus, applying the Test of Soundness can be problematic when the data and the warrants include these types of statements. It is difficult to detect the influence of these assumptions, except perhaps when one visits another culture or comes to know well how a person from another culture perceives our realities. James Howard Griffin's extraordinary book, *Black Like Me*,[166] described such an experience, namely what it was like to live as a black in America's deep south in the late 1950's. There are too many other powerful examples in literature and film for us to say that we can never possibly know what the world is like from another's perspective. But, it is not at all easy to achieve those other perspectives.

Metaphysical assumptions about groups of people, values, politics, and the like most frequently operate as warrants in arguments. Because of this, they can lead people to believe they must decide or act in one certain way and that all other considerations must be in error or even in opposition to their values, politics, and ethical views. When mapping an argument exhibiting axiomatic reasoning, the claims serving as warrants which are assumed to be true in such a fundamental way – in the mind of the decision maker –are not questioned. The speaker does not explain or give reasons for these broad generalizations; rather, she or he treats them as the basis for the claims being made about what to decide to do. One will often find a certain internal consistency to this approach, but that internal consistency may not mean very much. When beliefs about the world, about other people, and about values, goals, and priorities are treated as "givens" and not checked against the facts or the practical realities of a given situation, they can result in decisions which are unsound, unwise, or unworkable.

The four tests of the quality of arguments can be helpful to some extent in evaluating axiomatic inferences: Are the arguments (1) logically strong, are the (2) premises true, are the (3) reasons relevant to the claim being made, and is the (4) argument non-circular? As a general rule one will find that the logic may be strong – which is the internal consistency we spoke of earlier. But in those cases where there are internal contradictions in the system, the proponents often have anticipated this and prepared an escape clause: "Well we call that a mystery." Or, "If your faith were stronger you would understand." And if the source of the veracity of any of non-contestable "givens" is challenged, proponents are often defend these generalities with vague or unverifiable assertions such as: "It's just common sense, everyone know that..." "Our tradition has always taught that..." "It is a fundamental tenant of our founders that ..." "Inspiration and revelation are the sources of ..." But, that said, at a fundamental level axiomatic a priori reasoning generally abhors internal inconsistency. When inconsistencies are found, there is a strong tendency to reframe the definition of key terms and reformulate presuppositions about fundamental relationships to resolve and remove the "apparent" contradiction.

The test for the truth of the premises can be problematic. Typically the proponents would maintain that there cannot in principle be counter examples to falsify their broadest generalizations and first principles. Evidence is seldom used to unseat one of a person's fundamental metaphysical beliefs about the world: What facts would lead one to abandon the notion that each human life is valuable? What would a computer have to do to convince us that the machine can actually think for itself? How many genetic and psychosocial similarities between humans and chimpanzees would we have to identify in order to think of the members of that other species as having rights? How many generous policies would management have to enact and how much initiative and productivity would the workers have to demonstrate in order for labor and management not to view one another as adversaries? Equally troubling is the challenge of applying the Test of Soundness to check specific facts. Axiomatic reasoning often defines the categories of thought so as to establish its own set of "facts." Again, when the facts do not cooperate, proponents of axiomatic reasoning often seek recourse to the escape clauses of "mystery" and "faith." Here too, however, axiomatic reasoning, if it is not 100% *a priori*, can often be improved by internal and external critics who are able to appeal to well understood and indisputable facts.

The larger in scope the axiomatic system, the more likely the third test will yield unambiguously positive results. Why? Because large scale systems, like religions, metaphysical world views, political and economic world views, and the like are declared by their proponents to be relevant to everything. The problems that the Roman Catholic Church had with Galileo and Darwin, for example, grew out of a belief system which presumed that the Bible should be taken as delivering astronomical, geological, and biological truths. The fourth test, non-circularity, produces consternation as well. One often gets the impression when dealing with some of the longer standing axiomatic *a priori* systems of belief that one is either riding on a merry-go-round or watching people ride on a merry-go-round. To those watching from the side, the riders appear to be going no place fast but generally enjoying the experience. To those riding, the spectators seem to be rushing by, while the merry-go-round represents the steady and predictable force in the universe of their own experience.

Why human beings by the millions feel so good about living their lives on the basis of metaphysical assumptions that, on close analysis, reveal themselves not to be consistent, well-founded, or warranted? Could it be that our species is hopelessly irrational at some very fundamental level? Theologians may seek to explain some of the apparent irrationalities in terms of Divine Mystery – for "Who can know the mind of God?" Psychologists may be more inclined to talk about defense systems as a way of understanding the appeal of axiomatic *a priori* systems of belief. Cultural anthropologists and sociologists might speak about shared cultural understandings. And yet, none can deny the distress which reasoning based on axiomatic *a priori* systems of belief have caused believers and non-believers on numerous occasions.

Appendix E:
Scientific Reasoning and Investigatory Processes

Empirical models and metaphors may suggest fruitful lines of scientific inquiry, but they are only the beginning as far as the logic of scientific investigation is concerned. Our capacity as a species to anticipate "what comes next" and then to devise ways to affect the outcomes of events and processes is absolutely fundamental to our survival and our current planetary dominance. We look for cause and effect relationships in order to explain, and hence to predict and control. The opening sequence of *2001 A Space Odyssey*[167] dramatizes the basic idea: You hit your rival over the head hard enough and he dies! But your arm is not long enough and your fist is not hard enough, so you make a tool, a club, to get the job done. Progress from the bone used as a club to interplanetary space travel is simply a matter of filling in the blanks.

Thousands of years later we are still working on filling in those blanks. Using the map of the human genome and using gene expression research as a potential basis for a genetic counter-attack on diseases like cancer and malaria are not trivially easy undertakings. What makes a cancerous cell's DNA express itself in different ways at different points in the tumor's growth? What are the mechanisms that turn off and on the protein receptors and, hence, make one kind of therapy effective and another ineffective at different points along the way? The answers to these questions are empirical arguments. To apply the Test of Soundness to the evaluation of an empirical argument, we must ascertain the truth or falsity of the empirical statements used in the argument. The truth or falsity of those statements is not a matter of opinion, but rather a matter for scientific investigation, evidence, and testing. To answer empirical research questions, investigators examine the data gathered using instruments specifically designed to find the kinds of data that they expect might exist. They use these observations to test their inferences, with varying levels of confidence, regarding the probable truth of their hypotheses.[168,169]

Hypothesizing About Experience

Called the "hypothetico-deductive method," the basic building block of empirical investigation can be outlined as follows: It begins with an hypothesis. "If things of kind-K are under conditions C_1, C_2, ... C_n, then they would behave in a way B or manifest evidence of behavior B." Here are some example hypotheses.

> If the salmonella bacterium is exposed to temperatures greater than 140-Centrigrate for more than thirty seconds, it will die.

> The reflexes of a person who drives a motor vehicle five or more hours without a rest period will have deteriorated by 30% or more as compared to their reflexes after only 1 to 4 hours of driving.[†]

> In our new program we train sixth graders to tutor third graders in reading and math. Our hypothesis is that the test scores of both groups will be significantly higher than the scores of their peers who were not involved in this tutoring program.

> Green is big right now. So if we promote the belief in the general public that our company has a sincere concern for the environment, we will see an increase in our market share.

> If the Federal Reserve reduces the prime interest rate, there will be a proportional reduction in short term interest rates on consumer credit card purchases. And, if this happens, it will stimulate the economy, since consumers will tend to spend more, thus leading to an increase in manufacturing and the creation of more jobs.

The logic of scientific reasoning joins plausible hypotheses like these with a number of statements describing particular states of affairs that the scientists endeavor to bring about experimentally or to measure in their natural settings. The advantage of creating the conditions in the lab is that potential influences of extraneous factors can be reduced, yet that tends to weaken the generalizability of the findings.

[†] It is not necessary that a hypothesis be expressed as an "if...then" statement, only that it can be converted into one. For example, "The reflexes of a person who drives a motor vehicle five or more hours without a rest period will have deteriorated by 30% or more as compared to their reflexes after only 1 to 4 hours of driving" can be rewritten as "If a person drives motor vehicle five or more hours without a rest period, then the person's reflexes will have deteriorated by 30% or more as compared to after only 1 to 4 hours of driving."

Rather than risk accidents on the open road where our subjects and other people as well might be injured or killed, we can check the reflexes of men and women of different ages by having them drive on a closed track in dry weather. Of course, driving on a closed track is boring by comparison to driving on the open road under differing weather and traffic conditions.

If we divide the sixth graders and third graders into two groups each, we can train one group of sixth graders to tutor one group of third graders. If we assure that all other known relevant factors are held constant (for example, that otherwise they receive instruction in the same subjects and by equally competent teachers and in identical learning environments), then we should see statistically significantly higher test scores for the experimental group students [third graders who were tutored and their sixth grade tutors] as compared to the control group students [third graders who were not tutored and sixth graders not in the tutoring program].

The basic formulation of the experimental effort's logical structure is: "Items in Set-A suitably represent items of kind-K. If we create conditions such that the items in Set-A are under conditions C_1, C_2, ... C_n, then behavior B will occur or evidence of B will be manifested. If the subsequent findings do not include B or evidence of B, good reasoning allows us to infer that the hypothesis being tested is probably false. Assuming, of course, that there were no technical errors in creating the exact conditions C_1, C_2, ... C_n, in finding manifestations of B, in building and calibrating the devices used to measure the manifestations of B, or in the application and interpretation of the appropriate statistical tests.[170,171]

Calculated Confidence

If the findings turn out as predicted, then the investigator may have more confidence in the truth of the inferences, and yet, the hypothesis might still turn out, on further examination, not to be true. Rather, it may simply have been a coincidence that B resulted. In scientific inquiry, one's confidence in the truth or falsity of the relationship that one has hypothesized to exist is carefully calculated. Different statistical tests and methods of analysis are appropriate for application under conditions that are specific to the experimental data gathered in research with differing design features.

Technically speaking, statistical analyses do not confirm the inference that there is a relationship between two variables, rather they indicate the degree of confidence with which the null hypothesis can be ruled out. The null hypothesis is usually the assertion that two variables are unrelated. The factor considered to be related or the potential causative agent is not related, either positively or negatively, to the factor considered to be the effect of that hypothesized cause. Typically, experimental situations admit of degrees of confidence in the inference being made such that the null hypothesis (that there is no relationship) is to be rejected with a 5% or 1% or even smaller chance of error.

Scientific Reasoning as Extended Arguments

A full argument map of scientific reasoning would be far more than a list of conditions under which an item of kind, K, will manifest behavior, B. We must find a theory, T, which purports to explain the causal relationships of interest. Our amended claim is: "Given theory T, if things of kind K are under conditions C_1, C_2, ... C_n, then they would behave in a way B or manifest evidence of behavior B." The reasoning strategy at this point calls for designing an experiment that will falsify this claim. If we succeed in crafting such an experiment, the normal pursuit of scientific research then allows certain logical moves to advance our understandings. We can modify conditions C_1, C_2, ... C_n or we can look for slight but important differences in various items of kind K, thus creating sub-classifications of K, or we could amend theory T. Eventually, with enough refinements at the theoretical and technical levels, the investigation should lead to claims about the behavior of objects of the kind K (or an important sub-class of K), under certain conditions that can reliably be predicted to manifest B, if the hypothesis was fundamentally right in the first place.[172] The argument map would show the refinements which have been attempted. The factors which might threaten the validity of the experimental situation could be envisioned as watershed considerations, with the controls that mitigate each threat put in as counter-arguments.

History is replete with examples of unwarranted jumps from coincidence to causality. The untrained mind too readily believes that because first one event occurs then another event occurs that the second event was caused by the first. Poor inferences of this kind indicate a failure to satisfy the Tests of Logical Strength and the Test of Relevance. There has to be some warrant for thinking that the two phenomena are somehow related by more than mere chance. For example, we know that the incidence of heart disease is statistically correlated positively with aging. But it would be a profoundly unhelpful mistake to jump to the conclusion that aging alone causes heart disease. There are too many counterexamples walking around; older people with healthy hearts and younger people with heart problems. And, from the point of view of gaining a measure of control over the leading cause of death in our culture, namely heart disease, it is not at all productive to link the problem with a single factor that we can do very little about, namely, aging. We can, however, do things about other contributing factors, such as diet, weight, exercise, and infections. And we can manage some of the physical factors, for instance hypertension or valvular stenosis, with surgery and medication. But, just having the opinion that something should be true or that some intervention will work is not nearly adequate, for in science the standard is that one should expect to be required to justify each argument at every step in the process. And, further, that each of those steps and their justifications are open to thorough and independent scrutiny as well as replication by other scientists. In theory, the full argument map would show how the scientific investigator considered and resolved each of the questions raised at every step in the process.

Conducting an Investigation Scientifically

Setting out to investigate an empirical question logically and systematically, and in a way that allows others in the scientific and professional community to verify the results through replication, involves a number of steps. Any place along the way an investigator can introduce error though technical, conceptual, or reasoning mistakes. And yet, because the process can be monitored and corrected by the investigator or others on the research team, it is exceptionally robust from the perspective of the reasoning inherent in the process. Table 11 is an extended example that identifies the various steps in the process.[173,174,175,176] In every step, arguments are being made that can be analyzed using the A&H Method into reasons and claims. Each of these arguments can be evaluated for their logical merits. The truth or falsity of the data and warrants can be investigated, for example, in order to determine the soundness of the reasoning at each step in the scientific process.

TABLE 12: THE ARGUMENTS TO BE MADE AT EACH STEP OF A SCIENTIFIC INVESTIGATION

The Steps in the Investigatory Process		The Investigator's Argument Responsibilities
Identify a problem of significance. E.G., How does the workplace environment affect the productivity and job motivation of administrative assistants?	(1)	Explain why knowing the nature of this relationship, if it exists, is of benefit either as basic research or because of the potential application to a larger concern.
Form a hypothesis based on a relevant testable set of theories regarding the problem. E.G., Administrative assistants at workstations in noise-distraction-limited environments, with moderate privacy, a window, and one or two family pictures or other personal items on their desks are more productive than those who work at noisier, more public, windowless, less personalized workstations.	(2)	Set up the overall argument: The set of applicable theories (about the influences on human motivation and productivity) serves as the warrant. The data are the points of information gathered about the environment of the workplace and about the productivity and motivation of the administrative assistants. The claim is the hypothesis that there is a relationship that is a significant relationship.
Thoroughly review the scientific literature in order to identify and examine relevant prior studies of similar or related hypotheses. E.G., There were four relevant studies published. One dealt with noise, privacy, and job satisfaction. Another with visual distractions, including windows, and interruptions, such as in-coming phone calls. Two focused on personalizing the workplace. One was a quantitative study showing an inverse statistical relationship between productivity and workplace noise. The other was based on qualitative interview data. The administrative assistants interviewed indicated high levels of frustration and dissatisfaction with depersonalized work environments	(3)	Before accepting its conclusions, evaluate the scientific merit of the each study reviewed. Are the data and warrants used true? Are the arguments logically strong? Were there any problems with the validity or reliability of the data gathering methods? Were the appropriate statistical tests applied and were they applied correctly? Is the chain of scientific reasoning complete and unbroken? Given all the relevant theories and other things we know about the phenomena and the questions at hand, if one were to replicate the study how likely does it appear that essentially the same findings would result? Are the findings of these studies consistent with other studies of the same or very similar phenomena?

and they reported feeling less motivated to give their best efforts to those employers. Nothing in the literature combined all the factors being considered here.		
Identify all the variables that it will be important to measure, control, or monitor. E.G., work productivity, noise, privacy, personal items displayed, access to window, time at the workstation without a break, years of comparable work experience, personal sense of the value of the work, baseline productivity, and the administrative assistants' knowledge of the experimental situation.	(4)	Consider each variable and justify the decision regarding why that variable should either be allowed to vary or should be controlled. For example, we should control for hours worked per day or else those who work longer hours are likely to be more productive. But our aim is to find out if distractions affect productivity, other things (such as hours worked per day) being equal.
Make the variable measurable. E.G., noise will be measured as decibels, productivity as phone and e-mail messages sent and received in a randomly selected one hour period, windows as simply the presence or absence of an unobstructed view out of an exterior building window located within seven feet of the person's chair. Personal sense of the value of the work will be derived from interview data and from survey questionnaires.	(5)	Justify the chosen method of making each variable operational by explaining the relevance of the data captured. For example, why it is reasonable to operationalize productivity as e-mail and phone messages sent and received within the period of one hour?
Assure that the experimental conditions can be met. E.G., Determine that there will be a sufficient number of administrative assistants about whom data can be collected, that their supervisors have authorized the research, that the research has been reviewed and approved by relevant human subjects review boards, that the	(6)	Answer why and how questions for every decision made about setting up these experimental conditions. E.G., Why the sample was chosen this way, instead of by some other process? How was it determined that the number of administrative assistants about whom data will be collected is, in fact, a sufficient number for purposes of the kind of questions being asked? How

provision has been made to secure the informed consent of the persons who will be the experimental subjects, that the specific hypothesis under investigation will not be revealed to the administrative assistants who are subjects of the study, that the relevant demographic data (overall work experience, experience on the particular job, age, etc.) can be gathered. Decide how many persons will be interviewed, who will interview them, how the interviewers will be trained, what questions they will use to prompt the persons to talk about the value that they place in the work they are assigned to do, Etc.		have the rights of human subjects been protected? Why will the specific hypotheses under investigation not be revealed to the subjects of the study? Why is the demographic data being collected relevant? How will the interviewers be trained, why that way, why not some other way? How were the questions and prompts selected, how were they validated, and why do we think that the answers the subjects give will be reliable?
Design the experimental data generating strategy. E.G., Subjects will be randomly divided into three equally sized groups: Group-A will remain at their current workstations and data regarding noise, personal items, distance from exterior windows, and productivity will be gathered without any change in their work environments. Group-B will be assigned new workstations that are optimally configured for the purposes of this study and encouraged to personalize those workstations to suit their own tastes. Group-C will be assigned new workstations that are negatively configured according to the hypothesis of this study (noisy, no-window, not private) and be advised that they are not allowed to personalize those workstations.	(7)	Explain why the findings derived will not be spurious. In other words, justify each decision about how groups will be divided, what they will do, where they will go, what they will be assigned to do, how they will be assigned, etc. The arguments here are intended to establish that the investigator has considered all the ways that the data being gathered might be discounted as irrelevant or as misleading, and then has taken steps to guard against that threat to the validity of the investigation. For example, Group-A will remain as it is so that we can establish baseline measures. Group-B will be optimally configured and Group-C negatively configured so we can see what the full possible range of variance might be in work productivity.
Construct reliable measuring	(8)	Demonstrate that the apparatus, the

devices and Validate them. E.G., Interviews will follow such and such a protocol of questions to be asked, data will be tape-recorded and transcribed. Questions for the survey instruments will be independently pilot-tested. E-mails processed will be measured by an automated count of messages opened and messages sent from each person's desktop PC trough the network servers. Messages greater than 100 words will be counted as 1.5 messages. Privacy will be measured by counting the number of persons who pass within three feet of the person's chair, etc.		survey, and the interview questions are valid measures of the intended phenomena. Demonstrate that whatever amounts of error the tools may introduce is an acceptably small amount. Demonstrate that each time these tools are used their results can be relied upon if the tools have been used correctly.
Conduct the experiment and gather the data. E.G., The investigator, working with the supervisors, arranges for the administrative assistants to be divided into the three groups and for those in Groups B and C to be assigned to their new workstations. Personnel trained in the use of the various measurement tools gather the data on noise, measure the distances to the windows, count the people that pass within three feet of desks, conduct the interviews, have the administrative assistants fill out.	(9)	Anticipate problems and justify the decisions about practical problems that come up in conducting the experiment. In justifying those decisions the claim each time is that the practical adjustments made were the most reasonable under the circumstances. The investigator will have to explain how the scientific integrity of the investigation was maintained, why the adjustments did not significantly alter the experiment, and how they did not compromise the quality of the data or influence the test of the hypothesis one way or the other.
Conduct appropriate analyses of the data. E.G., The productivity comparison showed that Group B's productivity was statistically significantly greater than Group C's (confidence level .05). Or, noise in conjunction with lack of privacy accounted for 16% of the variance in productivity between those in distraction-rich environments and	(10)	Demonstrate that the data was handled correctly. E.G., that narrative data was completely and correctly transcribed and analyzed by properly trained and supervised raters, that those statistical tests that were applied were the appropriate tests to use with the kind of data that had been gathered, that they were the correct tests to use to examine the kind of question being investigated,

those in distraction-limited environments. Or, no quantitative differences were detectable when comparing window and non-window workers, when all the other variables measured are held constant. However interview data shows much higher work satisfaction and a strong, positive motivation to work hard among those with windows.		and that any technical conditions for their application had been satisfied.
Interpret the findings and discuss their significance. E.G., If workplace distractions can be limited, noise is reduced, and privacy is assured, then one can expect modest increases in the productivity of administrative assistants, regardless of whether they are working in windowed or windowless offices. However, motivation is higher among those working in offices with windows. These findings are of significance for managers and for interior design architects engaged in workplace configuration. In the light of this study, there are some things managers should consider to increase productivity and satisfaction. Cite relevant studies that show that that positive motivation is associated with loyalty and effort. These, in turn, contribute to sustained productivity.	(11)	Demonstrate that the interpretations being made are reasonable and justifiable, given the data. The claims at this point must not exaggerate the findings. Findings that may be statistically significant but which are otherwise trivial at the practical level should be described as such. Differences perceived in the data that go beyond mere numerical significance and have a degree of practical importance should be identified. E.G., What do the data tell us about how managers might bring about greater productivity and satisfaction in the workplace? Are the variables that appear to influence satisfaction and productivity within the control of managers or of those who configure the places where adminsitrative assistants will be stationed to do their work?
Extend the research by articulating new hypotheses. We might hypothesize that data gathered at longer intervals, for example, six months, one year, and two years, will reveal that the productivity of windowed workers remains constant or increases whereas the productivity of windowless workers	(12)	Explain why the additional research would be valuable in its own right or because of its potential to refine applications of the current findings. On which un-answered questions might further studies shed light? How would future research go beyond the current study and other studies in the literature? What would the hypotheses be that

deteriorates over time. The strategy used for measuring productivity failed to account for the quality of the work produced. Measures of client satisfaction, revenue generated, and clerical error rates should be added to future studies. The significance of this work is directly related to maximizing worker productivity and employee satisfaction while minimizing errors. This, in turn, It is also related to reducing costs of employee recruitment through increased retention of productive workers potentially by increasing the ratio of workers to supervisors, on the assumption that the number of productive and satisfied workers will be higher if workstation environments are configured in the ways suggested by this research.		required further investigation?
Publish the research. Make known to others in the scientific and professional community the hypothesis tested and the experimental methodology used, the findings, and their interpretation and potential significance. Typically this is done by submitting a written report to a scientific journal. The editor of the journal would send that manuscript for external review by one's scientific peer. They will render an independent judgment on the scientific merits of the project. Publication in the journal will depend on positive reviews, and often on revisions and on further scientific refinements as may be recommended by the reviewers.	(13)	The investigator must reason through questions such as "who may need to see the results of this investigation?" in order to decide on an appropriate scientific or professional journal in which to seek publication. If the study is large, the investigator may have to decide how to divide the research and present it in pieces in more than one publication, demonstrating in each the scientific integrity of that piece as being derived from the integrity of the overall investigation. The investigator will have to decide how best to communicate the findings, that is, how to write up the research report so that it is clear, objective, and strong enough to stand on its own merits as an accurate report of scientific research. Each of these decisions, like all those that have come earlier, must be justified by well reasoned arguments.

The scientific approach is exhaustively systematic, unwavering in the honesty of the inquiry. It anticipates the consequences of choices and intermediary judgments and decisions, demanding well reasoned justifications at every step from the beginning through all the intermediary stages in the investigation, all the way to the interpretive and expository presentation of the results. The cognitive skills required are the critical thinking skills of analysis, interpretation, drawing reasoned inferences, explanation, evaluation, and reflective self-correction. The habits of mind, such as following reasons and evidence wherever they lead, courageously pursuing the inquiry, being systematic, being confident in the power and process of reasoned inquiry, etc., are the ideal attributes of a critical thinker.†††††††††[177,178]

Science progresses when the entire scientific community can evaluate the merits of a scientific investigation and can seek to confirm or disconfirm its findings by replicating that investigation. This capacity of a community of investigators to engage objectively in self-monitoring and the self-correction of the findings of any member of the community, including correcting one's own prior work, gives scientific inquiry the advantage over the analogical and the axiomatic modes of reasoning. Scientific reasoning calls for the application of the four tests of the logical quality of arguments at every stage of scientific investigation. The results are evident in our increasing knowledge of the how the natural world works, and in the technological, biomedical, and engineering benefits humans have achieved over centuries by using scientific inquiry.

---

††††††††† Critical thinking skills and sub-skills and the different aspects of the disposition toward critical thinking are discussed in detail in Chapter 5. As we shall see, critical thinking skills, and the strong disposition to apply them, are of major significance not only to the quality of scientific inquiry, but, more generally, for all of problem solving and decision making.

REFERENCES

[1] Katapodi, M. C., Facione, N. C., Humphreys, J. C., and Dodd, M. J. (2005). Perceived breast cancer risk: Heuristic reasoning and search for a dominance structure. *Social Science and Medicine*, 60(2), 4121-32.

[2] Nosarti, C., Craford, T., Roberts, J. V., Elias, E., McKenzie, K., and David, A. S. (2000). Delay in presentation of symptomatic referrals to a breast clinic: patient and system factors. *British Journal of Cancer*, 82(3), 742-48.

[3] Facione, N. C. and Dodd., M. J. (1995). Women's narratives of help-seeking for breast cancer. *Cancer Practice*, 3(4), 219-25.

[4] Svenson, O. (1989). Eliciting and analyzing verbal protocols in process studies of judgment and decision making. In H. Montgomery and O. Svenson (Eds), *Process and structure in human decision making,* (pp. 65-81). Chichester, UK: John Wiley & Sons.

[5] Montgomery, H. (1989). From cognition to action: the search for dominance in decision making. In H. Montgomery and O. Svenson (Eds), *Process and structure in human decision making,* (pp. 23-49). Chichester, UN: John Wiley & Sons.

[6] Montgomery, H. and Svenson, O. (1983). A think aloud study of dominance structuring. In R. Tietz (Ed), *Aspiration levels in bargaining and economic decision making.* Berlin, Germany: Springer.

[7] Toulmin, S. (1958, 1969). *The uses of argument.* Cambridge, UK: Cambridge University Press.

[8] Facione, N. C. and Facione, P. A. (2006). The cognitive structuring of patient delay. *Social Science & Medicine,* 63(12), 3137-49.

[9] Katapodi, M. C., Facione, N. C., Humphreys, J. C., and Dodd, M. J. (2005). *op cit.*

[10] Gilovic, T, Griffin, D, and Kahneman, D. (2002). *Heuristics and biases: The psychology of intuitive judgment.* Cambridge, UK: Cambridge University Press.

[11] Slovic, P., Frishoff, B., and Lichtenstein, S. (1977). Behavioral decision theory. *Annals of the Review of Psychology,* 28,1-39.

[12] Gilovic, T., et al. (2002), *Op cit.*

[13] Kahneman, D., Slovic, P. and Tversky, A. (1982). *Judgment under uncertainty: Heuristics and biases.* Cambridge, UK: Cambridge University Press.

[14] Kahneman, D., Slovic, P., and Tversky, A. (1982). *Op cit.*

[15] Janis, I.L. and Mann, L. (1977). *Decision Making: A Psychological Analysis of Conflict, Choice and Commitment,* (pp. 1-41). London, UK: Collier Macmillan Publishers.

[16] Montgomery, H. (1989). From cognition to action: The search for dominance in decision making. In H. Montgomery and O. Svenson (Eds), *Process and Structure in Human Decision making,* (pp. 23-49). Chichester, UK: John Wiley & Sons.

[17] Taylor, S. E., and Brown, J. D. (1988). *Psychological Bulletin,* 103(2), 193-210.

[18] Thompson, S. C., Armstrong, W., and Thomas, C. (1998). Illusions of control, underestimations, and accuracy: A control heuristic explanation. *Psychological Bulletin,* 123, 143-61.

[19] Tversky, A., and Kahneman, D. (1973). Availability: A heuristic for judging frequency and probability. *Cognitive Psychology,* 5, 207-32.

[20] Gilovic, T., et al., 2002. *op cit.*

[21] Kahneman, D., Slovic, P., and Tversky, A. 1982. *Op cit.*

[22] Salomon, S.A. (2002). Two Systems of reasoning. In T. Glovitch, D. Griffin, D. Kahneman (Eds*), Heuristics and Biases: The psychology of intuitive judgment ,* (pp. 379-96). Cambridge, UK: Cambridge University Press.

[23] Kahneman, D. and Miller, D. T. (2002). Norm theory: comparing reality to its alternatives. In T. Glovitch, D. Griffin, D. Kahneman (Eds*), Heuristics and Biases: The psychology of intuitive judgment,* (pp. 348-66). Cambridge, UK: Cambridge University Press.

[24] Facione, P. A. (2007). *Critical thinking: what it is and why it counts – 2007 Update.* Millbrae, CA: The California Academic Press LLC. www.insightassessment.com.

[25] Toulmin, S. E. (1969). *Op cit.*

[26] Toulmin, S., Rieke, R. and Janik, A. (1979). *An Introduction to Reasoning.* New York: Macmillan Publishing Co., Inc.

[27] Svenson, O. (1989). *Op cit.,* pp.65-81.

[28] McCracken, G. (1988). The long interview. *Qualitative Research. Methods Series* 13, San Francisco, CA: Sage Press.

[29] Michler, E. G. (1986). *Research Interviewing: Context and Narrative.* Cambridge, MA: Harvard University Press.

[30] Mishler, E. G. (1986). The analysis of interview narratives. In T. R. Sarbin (Ed), *Narrative Psychology: The Storied Nature of Human Conduct,* (pp. 233-55). New York: Praeger.

[31] Personal Narratives Group. (1989). *Interpreting Women's Lives. Feminist Theory and Personal Narratives.* Indianapolis: IN: Indiana University Press.

[32] Reissman, C. K. (1993). *Narrative Analysis: Qualitative Research Methods.* Newbury Park: Sage.

[33] Labov, W., and Waletzsky, J. (1967). Narrative analysis: Oral versions of personal experience. In J. Helms (Ed), *Essays on the Verbal and Visual Arts.* Seattle: University of Washington Press.

[34] Baumeister, R.F. and Newman, L. S. (1994). How Stories Make Sense of Personal Experiences: Motives that Shape Autobiographical Narratives. *Personality and Social Psychology Bulletin,* 20, 676-690.

[35] Heatherton, T. F., and Nichols, P. A. (1994). Personal accounts of successful versus failed attempts at life change. *Personal and Social Psychology Bulletin,* 20, 664-75.

[36] Newell, A. (1990). *Toward Unified Theories of Cognition.* Cambridge, MA: Harvard University Press.

[37] Crowne, D.P., and Marlowe, D. (1960). A new scale of social desirability independent of psychopathology. *Journal of Consulting Psychology,* 24, 349-54.

[38] Reynolds, W.M. (1982). Development of reliable and valid short forms of the Marlowe-Crowne Social Desirability Scale. *Journal of Clinical Psychology,* 38, 119-24.

[39] Prochaska, H., Velicer, W.F., Rossi, J.S., Goldstein, M.G., Marcus, B.H., Rakowski, W., et al. *(1994).* Stages of change and decisional balance for 12 problem behaviors. *Health Psychology,* 13(1), 39-46.

[40] Triandis, H. C. (1980). Values, attitudes and interpersonal behavior. In H. E. Howe (Ed), *Beliefs, Attitudes, and Values. Nebraska Symposium on Motivation.* Lincoln, NB: University of Nebraska Press.

[41] Ajzen, I. and Fishbein, M. (1980). A theory of reasoned action: Some applications and implications. In H. E. Howe (Ed), *Beliefs, Attitudes, and Values. Nebraska Symposium on Motivation.* Lincoln, NB: University of Nebraska Press.

[42] Kreuger, R.A. (1988). *Focus groups: a practical guide for applied research.* London: Sage.

[43] Gibbs, A. (1997). *Focus groups. Social Research Update.* A publication of the Department of Sociology, University of Surrey, UK.

[44] Facione, N. C. and Giancarlo, C.A.F. (1998). Narratives of breast symptom discovery and cancer diagnosis: Psychologic risk for advanced cancer at diagnosis. *Cancer Nursing,* 21 (6), 430-40.

[45] Facione, P.A., Facione, N.F., and Giancarlo, C.A. (2000). The disposition toward critical thinking: Its character, measurement, and relationship to critical thinking skill. *Journal of Informal Logic,* 20 (1), 61-84.

[46] Facione, N.C. and Facione, P.A. (2002). Analyzing explanations for seemingly irrational choices: Linking argument analysis and cognitive science. *International Journal of Applied Philosophy.* 15(2), 267-286.

[47] Facione, N.C. and Facione, P.A. (2006). *Op cit.*

[48] Facione, P.A., and Scherer, D. (1978). *Logic and Logical Thinking,* McGraw Hill: New York.

[49] Victor, J., Krimerman, L. I., Elder, S. T., and Miremont, L. P., Cieutat, V.J. (1969). *Traditional Logic and the Venn Diagram: A Programmed Introduction.* San Francisco, CA: Chandler Publishing.

[50] Toulmin, S.E., (1969) *Op cit.*

[51] Toulmin, S.E., Rieke, R. and Janik, A. (1979). *Op cit.*

[52] Seech, Z. (1987). *Logic in Everyday Life: Practical Reasoning Skills*. Belmont, CA: Wadsworth, Inc.

[53] Fisher, A. (2000). *The Logic of Real Arguments*. Cambridge, UK: Cambridge University Press.

[54] Thomas, S.N. (1996). *Practical Reasoning in Natural Language*. Englewood Cliffs, NJ: Prentice-Hall.

[55] Browne, M. N., and Keeley, S.M. (2007). *Asking the Right Questions: A guide to Critical Thinking*, 8th Edition. Englewood Cliffs, NJ: Prentice-Hall.

[56] Missimer, C. A. (1994). *Good Arguments: An Introduction to Critical Thinking*, Englewood Cliffs, NJ: Prentice-Hall.

[57] *San Francisco Chronicle*. (November 13, 2003) Opinion Page A22.

[58] Ajzen, I. and Fishbein, M. (1980). *Op cit.*

[59] Triandis, H. (1980). *Op cit.*

[60] Gigerenzer, G., Todd, P.M., and the ABC [Center for Adaptive Behavior and Cognition] Research Group. (2000) Simple heuristics that make us smart. *Journal of Bioeconomics*, 2(1), 89-92.

[61] Toulmin, S. (1969). *Op cit.* pp. 94-146.

[62] Seech, Z. (1987). *Op cit.* pp. 136-57.

[63] Slovic, P., Frishoff, B., and Lichtenstein, S. (1977). Behavioral decision theory. *Annals Review of Psychology*, 28,1-39.

[64] Prior, A., Lejewski, C., Staal, J. F., Gram, A. C., et al. (1967). The history of logic. In P. Edwards (Ed), *The Encyclopedia of Philosophy*. New York: Macmillan Publishing. Vol. 4, pp. 513-71.

[65] Copi, I., and Cohen, C. (1990). *Introduction to Logic*. New York: Macmillan Publishing.

[66] Facione, P., and Scherer, D. (1978). *Op cit.*

[67] Copi I, and Cohen C, 1990. *Op cit.*, pp. 52-3.

[68] Jenicek, M. (Under editorial review). *Medicine without Fallacies: Improving Reasoning, Communication, and Decision Making in Clinical Practice and Research*. Chicago: The American Medical Association.

[69] Aristotle. (350 B.C.E.) *De Sophisticis Elenchis [On Sophistical Refutations]* Translated by W. A. Pickard. Cambridge. URL: http://classics.mit.edu/Aristotle/sophist_refut.html

[70] Machie, J. (1967). Fallacies. In P. Edwards (Ed), *The Encyclopedia of Philosophy*. New York: Macmillan Publishing. Vol. 3(1). Pp. 179-79.

[71] Hamblin, C. (1970). *Fallacies*. London: Methuen & Co Ltd.

[72] Facione, P. and Scherer, D. (1978). *Op cit.*, pp. 287-365.

[73] Searle, J. (1969). *Speech Acts: An Essay in the Philosophy of Language*. Cambridge UK: Cambridge University Press.

[74] Yarrow, P. and Yardley, S. (1967). "If I had wings". Pepamar Music Corp. *Album 1700*. Los Angeles: Warner Bros. Records Inc.

[75] Simon, H. (1957). *Models of Man: Social and Rational*. New York: Wiley.

[76] Taylor, S.E. (1982). The availability bias in social perception and interaction. In D. Kahneman, P. Slovic, and A. Tversky (Eds), *Judgment under Uncertainty: Heuristics and Biases* (pp. 190-200). Cambridge, UK: Cambridge University Press.

[77] Fischhoff, B. (1976). Attribution theory and judgment under uncertainty. In N. H. Harvey, W. J. Ickes, and R. F. Kidd (Eds), *New directions in attribution research*. Hillsdale New Jersey: Erlbaum.

[78] Simon, H. (1957). *Op cit.*

[79] Gigerenzer, G., Czerlinski, J., and Martignon, L. (2002). How good are fast and frugal heuristics? In T. Gilovich, D. Griffin, and D. Kahneman (Eds), *Heuristics and Biases: The Psychology of Intuitive Judgment,* (pp. 559-81). Cambridge, UK: Cambridge University Press.

[80] Slovic, P., Finucane, M., Peters, E., and MacGregor, D. G. (2002). The affect heuristic. In T. Gilovich, D. Griffin, and D. Kahneman (Eds), *Heuristics and Biases: The Psychology of Intuitive Judgment,* (pp. 397-420). Cambridge, UK: Cambridge University Press.

[81] Schwarz, N. (2002). Feelings as information: Moods influence judgments and processing strategies. In T. Gilovich, D. Griffin, and D. Kahneman (Eds), *Heuristics*

and Biases: The Psychology of Intuitive Judgment, (pp. 534-47). Cambridge, UK: Cambridge University Press.

[82] Huber, O. (1989). Information-processing operators in decision making. In H. Montgomery, and O. Svenson (Eds), *Process and Structure on Human Decision Making* (pp.3-21). Chichester, UK: John Wiley & Sons.

[83] Newell, A. and Simon, H. A. (1972). *Human Problem Solving*, Englewood Cliffs, N.J: Prentice Hall.

[84] Slovic P., Finucane, M., Peters, E., and MacGregor, D.G. (2002). *Op cit.*

[85] Waite, P.S. (2007). Campus landscaping in recruitment and retention: The package is the product. Presented at the 2007 the annual Noel Levitz conference on enrolment management. Orlando, FL.

[86] Facione, P.A., Facione, N. C., Giancarlo, CA, (2000). *Op cit.*

[87] Koehler, D. J. (1991). Explanation, Imagination and Confidence in Judgment. *Psychological Bulletin*, 110, 499-519.

[88] Koch, S. J. (1984). Availability and inference in predictive judgment. *Journal of Experimental Psychology: Learning, Memory and Cognition*, 10, 649-62.

[89] Kahneman D, Slovic P & Tversky A. (1982). *Op cit.*

[90] Tversky, A. and Kahneman, D. (1973). Availability: A Heuristic for Judging Frequency and Probability. *Cognitive Psychology*, 5, 207-32.

[91] Bandura, A. (1977). Self-Efficacy: Toward a Unifying Theory of Behavioral Change. *Psychological Review*, 84(2), 191-215.

[92] Bandura, A. (1989). Self -Efficacy Mechanism in Physiological Activation and Health-Promoting Behavior. In J. Madden, IV, S. Matthysse, and J. Barchas (Eds), *Adaptation, learning and effect*. New York: Raven Press.

[93] Schwarz, N. and Vaughn, L A. (2002). The availability heuristic revisited: Ease of recall and content of recall as distinct sources of information. In T. Gilovich, D. Griffin, and D. Kahneman (Eds), *Heuristics and Biases: The Psychology of Intuitive Judgment*, (pp. 103-19). Cambridge, UK: Cambridge University Press.

[94] Kahneman D, Slovic, P, Tversky A. (1982). *Op cit.*, p. 11.

[95] Kahneman, D., Slovic, P., and Tversky, A. 1982. *Op cit.*

[96] Janis, I. L. and Mann, L. (1977). *Op cit.*

[97] Rozin, P. and Nemeroff, C. (2002). Sympathetic magical thinking: The contagion and similarity "heuristics." In T. Gilovich, D. Griffin, and D. Kahneman (Eds), *Heuristics and Biases: The Psychology of Intuitive Judgment*, (pp. 201-16). Cambridge, UK: Cambridge University Press.

[98] Kahneman, D. and Frederick, S. (2002). Representativeness revisited: Attribute substitution in intuitive judgment. In T. Gilovich, D. Griffin, and D. Kahneman (Eds), *Heuristics and Biases: The Psychology of Intuitive Judgment*, (pp. 49-81). Cambridge, UK: Cambridge University Press.

[99] Berreby, D. (2005). *Us and Them: Understanding Your Tribal Mind*. New York: Little, Brown and Company.

[100] Robinson, R. J., Keltner, D., Ward, A, and Ross, L. (1995). Actual vs. assumed differences in construal: "Naïve Realism" in intergroup perception and conflict. *Journal of Personality and Social Psychology*, 68, 404-17.

[101] Tversky, A. and Kahneman, D. (1974). Judgment under uncertainty: heuristics and biases. *Science*,185, 1124-31.

[102] Chapman, G. B., and Johnson, E. J. (2002). Incorporating the irrelevant: Anchors in judgments of belief and value. In T. Gilovich, D. Griffin, and D. Kahneman (Eds), *Heuristics and Biases: The Psychology of Intuitive Judgment*, (pp. 122-38). Cambridge, UK: Cambridge University Press.

[103] Facione, P.A., Facione, N. C., and Giancarlo, C. A. (1996). The motivation to think in working and learning. In, Elizabeth Jones (Ed.), *Preparing Competent College Graduates: Setting New and Higher Expectations for Student Learning. Series: New Directions for Higher Education*, (pp. 67-79). San Francisco, CA : Jossey-Bass.

[104] Facione, N.C., and Facione, P.A., and Sánchez, C.A. (1994). Critical thinking disposition as a measure of competent clinical judgment: The Development of the California Critical Thinking Dispositions Inventory (CCTDI). *Journal of Nursing Education*, 33(8), 345-50.

[105] Thompson S.C., Armstrong, W, and Thomas, C. (1998). Illusions of control, underestimations, and accuracy: A control heuristic explanation. *Psychological Bulletin*, 123(2), 143-61.

[106] Schultz, T. R., and Wells, D. (1985). Judging the intentionality of action-outcomes. *Developmental Psychology*, 21, 83-9.

[107] Fischhoff, B., and Beyth, R. (1975). "I knew it would happen" – Remembered probabilities of once future things. *Organizational Behavior and Human Performance*, 13, 1-16.

[108] Janis, I. L. and Mann, L. (1977). *Op cit.*

[109] Kahneman D, Slovic, P, Tversky A. (1982). *Op cit.*

[110] Thompson, S. C., Armstrong, W., and Thomas, C. (1998). *Op cit.*

[111] Weinstein, N. D., and Klein, W. M., (2002). Resistance of personal risk perceptions to debiasing interventions. In T. Gilovich, D. Griffin, and D. Kahneman (Eds), *Heuristics and Biases: The Psychology of Intuitive Judgment*, (pp. 313-23). Cambridge, UK: Cambridge University Press.

[112] Fischhoff, B., Bostrom, A., and Quadrel, M.J. (1993). Risk perception and communication. *Annual Review of Public Health*,14, 183-203.

[113] Weinstein, N.D. (1982). Unrealistic optimism about susceptibility to health problems. *Journal of Behavioral Medicine*, 5, 441-60.

[114] Weinstein, N.D. (1980). Unrealistic optimism about future life events. *Journal of Personality and Social Psychology*, 39, 806-20.

[115] Slovic, P. (1989). Perception of risk. *Science*, 236, 280-85.

[116] March, J. G. and Heath, C. (1994). *A Primer on Decision Making: How Decisions Happen.* New York: Free Press.

[117] Kahneman D, Slovic, P, and Tversky A. (1982). *Op cit.*

[118] Janis, I.L. and Mann, L. (1977). *Op cit.*

[119] Slovic, P. (1989). *Op cit.*

[120] Kahneman, D. and Tversky, A. (2000). *Choices, Values, and Frames.* Cambridge, UK: Cambridge University Press.

[121] Slovik, P. (1971). Limitations of the Mind of Man: Implications for Decision making in the Nuclear Age. *Oregon Research Institute Bulletin*, 11, 41-9.

[122] Tversky A. (1972). Elimination by aspects: A theory of choice. *Psychological Review*, 79(4), 281-99.

[123] Montgomery, H. and Svenson O. (1983). A think aloud study of dominance structuring in decision processes. In R. Tietz (Ed), *Aspiration Levels in Bargaining and Economic Decision making.* Berlin: Spanger.

[124] Slovic, P., and Frishoff, B., and Lichtenstein, S. (1977). Behavioral decision theory. *Annals of the Review of Psychology*, 28, 1-39.

[125] Tversky, A., and Khaneman, D. (1974). *Op cit.*

[126] Newell, A. and Simon, H. A. (1972). *Op cit.*

[127] Slovic P, Fischhoff B, Lichtenstein SC. (1976). Cognitive processes and societal risk taking. In J. S. Carroll, and J. W. Payne (Eds), *Cognition and Social Behavior*, Hillsdale, NJ: Erlbaum.

[128] Spitzer, M. (1999). *The Mind within in the Net*, Cambridge: MIT Press.

[129] McClelland, J. L., McNaughton, B. L., and O'Reilly, R. C. (1995). Why are there complementary learning systems in the hippocampus and neocortex: Insights from the success and failures of connectionist models of learning and memory. *Psychology Review*, 102, 419-57.

[130] Segal, Z. V., Williams, J. M., Teasdale, J. D., and Gemar, M. (1996). A cognitive science perspective in kindling and episodic sensation in recurrent affective disorder. *Psychological Medicine*, 26, 371-80.

[131] Bower, G. (1981). Mood and Memory. *American Psychologist*, 36, 129-48.

[132] Fischhoff, B. and Beyth R. (1975). "I knew it would happen" – Remembered probabilities of once future things. *Organizational Behavior and Human Performance*, 13, 1-16.

[133] Montgomery, H. (1989). From cognition to action: The search for dominance in decision making. In H. Montgomery, and O. Svenson (Eds), *Process and Structure in Human Decision Making*, (pp. 23-49). Chichester, UK: John Wiley & Sons.

[134] March, J. G. and Heath, C. (1994). *A Primer on Decision Making: How Decisions Happen*. New York: Free Press.

[135] Janis, I. L. and Mann, L. (1977). *Op cit.*

[136] Kahneman, D., Slovic, P., and Tversky, A. (1982). *Op cit.*

[137] Kahneman, D. and Tversky, A. (2000). *Op cit.*

[138] Slovic, P., Fischhoff B, Lichtenstein SC. (1976). *Op cit.*

[139] Montgomery, H. (1989). *Op cit.*

[140] Montgomery, H. (1989). *Op cit.*, p. 31.

[141] Montgomery, H. (1989). *Op cit.*, p. 30.

[142] Montgomery, H. (1989). *Op cit.*, p. 24.

[143] Montgomery, H. (1989). *Op cit.*

[144] Montgomery H. (1983). Decision rules and the search for a dominance structure: Towards a process model of decision making. In P. Humphreys, O. Svenson and A. Vari (Eds), *Analyzing and Aiding Decision* Processes (pp. 343-69). North Holland and Hungarian Academic Press, Amsterdam/Budapest.

[145] Montgomery, H. (1989). *Op cit.*, p. 26.

[146] Montgomery, H. (1983). Op cit. pp. 343-69.

[147] Montgomery, H. (1989). *Op cit.*, p. 25.

[148] Huber, O. (1989). Information-processing operators in decision making. In H. Montgomery, & O. Svenson (Eds), *Process and Structure on Human Decision Making* (pp.3-21). Chichester, UK: John Wiley & Sons.

[149] Facione, P. (1990). *Executive Summary of Critical Thinking: a Statement of Expert Consensus for Purposes of Educational Assessment and Instruction (p. 2).* "The Delphi Report." Millbrae, CA: the California Academic Press. ERIC Doc. No. 315 423.

[150] Janis, I. L. *Groupthink*, (pp. 174-197). New York: Houghton Mifflin, 1982.

[151] Giancarlo, C. and Facione, P. (2001). Undergraduate Critical Thinking Dispositions. *The Journal of General Education*, 50(1), 29-55.

[152] Luger, G., and Stubblefield, W. (1989). *Artificial intelligence and the Design of Expert Systems*. Redwood City, CA: The Benjamin-Cummings Publishing Company, Inc.

[153] Dean, T., Allen, J., and Aloimonos, Y. (1995). *Artificial Intelligence: Theory and Practice*. Redwood City, CA: The Benjamin-Cummings Publishing Company, Inc.

[154] Quine, W. (1959). *Methods of Logic*, (p. 198). New York: Holt, Rinehart and Winston.

[155] Kneale, W., and Kneale, M. (1971). *The Development of Logic*. Oxford, GB: Clarendon Press.

[156] Johnson, R., and Blar, A. (2000). Informal logic: an overview. *Informal Logic: Reasoning and Argumentation in Theory and Practice*, 20(2), 93-108.

[157] *The San Francisco Chronicle*, Section A, p.16. (September 21, 2001).

[158] *Traffic 2000*. (2007). Steven Soderberg, Director. Hollywood, CA: Universal Studios. Michael Douglas, Don Cheadle, Benicio Del Toro, Dennis Quaid, Catherine Zeta-Jones.

[159] Newell, A. 1990. *Op cit.*

[160] Genesis 1:24. In A. Jones (Ed), *The Jerusalem Bible*. New York, Doubleday & Company, Inc., 1966.

[161] Rock, C. (1999). *Chris Rock: Bigger and Blacker*, HBO productions. Rock, C., writer and performer.

[162] Scriven, M. (1976). *Reasoning*. New York: McGraw Hill.

[163] Locke, J. (1690). Of wrong assent or error. In *Essay Concerning Human Understanding*, Book IV, Chapter XX.

[164] Plato. (380 B.C.E.). *Euthyphro,* translated by Benjamin Jowett. URL: http://classics.mit.edu/Plato/euthyfro.html

[165] Kidd, I. (1967). Socrates. In P. Edwards (Ed), *The Encyclopedia of Philosophy*, (Vol. 7, pp. 480-86). New York: Macmillan Publishing.

[166] Griffin, J. (1961). *Black Like Me*, New York: Signet.

[167] *2001: A Space Odyssey*. (1968). Stanley Kubrick, Director. Warner Brothers Studios. Gary Lockwood, Keir Dullea.

[168] Hempel, C. (1966). *Philosophy of Natural Science*. Englewood Cliffs, NJ: Prentice-Hall, Inc.

[169] Toulmin, S. (1953). *The Philosophy of Science*. New York: Harper & Row.

[170] Wampold, B. and Drew, C. (1989). *Theory and Application of Statistics*. New York: McGraw Hill.

[171] Larson, R. and Marx, M. (1989). *An Introduction to Mathematical Statistics and its Applications*. Englewood Cliffs, NJ: Prentice-Hall.

[172] Kuhn, T. (1962). *The Structures of Scientific Revolutions*. Chicago: Phoenix Books. The University of Chicago Press.

[173] Miller D. (1991). *Handbook of Research Design and Social Measurement*. Fifth edition. Newbury Park, CA; Sage.

[174] Strauss, A. *Qualitative Analysis for Social Scientists*. New York: Cambridge University Press, 1990.

[175] Patton, M. (1990). *Qualitative Evaluation and Research Methods*. Newbury, CA: Sage.

[176] Nunnally, J. (1978). *Psychometric Theory*. New York: McGraw Hill.

[177] Facione, PA, Facione, NF, Giancarlo, CA, (2000). *Op cit*.

[178] Facione, P. A., (1990). *Op cit*.